THE GREATEST STORY
OVERSOLD

THE GREATEST STORY
OVERSOLD

Understanding Economic Globalization

STAN G. DUNCAN

ORBIS BOOKS
Maryknoll, New York 10545

Founded in 1970, Orbis Books endeavors to publish works that enlighten the mind, nourish the spirit, and challenge the conscience. The publishing arm of the Maryknoll Fathers and Brothers, Orbis seeks to explore the global dimensions of the Christian faith and mission, to invite dialogue with diverse cultures and religious traditions, and to serve the cause of reconciliation and peace. The books published reflect the views of their authors and do not represent the official position of the Maryknoll Society. To learn more about Maryknoll and Orbis Books, please visit our website at www.maryknollsociety.org.

Library of Congress Cataloging-in-Publication Data

Duncan, Stan G.
    The greatest story oversold : understanding economic globalization / Stan G. Duncan.
      p. cm.
    Includes bibliographical references.
    ISBN 978-1-57075-883-6 (pbk.)
    1. International economic relations – Religious aspects – Christianity. 2. International finance. 3. International trade. 4. Globalization – Economic aspects. I. Title.
    HF1359.D856 2010
    261.8′5 – dc22
                                      2010009725

Contents

Preface

Back in 1981, I was at a breakfast sponsored by the Disciples Peace Fellowship in San Antonio, Texas. It was a part of the annual Christian Church (Disciples of Christ) General Assembly. Our keynote speaker that morning was William Sloane Coffin, the late preacher, chaplain, writer, and activist. I had just read an article in *Newsweek* about Central America, and he had just returned from two weeks in Nicaragua, so I, of course, believed that we both knew nearly the same amount about the area. He set me straight, of course. In fact he told me that I didn't really know a damn thing about Central America and that I ought not to talk about such a complicated subject until I had gone there, walked around, and had done my homework. And that was that. Bill never was known for his tact.

As soon as I got home from that event I started making phone calls to friends and strangers about ways that I might do what he said and get myself down there. I eventually put together the first of what turned out to be fifteen delegations to countries in Latin America over the next twenty-five years. As a result of those experiences I also enrolled in a master's program in third world development economics and eventually moved to Guatemala in order to coordinate research on a series of handbooks on development in the larger region. In no small way, then, I can say today that that uncomfortable put-down by Bill Coffin back in the early 1980s was the first step in the writing of this book. If it hadn't been for our uncomfortable encounter, much of my life would have gone in a very different direction, and this book would never have been written.

Some parts of the chapters included here were written originally for other purposes. The introduction to globalization was prepared first for the United Church of Christ's Economic Globalization Task Force. The section on the international debt crisis was for a packet of resources following the passage of a UCC resolution on debt cancelation. The section on NAFTA was delivered at a workshop on trade. And parts of the final chapter on debt and trade in ancient

Israel was written originally as a biblical resource for Jubilee Sunday services. Taken together, they bring under one "roof" background information, worship materials, and faith-based activist resources to help ordinary people in churches learn at least the basics of one of the most important developments of our time. Our rapidly integrating global economy, with its winners and losers and peaks and valleys is daunting for most of us, and this book attempts to help us understand it, address it, and change it from the perspective of faith.

Insofar as that happens, Bill Coffin, may he rest in peace, should get at least some of the credit.

Acknowledgments

There are too many people to thank for helping bring this book to completion. There were biblical and economic writers who taught me, and activists and "laborers in the vineyards" who inspired me, some of whose stories are retold here.

Specific thanks need to go to the truly wonderful people who read early drafts of the manuscript and offered comments that made the final version better: Rev. Derrick Boykin, Peter Buck, John Will, Glen Bays, Fr. Tom Massaro, Rabbi Michael Lerner, John Anthony, Neil Watkins, and Rev. Phil Hardwick. I don't know what I would have done without them. It's unfortunate that no women are represented on this list, but it doesn't reflect the intellectual and emotional support that I have received from a number of female scholars and activists over the years. But it was simply the "luck of the draw" that none were available as readers when the manuscript was.

Special thanks to my brother-in-law and good friend Capt. William "Biff" Holt, whose gentle nudging and encouragement launched and nourished this project over many difficult years.

And finally, my wife and three children, whose love and trust and forgiveness have kept me alive during difficult times and given me the spiritual joy that empowers my writing.

Taken together the faith and encouragement of all these people helped me see that the Spirit of the Lord is in fact upon us, bringing good news to the poor, release to the captives, sight to the blind, and liberty to the oppressed.

ONE

An Introduction

Some men rob you with a six gun; others with a fountain pen.
— Woody Guthrie

This book is essentially about three things: economic globalization, various problems and issues related to globalization, and faith. By "faith" more specifically I mean possible responses of faith communities to the first two topics. It is intended as a helpful handbook of concepts and histories about some of the major international economic justice issues of our time, and faith-full ways that we can be involved, become activists, and make a difference.

Is This a "Religious" Book?

The short answer is yes. In spite of the occasional use of economic jargon, the thoughts, ideas, and perspective of this book are still fundamentally religious though it may not always seem so to readers from a more doctrinal, credal background. Much of the book is intended for activists from broad religious or spiritual backgrounds who want to gain a deeper look at some of the critical economic justice issues of our day, but have no previous in-depth knowledge of economics. Many of the early chapters were written originally for religious activists and not for people with previous in-depth knowledge of economics. And at the end we have added a biblical, theological chapter that tries to lift up themes and messages in the Hebrew and Christian scriptures that address theologically something like the "economic globalization" of their day.

However, there is more to writing from a religious perspective than including Bible studies. The Bible is enormously complex and how one understands its origins and meaning has much to do with how it is used in contemporary moral, ethical, and political decision making. There are two types of writings in the Bible that may be of most help to us as interpreters of contemporary issues. The first are parallels and the second are principles, and they should be distinguished. Parallels are stories (historical or in parables) of hunger or poverty or oppression that, however roughly, parallel conditions in our world today. Examples would be stories of the rise of poverty and social unrest in ancient Israel that grew as its own involvement in international trade grew. We could ask then, What did the prophets say about that? How did the oppressed and those who aligned themselves with the oppressed respond to it? The answers to those questions can be helpful in understanding and critiquing current situations. Principles, on the other hand, are broader, more general interpretive teachings or paradigmatic stories that give us guidance in a larger sense. A frequently used example is the story of God through Moses liberating the Hebrew people from slavery in Egypt. A principle based on that story is that since God freed us, it is therefore our duty and responsibility to free others. This thread is found throughout the Bible, especially in Exodus and Deuteronomy and the teachings and parables of Jesus, and has had a profound influence on liberation movements all over the world.

So while it is true that the Bible will be of little help if we are trying to decide how high to set the Federal Reserve overnight discount rates or whether there should be a tax on currency exchange rates, it can and should give us guidance on a larger perspective that we as people of faith should have when making those decisions ourselves. If we believe, as the Bible seems to believe, that God has a special interest in the poor, the weak, and the oppressed, then the first questions people of the Bible should be asking themselves are: How many marginalized and weak people will be hurt or helped by this or that policy? How many wealthy and powerful will it help? If the policy is designed to bail out banks, for example, by cutting price supports for third world farmers, then it is probably a policy that stands outside of our biblical and faith tradition.

Why This Book, Now?

At the time this book was being written, the United States had just fallen into a deep recession, which lasted for months and its aftereffects for years. One thing that made this recession different from any other in the past was the intense interconnectedness of our global economies. That means that today when the United States sinks the rest of the world sinks with it. Our problems and mistakes will be carved on the foreheads of suffering children in hundreds of countries for a generation, and decisions that our leaders made to pull us out of the recession will have a tremendous impact on what kind of nation we will be and what kind of global society we will have in the future. Today, more than ever, we are all in this together. The saying that when a butterfly bats its wings in Taiwan a monsoon is caused in Brazil, has never been more true. We might change the saying slightly to say that when brokers on Wall Street place bets on whether commodity futures will go up or down, cotton farmers in Bangladesh hang on the outcomes. A common practice is to pull certain commodities like cotton off the market, which drives up the price (called "forward-pricing"), which may create a slight financial pinch for the rich but puts the commodity out of reach of the poor, and commodities dealers make a profit.

The oil price spike in the summer of 2008 was driven in part by oil investors like Andrew J. Hall, who was under contract to Citigroup to place bets on future prices of oil. In recent years he has placed so much money on the table betting that oil prices would go up that he in fact influenced their going up. It is estimated that his gambling on oil prices caused as much as 10 percent of its final increase.[1] To most of us, that was a hit in our pocketbooks. But in Honduras and Bolivia, tractors and trucks went idle and families went hungry. Similarly, the new wealthy classes in China have been eating more meat in the last twenty years, trying to imitate their rich-country colleagues. But when they did that, it pulled more and more meat out of the market and the regional supply went down, driving up prices and effectively pricing it out of the reach of poor urban families. Beef, as you probably know, takes about 200 pounds of grain to produce 175 pounds of meat. So the more meat China's wealthy eat, the less grain there is on the market. The less grain on the market, the higher its price. The higher its price means the higher the level of hunger in the world. This complex web of interlocking economic, political, and ideological forces means that more than at any other time in our history we are all winning together or losing together.

One of the problems with these connections between cause and effect is that the people who are affected by them seldom see them. During the 1990s and early years of the new millennium, for example, small coffee farmers in the Alto Occidente region of Colombia experienced a rapid decline in profits, which drove thousands of them from their homes and farms and into the harsh ghettos surrounding Bogotá looking for work. That, by the way, was when the company that sponsored the famous "Juan Valdez" commercials went bankrupt. In the spring of 1999 I was in Colombia for a couple of weeks and attended a Mass in Ciudad Kennedy (yes, named after *that* Kennedy) in southeastern Bogotá, and by coincidence several of the people sitting around me were families of coffee farmers. After church we chatted for a while and I discovered that most of them were doing poorly financially. Two or three of the men in the group had quit their farms altogether and had moved with their families into the city looking for work.

I had my suspicions about what was causing their hard times, but I asked them why they thought the business was doing so poorly. Almost to a person, the answers I received were individual and local. The seasons had not been good to them. The blight on coffee trees had been terrible for several years in a row. The rains had been long and were hard on the coffee cherries. The local *coyotes* (mediators) no longer offered them a fair price. And so on. Not a one of them mentioned the small clutch of Americans in $2,000 suits who had been gambling with coffee prices on the New York Coffee, Sugar, and Cocoa Exchange, the one constant that had more to do with their farms and livelihoods than the last seven years' worth of blight. Nor did they mention the international banks and multilateral financial institutions thousands of miles away that made far too many farm loans in other countries to increase coffee production, and in so doing drove down profits for individual farmers. And how could they have known those things? How could they have had any way of knowing the international "principalities and powers" that had such a profound influence on their daily lives?

More recently, during the rising global food crisis, how many of the tens of thousands of people who protested the soaring prices realized that at least one of the causes of their misery was geopolitical and ideological? Dropping tariffs on incoming corn in one country, for example, which allows cheaper corn imports from another country, which drives corn producers out of business in the first country. The social-political impact of these acts has been brutal on some countries. Haiti exploded in mass demonstrations and food riots in March 2008. Five people died (including a UN staff member), the government fell, the prime minister was ousted, the World

Bank rushed in with loans for food, and the World Food Programme called for international aid. There are a number of reasons for the price increases, but one that is key began a decade ago when the United States pressured Haiti to drop its tariffs on imports, such as rice, in order to allow in subsidized U.S. rice, which then destroyed Haiti's rice farmers and forced Haitian consumers to become dependent upon imported rice. Then, in 2007, when the price of U.S. rice rose to triple digit highs, people in Haiti suddenly experienced absolute starvation for the first time in decades. They had turned over food production to the United States, and then when prices went up they found that they were no longer equipped to feed themselves. How many hungry people in Haiti do you suspect could connect the dots to see how their local story fits into the global story?

German biblical scholar Ulrich Duchrow has argued that the ignorance of the poor regarding the global forces that control them is not unintentional. "Hardly anyone tells them that they are victims of a whole interconnected system extending all over the globe and varying only in degree," he says, because "if they heard, they might join forces!"[2] However, today might be different. With the possibility of a looming global food shortage and steadily declining oil reserves, we might be approaching a crisis that touches the developed world as well as the undeveloped, and we may for the first time in history be witnessing a time in which the poor and hungry do in fact begin to join forces.

Why Addressed to People of Faith?

People of faith need to be a part of the work to make these connections and help our congregations and faith groups learn about them. Part of what comes from a belief in the God of all creation is a commitment to stretch ourselves to where we can view issues "from above" and not just "from below." That is, we need to lift our perspectives from a "me first" level to as high as our human limitations can take them. Part of what happens when my life is intertwined with the spirit of the God of Abraham, Moses, and Jesus is that I am no longer solely concerned with just my own life but also with the lives of the rest of the global, universal, eternal family of God.

Additionally, weakened though they are of late, religious congregations remain among the few institutions still standing that have the perspective and ability to offer a sustained moral critique of the political and market forces that are tearing us apart. Churches and other religious organizations need to help people make those connections and to face up to their own responsibility for the damage done. Perhaps we have fallen down on that task because we are too complicit in the crime. Perhaps we subconsciously feel it would hurt too much and cost too much. But it has to be done.

To be fair to our human frailties, this is an enormously difficult task. The media will not help. The politicians who set the national conversation agenda will not help. Their reelections are financially tied to the very people who wish to keep these kinds of connections secret. Only such things as diligence, persistence, study, advocacy, and faithful commitment to see the issues from above and from love will do it. The Holy Spirit is not on the side of oppression or starvation. The Holy Spirit is on the side of liberation, democracy, wholeness, and the abundant life.

Obviously this one book or others like it cannot do everything. But what we can do is to supply some of the background material that might help the reader understand the framework of the various global economic forces and make some of the connections between what happens "here" and what happens "there." It can help create a framework through which these and future issues like them can be viewed. We can't start everywhere, but we must start somewhere.

Is This Book Biased?

The short answer is yes. But it's more complicated than that. First, I want to say firmly that there is much about economic globalization (and globalization in general) that is positive. I believe it is beyond debate that today's rapid, global movement of goods and services can — and in many cases does — help feed the poor, increase democracy, and lower human rights abuses. One of the most accessible books that makes that case with numerous heartening and engaging stories is Thomas Friedman's *The Lexus and the Olive Tree*.

On the other hand, I also believe that all writing is biased. Friedman's work is biased toward globalization, just as David Korten's *When Corporations Rule the World* (as one can tell from the title) is biased against it. The truth is that globalization is a mixed bag. In addition to its frequently proclaimed values, there is much about it — at least in the form that it is now taking — that is damaging both in poor countries and in rich. For example, the present reigning model of globalization requires a constant downward pressure on wages that results both in the increased poverty of workers and the increased mobility of corporations seeking cheaper wages. This darker side of economic globalization is seldom discussed on the business pages of our local papers. Until it is forced upon them through protests or presidential primaries, our national leaders and the mainstream media rarely comment on the loss of jobs in the United States, many of which are directly related to NAFTA and other trade deals. And when they do, they almost never discuss whether NAFTA has been good or bad to poor communities in Mexico or other countries that have followed the free market economic formula. Therefore, though parts of these chapters seem to overemphasize the negative aspects of globalization, in actual fact they are an attempt to bring balance to a story that most people have been told has only a positive side.

Having said that, it is also true that not much of the following will make sense unless the reader accepts the premise that there is something fundamentally wrong with our present global economic situation, that the corporate and political powers have contorted and stacked the decks of the financial machinery that runs the earth in such a way that rewards the rich and extracts payments from the poor. I will attempt to bring together evidence as we go along that will (in my opinion) make that case; but if you begin with the belief that things are fine and getting better (and that it will get better faster if the critics will just get out of the way and let the unregulated "free" market function), then most of what appears like evidence will be nonsensical.

We also need to agree that the Bible and Christian theology still have something to say to this situation. There are a number (in fact a growing number) of people who accept that the world's economy is dangerously skewed, but who also believe that religion is unhelpful to that issue, and may in fact be a contributor to the crisis. I don't believe that, and this work reflects a fundamental belief that we can find tools and insights to address our present situation in the stories and theological traditions of the Bible.

It is worth noting again that there are also clear biases in the existing rules of international finance. There does exist an ideology of inequality which drives the creation of the rules and by which the international financial system itself is ruled. The wealthy have not (usually) created this system that benefits them because they are mean people. They've done so because it is human nature to look out for oneself and one's class. It is not always evil (though, undeniably occasionally). Sometimes it is simply a blindness driven by class or race or gender. Once one has sworn allegiance to a god other than the God of all creation, then the rest is less voluntary. Worshiping gods of wealth and power and influence can become an authentic bondage, a bondage that blinds one from seeing and feeling a larger reality and blocks that reality from surfacing in one's consciousness.

TWO

Globalization:
The Greatest Story Oversold

I can calculate the movement of the stars, but not the madness of men.   —Sir Isaac Newton, after losing a fortune
in the South Sea financial bubble

There are only two families in the world, as my grandmother used to say: the haves and the have nots.
                                    —Sancho Panza, in
                                  Don Quixote de la Mancha

I once knew a woman in one of my churches who had never been to college, had two dear little daughters, and was not married. The father of her children (whom she never married) was in the family for a while, but when responsibilities of fatherhood got too large for him, he left. And because they were never married, he managed to avoid any child support or alimony payments. In fact, she was not even sure what state he now lived in, so tracking him down and demanding help was a little daunting. When I knew her she lived with her two children in a one room efficiency apartment, and she "made ends meet" by working three paper routes and spending very little. One of the ways she survived was by relying heavily on places like Wal-Mart for family clothes and household supplies.

Wal-Mart had been very good to her. She and her children lived on approximately $20,000 a year (with no benefits), which wasn't much even then. But at Wal-Mart she was able to buy clothes for both kids, plus toys and most of her groceries, all for under a hundred dollars a week. And she had been doing that for several years, ever since the father had left and they had fallen into their desperate situation.

One day, during our regular Wednesday morning Bible study, the subject of Wal-Mart came up. Someone in our group had seen a piece on TV about protests in Mexico City over Wal-Mart's plans to build a store on the site of an Aztec pyramid. I waxed eloquent for a moment about what little I knew about some of Wal-Mart's unsavory practices overseas. How it tries to portray itself as a "buy American" company, yet its private label clothes are manufactured in at least forty-eight countries around the world. How it imports a whopping 10 percent of all of the clothing that is produced in China. And how working conditions in China are among the worst in the world. Most of China's clothing is sewn by young girls (frequently fired at age twenty-five for being too old), who often work seven days a week, often past midnight, for twelve to twenty-eight cents an hour, and with no benefits. They are housed in crowded, dirty dormitories, fifteen to a room, and fed a thin rice gruel.[1]

My friend was stunned. "But Wal-Mart is a good place," she said. "I don't know what I would do without Wal-Mart. I don't know how I could survive without Wal-Mart. It *can't* be bad."

My friend's situation captures one of the real dilemmas in the discussions about economic globalization: The present model of international trade, which is practiced with a vengeance by the United States and other wealthy countries, clearly does harm to a great many people. Recent studies have shown that when countries follows their own path to development, they tend to develop more rapidly. But when they follow the reigning rules for growth, they in fact grow more slowly or in some instances even fall behind.[2] Those who are trying to change it, whether through protests in the streets or letters to elected leaders, have every reason to do so. However, for other poor people who legitimately need help, it just as clearly works for their good. Greater access to cheaper goods has been a tremendous benefit to families like my friend and her two girls. In many places around the globe, the growth in manufacturing and exports has created new jobs and helped lift many from poverty. And access to inexpensive cell phones, purchased in the Tehran equivalent of a Wal-Mart, allowed Iranian students to show the entire world the story of their regime's 2008 rigged elections and brutality.

It is safe to say that religious "liberals" tend to see mostly negatives in globalization, and conservatives see mostly positives, but the reality is much more mixed. However, it seems to me that for people of faith, ultimately the exact percentages are not important. Even if the present rules for governing the global economy benefited 90 percent of the world and harmed only 10 percent (and that would be a hard case to make), we should still be concerned. Our mandate is to stand with that 10 percent. It is a central plank of the Christian tradition that I come from that Jesus calls us to feed the hungry and clothe the naked, whether their numbers are high or low. And that call is similar in many other faith traditions. The *percentages* of suffering are not the issue; the *fact* of it is. That is helpful for me to keep in mind when discussing ways to "tweak" the system, change the system, or blow it up altogether.

Definitions

A short definition of economic globalization might be "The increase in trade and capital transfers across national boundaries." Let's define our terms. First, "trade," as most of us learned in our high school or college Econ 101 class, is simply the buying and selling of goods and services, in this case across national boundaries. To a greater or lesser degree, people have been doing this for thousands of years. The ancient Israelites were very involved in global trade, through the efforts of their most important trading partner, Phoenicia, directly to the north of them. Phoenicia, and its two main cities, Tyre and Sidon, was the largest and most advanced marketing economy of its era, reaching Spain and Portugal, perhaps even France, and it relied heavily on North Israel and Judah to supply raw materials for its exports. Today's international trade, however, is different from that of earlier ages, if for no other reason than its sheer size and impact on the nations involved, about which we will say more below.

The second item in our definition is "capital transfers," meaning the buying and selling and trading in money itself. Usually when we think of the global economy we think only of trade (commodities, cars, computers, and so on) and "free trade" deals (such as NAFTA, CAFTA). But what few of us realize is that financial trading and speculation on money itself is far larger. To get a sense of its size, the total amount of all global trade in early 2008 was about $15 trillion. That's a lot of money, but the portion of that that was trade in *finance* (insurance, credit, swaps, etc.) was about $10 to $12 trillion. That's roughly 80 percent of everything traded that year. Its impact on what we normally think of as basic buying and selling of goods and services is incalculable. That's why, in 2008, when the great financial institutions of the world were found to be nearly bankrupt, suddenly nobody could make or receive a loan and global commercial trade nearly collapsed.[3]

And the amount of money being traded around increases at an amazing rate. From 1980 to 2000 capital transfers from country to country grew by more than 6,500 percent.[4] It declined dramatically in 2008 and 2009, but (using taxpayer money) it soared back to "normal" levels again in 2010. So when we talk about the issues of trade and free trade treaties (central topics of this book), we need to remember that in many ways the transfer of money across borders is a far larger story than the transfer of goods.

Shell Game Finance

Here is a quick picture of how this trading back and forth in the value of money works. What most of us think of when we think of international trading is what is known as "foreign direct investment," as when, for example, a corporation in the United States spends money to purchase shares in a factory in a foreign country. However, in truth, the vast majority of international trade is simply speculation on the value of money, or bets on the future value of that money. It's old fashioned, "Old West"–style gambling. Some critics actually refer to it as "Casino Capitalism," and for good reason. Investors, speculators, currency traders, etc., will literally place bets on the rise (or fall) of the value of currency on the global markets, selling now when they think it is going to go down and buying when they think it will soon go up. Or even if there is a legitimate investment in the building of a new marina in Jakarta, there might be at least as much if not more money speculated on its success or failure, or insurance policies taken out on it, as there is in the project itself. Sometimes this is done by third parties that are not even involved in the project. This element in the global economy is seldom mentioned in the business pages of our local papers, but it is a phenomenon that has ballooned in recent decades as regulations on capital transfers have been reduced or eliminated all over the world. It is now larger than all of the other international financial transactions combined. It was a contributing factor in the worsening of Argentina's 1999–2002 recession and was the key factor in creating the horrendous collapse of many South East Asian economies in the late 1990s.

These countries had just restructured their economies in a number of ways to make themselves more attractive to Western investors, and then the financial world came to an end. Following the advice of the experts in the developed world and their banking allies, they eliminated restrictions on the flows of money in and out of their countries, they allowed high domestic interest rates (to make the return for foreign investors higher), and they pegged their currency to the U.S. dollar (to assure foreign investors against risks). In the short term, these measures resulted in an explosion of new money flowing into the countries, creating a sharp (but shallow) boom in economic growth. However, even though large amounts of foreign capital was rushing in, little of it ever made its way into the "real" economy, such as manufacturing or farming. Instead most of it went to high-yield, high-risk sectors like the stock market, consumer loans, and real estate. The economy looked good, but with so many of the controls and regulations on money flows eliminated, the boom was far more fragile than anybody thought. People were in effect betting on the growth of the growth, and — though Alan Greenspan frequently and characteristically denied it in our own country — that clearly created a "bubble." Things appeared good, so they invested in the appearances, not the reality, making the appearances, well, appear even better.

This kind of rapid slinging of money all around the world, borrowing, investing, insuring, and in fact *gambling*, looks a lot like the old shell game of our grandfathers. In that trick the magician claims he has eight peas covered by eight shells. He whirls them around rapidly, lifting one now, and then another, showing the pea underneath. But then at the end of the show you discover that it was all a sleight of hand and there were only two peas under two shells; all the others were empty. His hands covered it up and the speed blurred it, but in the end the abundance of peas was just an illusion. And like the shell game of global finance, if the "magician" keeps slinging peas around too long, eventually he'll make a mistake and some of the shells will flip over and we will discover that they were empty. And then everyone reaches for the two remaining peas and all hell breaks loose.

The government of Iceland got into the game in 2001 when it raised its bond interest rates to about 15 percent to encourage foreigners (mainly British) to invest in their country. It worked, and for a while in the mid-2000s they received tons of outside money. At the same time, the high interest rates raised the costs for local Icelanders wanting to borrow money, so a large percentage of them arranged home and car loans from sources outside of the country, which brought in even more foreign money. For about six years these factors were sucking in outside money and making Iceland look like it had a booming economy. Its financial planners were all considered wizards. But the whole shell game was based on borrowed money, shifted from shell to shell, and eventually when the global economy began to teeter, someone looked under the shells and saw there was little of substance there, and the whole charade evaporated. Interest on foreign loans for local Icelanders went up, foreign investments coming into the country went down, and the nation imploded. In 2008 their net losses were higher than their entire GDP. They became the first developed country to apply for IMF help in thirty years. It was a painful, terrifying disaster.

More recently, Greece got caught in a similar spiral of taking on debts and then betting that they could raise money fast enough to pay them all back. Our own Goldman Sachs played "enabler" for their gambling addiction by arranging a deal to swap $10 billion of Greece's debt, issued in dollars and yen, for what should have been a rough equivalent in euro debt. But they used a false exchange rate, which gave Greece (and Goldman) a huge profit in the swap. Then Goldman arranged a second deal, which allowed them to postpone paying anything back for several years, giving the illusion that the country actually owned all of that borrowed and traded money. That kind of swap is illegal today, but Goldman put it together for the Greeks just under the legal wire. As with Iceland, when the global economy began to sputter and Greece's "balloon note" came due, people looked under Greece's shells and found bupkis, not many peas but plenty of lies and cover-ups.[5]

Incidentally, when Greece's downward slide began to be inevitable, Goldman and several others created a European index, based in London, that allowed hedge funds, individual investors, and banks to make even more bets — called "credit default swaps" — on the point spread of Greece's decline. The more Greece fell behind on its debt payments, the more profit was made by financial traders. If it had collapsed altogether, doing immeasurable damage to the euro and the lives of millions of people in the European Community, they would have made a killing. To make matters even worse, when bond traders saw so many investors gambling on the demise of an entire country, they started holding off on buying Greece's bonds — or at least demanding lower prices and higher interest for them — making it even more difficult for Greece to pull out of its black hole. It was as though some of the firemen at a burning apartment complex were sitting in front of the flames placing bets on how many people were going to die, and the more firemen who entered the game, the fewer there were putting out the fire, making the gambling stakes even higher and more "exciting."

As you know, at the last minute — and very begrudgingly — Germany and others stepped in and bought up much of Greece's debts, thus averting an international disaster, but not before causing many global "white knuckle" moments and huge spikes in sales of saki, vodka, and gin all over the world.[6]

Though it seems impossible, the East Asian currency crisis of the 1990s was an even larger and darker crisis. When the countries dropped nearly all of the controls and regulations on money transfers and exchange rates, that allowed rapid new investments to come in when times were good, but it also allowed for rapid withdrawals when investors got jittery. And eventually they did. The Asian "Tigers" looked amazing during most of the 1990s as investors sought greater and greater returns on their money, again investing in the promise (or illusion) that the emerging economies would eventually be sufficiently productive to catch up, turn a profit, and make everyone rich. Nobody doubts that the countries of East Asia were growing, but force-feeding them money, long before they had developed an underlying productive economy, was a move straight from the gambling tables. It was "Casino Capitalism" all over again. And, as with any Ponzi scheme, the early investors did make miraculous amounts of money off of these promises, but it couldn't continue forever.

In 1997, the currency of Thailand, the *baht,* began to falter. Investors started questioning whether it was really worth what the government said it was. Gradually a few got nervous and began to pull their money out, which made other investors do the same, and within weeks the economy of Thailand dramatically crashed. In a nanosecond, there was a withdrawal frenzy across the entire region, with each investor racing to pull more and more of its money out with the smallest losses. In the process they created a cataclysmic currency implosion that nearly destroyed all of the economies of South East Asia. Within months millions of people lost their jobs; tens of millions had declines in income. Factories closed. Wages were cut. Food riots broke out. Hunger and even starvation became common. In Indonesia unemployment rose to 45 percent, and the government itself collapsed (which, by the way, was not an altogether bad thing). The IMF rushed in with the largest financial bailout in history (and made conditions worse with its usual people-punishing, business-rewarding strings attached). The crisis ricocheted across the globe and shook the ground under countries as different and as far away as Russia and Brazil (and once again shot up the sales of vodka and rum).

If all of this sounds a bit familiar, it's because you read our own version of this whole story recently in the United States during the unraveling of our own fast-and-easy money era. There were scores of Wall Street investors slinging buckets of money all over the world in insanely risky investments, gambling on potential changes in the exchange rates between various currencies, all claiming that their money was backed by this huge stash of peas they held in their vaults and under their shells. But then when their original source of money to play with, the shaky subprime mortgages, began to crumble, a few investors began lifting their shells and found barely anything there. The rest of us then began to stop spending what few peas we did have and the economy ground to a stop. And like the deep pockets of the IMF, the U.S. government stepped in with lots of cash to bail out and reward the investors who gambled away your grandmother's savings (and enabling them to return to the gambling tables within months).[7]

It's helpful to keep the stories of Asia, Greece, Iceland, and the United States in mind when you hear pundits on TV speak of "economic globalization" and mainly mean by that the rules governing *trade*. As we saw when our own financial problems flew rapidly around the world, the movement of money alone, and not just goods and services, can be a dramatic (and sometimes deadly) force in the global economy.

A Snapshot of Our Present Condition

The world has always known some level of cross-border international trade. We've noted the amazing distances that ancient Phoenicia went to trade and barter with its foreign neighbors, and there have been many other countries like it throughout history. In fact, even since the beginning of the so-called "modern" era of history (roughly since eighteenth-century European industrialization), our present burst of globalization is actually the *second* wave, not the first. The first was over a hundred years ago during the golden age of colonialization, when the world was in many ways more tightly integrated, or "globalized," than it is now. People could travel without a passport, the gold standard controlled international currency, and advanced technology (cars, trains, ships, and telephones) was making the world smaller at a rapid pace.

My great-grandfather was a product of that era. He was part of the great European migration of the later nineteenth century driven by economic upheaval, wars, and the redemptive "American Dream." Between 1850 and 1914 over thirty million people came to the United States, and many, like my great-grandfather, entered illegally. He hid out on a British-owned tramp steamer, traveling from southern France to New Orleans in 1855 without a passport or birth certificate or even seeing an immigration official. He got odd jobs and worked his way up the Mississippi River and out to the prairie of South Dakota where, with a shovel and an axe, he literally chopped up the sod and used it to build his first house. He then sent back to France for a wife, who arrived a year later, also without a passport.

His son, my grandfather, moved down to the Panhandle of Texas during World War I and got caught up in another global trade story. During World War I, Turkey broke ties with Europe and blocked wheat shipments into Europe from Russia. That caused a food panic throughout Europe, so the heads of state appealed to the United States for larger and larger shipments of grain. The United States responded by launching a campaign to send thousands of poor Americans (who knew nothing about farming) out to the prairie on a mission to grow wheat for our allies in Europe. "Plant more wheat! Plant more wheat! Wheat will win the war," was the chant of the time. What they created was an intense and complex form of economic globalization that involved millions of people in over thirty countries. Unsurprisingly, just as the cautionary voices of today's globalization are often ignored, the pleas of eighteenth-century agronomists, that "busting" up centuries of sod and planting crops foreign to the environment would eventually destroy the ecosystem and bring about nightmarish dust bowls, went totally unheeded. At the end of the Dust Bowl era, thousands of poor farmers lost their lives and even more lost their livelihoods.[8] My own grandmother got lost one day for several hours in one of the worst of the many "Black Devils" of the era and eventually lost one of her eyes from sand infection. I'm sure she went to her grave never realizing the connection between her blindness in Texas and a trade war in Europe.

The world's corporate and political leadership is undertaking a restructuring of global politics and economics that may prove as historically significant as any event since the Industrial Revolution. This restructuring is happening at tremendous speed, with little public disclosure of the profound consequences affecting democracy, human welfare, local economies, and the natural world.   —The International Forum on Globalization

---

But while there are similarities between early and modern "globalization," the differences are also very great. One difference is the sheer size of today's trade. No matter how much trade and transportation took place between nations in our ancient past, there has been nothing in the history of the world that has come anywhere close to the explosion in economic growth that has taken place since 1950. Before that date, not even the most powerful nations grew more than around 1 to 2 percent per year. But after that time a number of countries have doubled, tripled, and quadrupled that speed. Japan's leap was from 1950 to 1973, Korea's was from 1973 to 1990, and China's was from about 1990 to 2009 (when it slowed temporarily with the global downturn). The most recent wave of economic integration began in the 1970s with the accumulation of debt by developing countries and erupted with force in August 1982, when Mexico's near-default on its debt payments started the process of a complete restructuring of the global economic system, which will be the focus of a later chapter.

A second difference is the relatively small role being played today by individual nations themselves. It is impossible to overestimate how antigovernment and probusiness our world is today. Compared to our forebears, we live in an almost totally business-oriented and business-driven culture. So much so that many critics refer to our present international economic structure as "*corporate* globalization," not "*economic* globalization." The world is connected together following a corporation-determined model, not a social, or governmental, or especially *moral* model. Moral questions of right and wrong and good and evil are defined solely by whether they help or hurt the "business climate" of the wealthy classes of the world. The governing bodies of individual countries (whether dictators or democracies) play an increasingly weaker role in issues of trade and planning for growth, while independent, nontransparent, nondemocratically ruled corporations play an increasingly powerful one. It has come to be almost an article of faith of both political parties in the United States that huge, powerful, nontransparent, international corporate bureaucracies are better equipped to make economic decisions that affect human health and safety and the environment than democratically elected and accountable national officials. Following the financial disaster of 2007 and 2008, many pundits prophesied the end of influence of corporations on governmental decision making, but they were wrong. If anything, titans like Goldman Sachs and JP Morgan are even more powerful and, with their competition crippled or gone altogether, are even better positioned than before to influence votes in Congress to increase that wealth.

A clear example of that was the repeal of the Glass-Steagall act in 1999. For decades this law had kept insurance, commercial, and investment banks separate to prevent the kind of gambling with depositors' money that contributed to the crash of 1929. But in 1998, Citicorp (a commercial bank holding company) merged with Travelers Group (an insurance company) and created Citigroup, and then got the Treasury Department to give them a two-year forbearance while they arranged to have Congress change the law for them. It's helpful for the story to know that at that time the financial services industry was the largest contributor to Congressional campaigns in Washington and owned the largest army of lobbyists. In

1998 alone it spent more than $200 million for lobbyists. The new Citigroup spent more than $12 million that year on lobbyists and $5 million on campaign contributions to legalize its merger. In 1999 Congress came through and passed the "Financial Services Modernization Act," which allowed all types of financial institutions to merge, to invest together, and gamble together. As it turned out that act and the radical "Wild West" gambling that it made legal, was one of the major causes of the economic collapse of 2008.[9]

The fact that we live in a business-worshiping age also means that it is less common for one country to arrange trade deals with another, and it is more common for two (or more) corporations to arrange the deals and then go to their respective legislatures to have them sign off on or — if necessary — pass the laws to make the deals legal. It is also increasingly likely that the corporation itself will be stateless and not have a "home" country at all. A modern transnational corporation may have offices and production facilities in a dozen countries and swear allegiance to none. For example, most of us probably think a company named "Fresh Del Monte Produce" would be a venerable old U.S. company. However, today's Fresh Del Monte grows its produce in twelve countries, processes them in eight, and is owned by a Middle Easterner named Mohammad Abu-Ghazaleh, who doesn't live anywhere near the United States. The corporation does maintain an office in Coral Gables, Florida, but it is incorporated in the Cayman Islands to avoid paying U.S. taxes.[10] So what exactly is the "nationality" of this company? To whose laws is it accountable? And in our new hyperglobalized world, does anyone bother to care?

Trend Micro, producer of computer protection programs, is similar. It keeps its main virus response center in the Philippines, with six other labs scattered from the Far East to Munich. Its "official" financial headquarters is in Tokyo. Its product development is in Taiwan. And its major source of sales is in the United States. So, again, what is the nationality of this company?

The numerous financial crises of 2008 further dispersed ownership around the planet. During the 2008 global bank failures and bailouts, Banco Santander of Spain bought out America's Sovereign Bankcorp; Japan's Mitsubishi bank bought a major portion of Morgan Stanley; and three separate groups — Qatar, the Olayan family of Saudi Arabia, and Israel's Koor Industries — came together to purchase a controlling interest in Credit Suisse of Switzerland. In

August 2009 the U.S. FDIC actually paid Spanish banking giant Banco Bilbao Vizcaya Argentaria $9.7 billion and covered the losses of $11 billion in risky loans to get them to buy up the deeply indebted Guaranty Bank of Texas, giving it international giant status and making it a head-to-head competitor with its Spanish rival, Santander (which, as you recall, had already purchased U.S. Sovereign Bank).

In 2008 I purchased a new condominium arranged by a mortgage company in Weymouth, Massachusetts, which immediately sold the loan to a holding company in Florida, which then sold it to an investment firm on Wall Street, which bundled it with dozens of other loans and transformed all of them into securities (called "Collateralized Debt Obligations") and sold them in slices (called "tranches") to dozens of investors on the international market, who leveraged, sold, or invested them in numerous other projects. The actual servicing of my loan was contracted out to an entirely unrelated company that charged a fee to process the paperwork, but God only knows where the many fragments of the original loan are. It's likely that a portion of it (one of the "tranches") was purchased by the Republic of Iceland, which had wagered and lost eight times its gross domestic product on financial bets and had to be bailed out by Britain and the Netherlands in January 2009. Iceland used its bailout money as leverage to get another loan from the Royal Bank of Scotland, which it used to invest in a hedge fund in Thailand that insures subprime loans in southern California. If so, then who now owns my money?

In a very revealing case, in October 2009 a federal bankruptcy court in the Southern District of New York ruled that PHH Mortgage Company had no legal right to foreclose on a delinquent borrower's home because it couldn't prove it owned the note. In fact, the judge, Robert Drain, wiped out $461,263 in mortgage debt because no one could trace up the securities chain and prove ownership. Evidently, in that case at least, *nobody* owned the money. It moved into the international financial vapors and disappeared. Similarly, in September 2008, when then U.S. Treasury Secretary Henry Paulson went to Congress to ask for hundreds of billions of dollars to buy up bad home loans and insure them, he got immediately slapped in the face with this same reality: To whom does he make out the check? In what country will the bailout money reside after the rescue has been made? "We've got this great complexity," he said in an interview at the time. "Investors are scattered all around the world, and that makes decision making very complicated."[11] No kidding? Soon after receiving the money from Congress, Paulson changed course entirely and began targeting it to the ailing banks themselves rather than try to track down individual loan holders.

One of the most visible ways that the transnational nature of the modern corporation touches the lives of Americans is in "outsourcing," the sending of jobs to low-income countries to save money on health care, safety, labor, and, of course, taxes. It has been a growing part of the statelessness of the global market for some time. Fifty years ago we experienced an internal version of outsourcing when the urban "Rust Belt" states of the Northeast began moving textile and manufacturing jobs to the poor rural communities of the Southeast where labor, taxes, and safety regulations were cheaper. Then, beginning about the mid-1970s to the early 1980s, those jobs gradually began to be outsourced beyond our borders to poor communities in northern Mexico and, later still, all over the globe.

Today, with the rise in such things as college degrees and technology, job losses due to outsourcing have moved up the economic ladder and are affecting a wider range of mid-level professional positions. A neighbor of mine was once a highly respected commercial artist, the head of his division in a national T-shirt design company. But one day he was told that the company could cut costs and raise profits if they had equally competent artists in the Philippines do the same work. They could send their creations back and forth as email attachments, for one tenth of the cost. In fact, the demand for foreign graphic artists is so high that new firms have started up that do nothing but connect U.S. companies with willing, and low-salaried, artists in the Philippines.[12] *Business Week* journalist Kathleen Madigan has written that today over 30 percent of American private sector jobs are at risk of being shipped overseas. "And that doesn't count back-office functions such as accounts payable, marketing and sales, and human resources that exist in U.S.-grounded industries such as retailing, health care, and recreation. All of them could be shipped overseas in the name of cost-cutting."[13] Nearly everyone either feels personally that his or her job is precarious and exportable or knows someone whose is.

When you combine statelessness with vast wealth, you get institutions with incredible power and influence. They often have economies that are larger than the countries that host them. If we think of the gross sales of a corporation as roughly the equivalent of the gross domestic product (GDP) of a country, then among the world's one hundred largest "economies," fifty-one of them are actually businesses. The combined sales of the world's top two hundred corporations are equal to 28 percent of the total GDP for the whole world.[14] Corporations make their own trade policy; they effectively set their own domestic policy; and (though they are hesitant to admit it) they buy and sell votes of politicians to do their will. And they have no real concern about which party's vote they purchase. When Republicans controlled Congress, massive amounts of money from multinational corporations poured into the reelection campaigns of Republican legislators. But following the return to Democratic control in 2006, the money made a rapid shift to Democrats. Corporations are basically nonpartisan. They support whatever and whoever will increase their income. They are secret societies, nondemocratic in governing structure, and prefer nondemocratic countries in which to do business.[15]

Their above-the-law nature is an ongoing concern of many people of faith, consumer advocates, and human rights organizations; but in the corporate, governmental, and media communities their size and influence is consistently portrayed as a blessing that benefits us with a bounty of goods (that is, until their CEOs go to jail in scandals or bring down the global economy, but then only temporarily). Even today, following what was arguably the worst greed and corruption financial meltdown in our history, the titans of business have returned to their peaks of power and influence. No one knows exactly how far the 2010 Supreme Court decision allowing corporations unlimited financial influence over elections will allow them to go, but it's clear that their *intention* is to use their new freedom to acquire more power, more persuasion, and more wealth.

It is difficult for most of us in Middle America to see the extent of the power of major corporations over us, but in poor countries it is very clear. One illustration of that is a coffee purchasing arrangement between the giant Swiss corporation Nestlé and the countries of Mexico and Vietnam. When most of us think of Nestlé, we probably think of chocolate. If you are "of a certain age," you will remember their old jingle of the 1960s, singing the letters out loud, "N-E-S-T-L-E-S...Nestlé makes the very best...*choc*olate."

But today it is also the largest buyer of coffee in the world, especially for its instant brand, Nescafé (now "Nescafé Taster's Choice"). In a very telling story of their power and influence, in the late 1990s, Nestlé told its Mexican coffee suppliers that it was moving its accounts to Vietnam, where it could save money because labor was cheaper. Prices paid to Mexican farmers were already rock bottom, so initially Mexico decided to accept the loss of the Nestlé account. In anticipation of the new contracts and huge sales, Vietnam responded by putting millions into retooling its coffee plantations and they increased production that year by fifty-five thousand tons. Eventually, however, Mexico blinked and agreed to lower its prices (one more time) to coffee growers, so Nestlé pulled back on its Vietnam deal, purchased only forty-five hundred tons of Vietnamese coffee, and otherwise remained in Mexico. The end result was that Mexican farmers lost because of one more cut in prices, Vietnamese farmers lost because of overproduction, which drove down their profits, and Nestlé made a killing.[16]

Dollars without Borders:
The "Washington Consensus"

Over the years the present reigning model of economic globalization has acquired a variety of names: "Thatcherism" (after British prime minister Margaret Thatcher), "Reaganomics" (after President Ronald Reagan), "Friedmanism" (after University of Chicago economist and radical free market guru Milton Friedman), "Neo-liberalism," and others. But by the mid-1990s, perhaps the most frequently used name among pundits and politicians was the "Washington Consensus." That name emerged in the late 1980s when a Washington think-tank economist named John Williamson published an article for his colleagues that attempted to pull together a *consensus* of agreed-upon policy prescriptions of economic technocrats based in Washington, D.C. Hence the name, "Washington Consensus." His term (though not necessarily his specific meaning) took on a life of its own and became shorthand for a fairly radical vision of a deregulated and privatized free market that is now worshiped as divine truth by the major legislative, economic, and media powers of the West. They speak of it reverentially as though it is the only model for economic growth and happiness that God could or would have ever created. Though many developing countries have now turned their backs on some of its basic principles, it is still viewed by many as the primary path to the Kingdom or Nirvana (or both).

The fact that the Washington Consensus prescriptions actually failed in dozens of countries, causing poverty, suffering, and death, and that they exacerbated the problems in a number of other crises, has begun to wear even on some of the proponents of the Consensus dogma. Many developing countries that were sucked into its ideological pull from the 1980s to the early 2000s have recoiled from it today, and some have even voted in new governments whose main platforms were to oppose it. Because the rigid ideology of the Washington Consensus was tied so closely to country loans from the IMF, many middle-income countries have pushed themselves to pay off existing loans and then to back out of the international loan system altogether. Many countries in Latin America began coming together in the late 2000s to create a more humane version of the IMF, one that stresses people and the environment over corporate interests.

So many countries pulled out of the IMF that from 2004 to 2008, its loan portfolio dropped 90 percent. Before the international financial crisis, there was even talk of letting it deplete itself and die altogether. In the summer of 2009, the group of the world's eight wealthiest countries met to work out a consensus approach to the crisis. They wanted the IMF to help by injecting stimulus money into the economies of small countries. However, the fund was essentially broke, so in spite of their own local financial woes, the countries had to chip in extra money to the IMF to build it back up or else it could do nothing to help further their cause.

The term's fall from grace began with the painful Southeast Asian economic meltdown in the late 1990s, caused in large part by the slavish adherence of many countries to Washington Consensus policies. It was IMF guidance, following the rules of the Washington Consensus, that caused them to lower controls on the flow of capital in and out of their countries, which gave them a temporary appearance of wealth, but incredible human suffering when that money was sucked so rapidly back out of the countries again. And when the crisis hit, the IMF gave them such wrongheaded, punitive, punishing advice (raise taxes, cut salaries, lower social spending, sell off national assets, and open up financial markets to even further speculation) that when they finally began to get back on their feet again, they pledged to never touch the IMF or follow its "consensus" rules again. Martin Wolf, writing in the British *Financial Times,* described the IMF's policy prescriptions as "little more scientific than for a doctor to bleed his patients." It is estimated that in 1997 over $100 billion left the economies of Indonesia, the Philippines, Thailand, Malaysia, and South Korea, crippling their economies and driving tens of millions of people into poverty. That may not seem like much in comparison to the trillions that the United States has spent in order to save our own economy from collapse, but for developing countries over a decade ago, the loss was overwhelming.

Even the IMF itself, the most strident and demanding of the international financial institutions, eventually began to speak of softening its prescriptions and to be less heavy-handed about demanding their enforcement. However, skeptics have described the "new" IMF as "Washington Consensus Lite," meaning it makes the same demands, but with a more gentle face. For example, even though it changed the name of its harsh "Structural Adjustment Programs" to the "Poverty Reduction and Growth Facility," for the most part it still pushes the same gut-wrenching economic policies as before. In 2002 the IMF released new guidelines for the way it would impose debt relief conditions on poor countries. The language appeared to signal a change of heart toward more humane requirements, but in reality little changed. A report from EURO-DAD, the European Network on Debt and Development, found that, from 2002 to 2007, IMF conditions changed neither in number or in kind. "During the first two years after the Guidelines were approved," they wrote, "the Fund attached an average of 12 conditions per loan granted to a poor country. After the 2005 review, our research found that the number of conditions increased to an average of 13 conditions per loan."[17]

Williamson himself complained some years after his initial article that overzealous promoters in some of these financial institutions — those with a more radical ideological economic agenda — had taken over his term and contorted it into a much more harmful and punishing model than he himself had intended. He described their version of his program as "laissez-faire Reaganomics — let's bash the state, the markets will resolve everything."[18]

These policy prescriptions (coming mainly from the U.S. Treasury, the IMF, and the World Bank, but agreed to by many others) have frequently been described by both supporters and critics alike as harsh and painful, the difference being that supporters say that they will eventually produce great benefits and critics are not that certain. Today, after thirty years of forcing these prescriptions on poor and developing countries, there is increasing evidence (some of which will be discussed below) that those countries that followed the rules closely grew little or not at all and those that ignored them or adapted them to their local situation, grew a lot.

The "Rules" of Economic Globalization: Where Everyone but the Majority Wins

So what are some of the credal "beliefs" behind the "religion" of globalization? Williamson's original list had eight policy prescriptions (later others raised it to ten, then twenty) not all of which would be considered controversial by most mainstream economists. For example, some were designed to keep down inflation (which is bad because it depresses investment and growth) by limiting the printing of money or by having a realistic foreign exchange rate. Another was a requirement that a country not run too large a deficit as a share of its GDP. In times of financial crisis a country can (and should) increase deficit spending as a way of stimulating the economy and keeping people employed until the economy can get back on its feet again. But in "normal" times, in the colloquial words of Jim Weaver, a UCC pastor and economist at American University, you need to "cut your cloak to fit your cloth."[19] Some of these suggestions were so noncontroversial that a cynic might wonder why, during the big spending years of the last decade, our own federal government did not follow them.

However, there are other global economic "rules,"[20] the consensus that seemed to have been driven more by a theological ideology (for example, that "bashing the state" is the highest form of human good) than by empirical evidence or standard economic models. And these are the rules on the list that are of most concern to people of faith, development specialists, and justice activists in general.

The first is the "requirement" that a country open up its economy by eliminating quotas and tariffs and local subsidies so that their local fledgling businesses can compete on what was euphemistically called an "even playing field," against huge, often subsidized, multinational corporations. Putting it so bluntly sounds biased, but it is nonetheless what happens in practice. It's an odd fact of many international trade deals that poor developing countries are often required to lift their subsidies long before the wealthy developed countries follow suit. Mexico, for example, followed that pattern with the signing of the North American Free Trade Agreement (NAFTA), and within just a few years (among other things) its four-thousand-year-old history and culture of corn production was in ruins. Hard-working indigenous farmers found that, with their own subsidies eliminated, they could not compete with highly subsidized U.S. agribusiness farmers, who now dominate their market.[21] According to a study of the effects of NAFTA on Mexico

> two million campesinos were forced off their land in the first two years of NAFTA alone.... Accelerated imports of cheap corn made Mexico dependent on U.S. agribusiness for one-fourth of its consumption of basic grains. But these cheaper imports did not reverse the decline in per capita food consumption as incomes fell after an estimated one million workers lost their jobs in 1995.[22]

In India, the removal of quotas on European imported, subsidized commodities and the removal of domestic subsidies for local commodities had a viscerally tragic result. For the last ten to fifteen years, in the south central region of India there has been an epidemic of farmers committing suicide. For years newspapers carried grisly news reports of farmers who lost money on their crops year after year after year until finally, in that very traditional, honor-shame society, they began taking their own lives rather than face the shame of utter ruin, usually by eating their pesticides, sometimes falling on their hoe, sometimes worse. It's an epidemic that has lasted many years, and its toll is measured in the tens of thousands.[23]

Of course, there are many causes of poverty in places like Mexico and India, and not all of them relate to you and me, but this one clearly does. Our country and other developed countries, following the Washington Consensus principles, pushed developing countries to drop tariffs on imported goods and lower subsidies that helped local farmers, while at the same time we increased subsidies we paid to our own farmers. The difficulty in changing that imbalance was seen in a 2008 campaign to get Congress to overhaul the U.S. Farm Bill. The Farm Bill is where the numbers for these huge subsidies are set every four years, and that year social justice organizations launched a major national effort at making significant changes. However, after a tremendous amount of work by organizations such as Bread for the World, Church World Service, Catholic Relief, Jewish World Service, and others, with thousands of letters and phone calls and constituent visits by local activists, the U.S. Congress nonetheless increased the majority of financial subsidies on the very commodities that have undercut the prices of poor farmers around the world for decades.

It was a discouraging outcome, but perhaps not mysterious. Any discussion of local activists attempting to influence legislation has to take note of the powerful connections between huge subsidies and huge campaign contributions that politicians of both parties receive from agribusiness corporations. The "lion's share" of subsidies goes to the wealthiest 10 percent of Americans, who are almost always the most important donors to reelection campaigns. In 2008 agribusiness gave more than $65 million to Congress (38 percent to Democrats, 68 percent to Republicans), and most of that went to people on farm or agriculture-related committees. When the good people of a local Bread for the World chapter have a bake sale to pay for sending members to talk to Congressperson Henry Bonilla (R-TX), who until 2008 was chair of the powerful House Appropriations Subcommittee on Agriculture, how could they compete against the $250,414 in campaign donations he had just received from Cargill, ADM, and others to get him to vote against their proposal? When a delegation of Oxfam activists from Georgia pooled their resources to visit Sen. Saxby Chambliss (R-GA), who at the time was chair of the Senate Agriculture Committee, how could their voice compete against the $287,000 that he had just received from these same corporations? There's no way that bake sales and pools can compete with that.[24] The Presbyterian Church (USA) released a report following the 2004 election that found agribusiness donations to Congress at $52,593,698, the second highest after health institutions. By comparison, total donations from environmental protection organizations came in distantly at around $2,000,000.[25] As the old saying goes, it's hard to believe one way when your salary (or political office) depends on your believing another.

Precise numbers of how much the United States pays for subsidies are difficult to come by, but in 2005, during World Trade Organization negotiations, the United States offered to lower its overall subsidies to *only* $22 billion! That's a lot of money even today; and as it turns out in the end the United States failed to keep that promise.[26] The United States and other wealthy countries usually argue that subsidies are needed to protect our own poor farmers from the "dumping" of cheap products from poor countries grown by farmers who can undercut us because they make only a dollar a day. But in actual practice our subsidies do the opposite. They offer "free" money to our (usually large) farmers that encourages them to produce more than what the market can naturally absorb. The subsidies create an incentive for our farmers to overproduce a handful of select crops — mainly wheat, corn, rice, and soybeans — and then "dump" them on the world market at prices that can't be matched even by starving farmers in India, Africa, and Latin America.

Following a simple "supply and demand" principle, our overproduction puts too much of these products on the market, which then depresses world prices, which then out-competes the prices of poor-country farmers, which then lowers their incomes. If they sell their crops at all, they have to sell them at a price under our subsidized price, which slashes their already dismal profits. Ultimately, then, our program of subsidized overproduction is one of the contributing factors in the poverty of millions of farm families who are unable to compete with us.

A second "rule" in the Washington Consensus list is for a country to "liberalize" (open up) its financial markets and eliminate controls on capital ("money") flows in and out of the country. This is similar to the demands that countries lift tariffs and other controls on the flow of commodities into the country, but it has to do with money rather than physical products. It is an article of faith among globalism's supporters that deregulating the flow of money in and out of a country will increase foreign direct investment, promote economic growth, and lift the poor from their poverty. We've already seen how unregulated money flows in East Asia created dangerous and ultimately devastating unregulated risk. When fast unregulated investment money flowed into that region it was celebrated as a time of exciting and *irreversible* growth. But with no regulations on any of the financial transactions, what they also created was some very risky, unstable economies. When that same money was sucked out again in 1997, the region lost nearly 70 percent of its *claimed* wealth in less than a year. While those claims were more promises or "bets" than actual real money, still ordinary people were counting on that money when they took out loans for homes, cars, condos, and appliances, and when it disappeared, their hopes and dreams and livelihoods disappeared with it. More recently, we've seen how the great investment banks on Wall Street claimed to have trillions of dollars on hand, but when nervous investors attempted to pull their money out in 2007, they found that much of what was on their books were accounting tricks and no real money. As just one example, many banks frequently sold investors a type of security that was backed by risky subprime mortgage loans. They weren't worth much, so to attract buyers they added the proviso that if the underlying loans tanked, the bank would buy them back. And, of course, they did tank, and the banks had to buy them back just when their value was in a tailspin. However, to make their balance sheets look good, they would list the sale of these boomeranging securities, but not their repurchase. So their books showed a lot of sales at good prices, but not the rebuying at bad prices. Citigroup had billions of dollars of these essentially worthless pieces of paper. Bank of America had $2.1 billion in them at the end of 2006, and by September of 2007, when the defaults on mortgages began to rise, that number grew to $10 billion. And of course, when investors asked to see the books, the banks hauled out whitewashed versions that covered up the sleight of hand underneath them. It was all unregulated and all legal, but morally wrong. It all sounds a bit like the market traders in Amos's time who had one set of scales for buying and another for selling and, until their own financial crash came (about 700 B.C.E.), made a killing.[27]

This means that the basic premise — that liberalizing and deregulating international finance contributes to economic growth — may be flawed[28] because the high risk it creates may make the downsides more costly than the upsides. The volatility caused by radically deregulated global finance leaves a country vulnerable to extreme downswings when the inevitable crisis does occur. Governments, for example, usually feel compelled to step in to bail out the collapsing financial institutions (think of our own present situation again, and the Savings and Loan and Penn Square scandals of a generation ago). Bailouts in poor countries are invariably paid for by cuts in public expenditures, typically health care or education. In fact they are encouraged to do these things by the IMF and other outside "benefactors." The result is that the ones who pay the most for the bailouts are almost always the poorest people in the society.[29] The crisis in Thailand, in the late 1990s, led directly to an upswing in cases of malaria and HIV/AIDS. In Indonesia it contributed to widespread hunger and even cases of starvation.

In addition, during an economic crisis, high-income people have much better access than poor people to such things as "capital flight" with which to protect their money.[30] When the economy turns downward, the wealthy and well connected (usually the same people) can put their money in foreign banks, where the interest rates are typically still high, while poor people have no such resource. Following the deregulation of controls on financial flows in the 1980s, capital flight by wealthy people became a major drain on the economies of developing countries. Economists at the IMF (who recommended the deregulation) admitted at the time that lifting those regulations would result in the wealthy more easily sending their money abroad, but they claimed it was necessary for the long-term health of the global economy and that it would be a one-time-only occurrence. Both claims were later found to be incorrect. According to the EURODAD study mentioned above, after this type of economic restructuring took place, poor and developing countries lost roughly eight times as much money in capital flight as they received in foreign aid, and the trend has continued every year since. In fact, developing countries still lose between $500 to $800 billion annually. Not much compared, say, to the wars in Iraq and Afghanistan or Wall Street bailouts, but huge for poor and developing countries of the global south.[31]

At the UN's 2002 "Financing for Development" summit, the developed countries responded to the capital flight issue by pledging to work toward "an enabling domestic environment" for "mobilizing domestic resources, increasing productivity," and "reducing capital flight." In 2005 they met again and condemned it again, and urged the UN to "support efforts to reduce capital flight and (increase) measures to curb the illicit transfer of funds." So far, however, none of that has happened.

A third "rule" in the Washington Consensus list of prescriptions for globalization is that to compete in the global economy, a state must privatize all of its public assets. Again, many economists agree that some state enterprises in some countries are bloated and should be streamlined or sold to save money and to make them more competitive. But underlying the concept of privatization in the ideology of "market fundamentalism" seems to be a distaste for government of any kind. The movement's intellectual mentor, Milton Friedman, has gone so far as to call for the end of all government programs, except the military and police, including Medicare, Social Security, national postal service, minimum wage, national parks, public education, and even water.[32]

Williamson says that those with the "bash the state" mentality believe that by attacking the foundational structures of government itself, they are doing something noble. They believe they are, in his words, "storming the citadels of Statism."[33] National sovereignty, democracy, and government itself were all seen as simply evil on their face, while free markets and corporation-led globalization were totally good. "Efficient markets" should rule us, not governments. Economist Joseph Stiglitz says that "in this model there is no need for government — free, unfettered, 'liberal' markets work perfectly."[34] Unsurprisingly, the results of this policy of selling off public assets in developing countries were mixed. In countries where there were already solid financial institutions, sound information access, and complex market systems in place, it had some level of success. In poor undeveloped countries where none of these existed, the results were massive layoffs, sharp rises in prices of staples, and overall horrific suffering.

Even acknowledging that some governmental structures in many poor countries were often top-heavy and overly regulated, the fundamentalism doctrine of the Washington Consensus says they must be privatized radically and rapidly, a so-called "Shock Doctrine," which in the real world was dangerous. The consequences were often horror stories of too-rapid sell-offs at bargain-basement prices, without pausing to put in place the protections from the inevitable damage that resulted. The purveyors of this radical form of globalization seemed unconcerned about the potential damage. Canadian journalist Naomi Klein tells a story of a time in 1994, when Jeffrey Sachs, an economic advisor to Boris Yeltsin, addressed an international conference on the future of post–Soviet Union Russia. In the audience were distinguished economists and finance ministers from all over the world whose task was to hammer out the posture of their countries and the international financial institutions toward this new, but giant, nation. All who were present, including Sachs, were neoliberal, free market adherents. And all believed strongly that Russia must rapidly sell off all of its national assets in order to join the ranks of the capitalist countries of the world.

Sachs had just seen some success from giving similar advice to Poland and was prepared to try it again. However, he had also recently returned from Russia, where he had seen how precarious the society was, and he was concerned. He told them that in order for shock therapy to work, there had first to be an international infusion of aid, along the lines of the "Marshall Plan," which went to rebuild Germany and Japan following World War II. He said that only hundreds of billions of dollars would forestall an economic nightmare that might engulf the entire nation. That much aid seems high, he said, but would not be much if spread out among a number of countries, and the benefit would most likely be a rising star economy along the lines of what happened to Germany and Japan. On the other hand, he said, without such aid to cushion the blow and protect workers and food production during the transition, the results would be catastrophic. He mentioned the possibility of a Hitler-like despot coming to power, civil war, mass starvation, and remilitarization. He finished his speech, received applause, and sat down. And then the conference went on for four more days and not one speaker, or one workshop, ever again mentioned the possibility of financial aid to "cushion the blow" of privatization in Russia. The grim reality he discovered was that in this distinguished and influential community, the idea of protecting a nation from starvation or despotism was on nobody's mind, in nobody's heart. Helping markets function efficiently was their concern (something that could happen if a few "oligarchs" took over everything), but preventing a humanitarian disaster was not.[35]

In the first five years following the rapid sell-off of the state enterprises, more than 80 percent of Russia's farms went bankrupt; roughly seventy thousand state factories closed. Before shock therapy, 2 million people in the Russian portion of the USSR were living in poverty; after it, the number rose to 74 million. By 1996 almost 37 million were in desperate poverty. Not a shining legacy of how such a worshiped, accepted, and promoted economic theory is supposed to work in practice.[36]

Another moderate voice often ignored during the restructuring of Russia was that of Joseph Stiglitz, who once was a part of the World Bank decision-making apparatus. He has argued that large-scale privatization can be a good thing when done as a part of a comprehensive set of reforms that include new jobs for the laid-off government workers and new regulations on the management of the newly privatized companies. Without such conditions, he says, what is created is massive layoffs, a rise in fees, and a decline in services — the very things that did in fact happen in the case of Russia.[37] He says the problem is that international financial institutions like the IMF (and occasionally the World Bank[38]) focus their advice solely on saving money with which to balance the national "checkbook," while they should be looking at the overall results, which include unemployment, alienation, anxiety, increased street crime, and family violence.[39]

A Latin American example of a disaster of privatization took place when the World Bank pressured the government of Bolivia to sell off the public water system in the northern city of Cochabamba to a consortium of utility and engineering firms led by the California engineering giant Bechtel. Owner Riley Bechtel, you may recall, was appointed to President Bush's Export Council to advise the president on how to create markets for American companies overseas. The Bechtel company itself later received one of the largest no-bid contracts in history to help reconstruct war-damaged Iraq. Immediately after it took over the water system in Cochabamba, the price of water rose 35 percent, up to about $20 a month. That may seem small to us, but most of the residents of Cochabamba made less than $100 a month in total income, and $20 was more than they paid for food. Soon protests broke out. The government called in over a thousand heavily armed police. They fired into the crowds. Many were injured; some died.[40]

The good news in the Bolivian story is that at the end of the conflict, the popularity of the government then in power plummeted and an indigenous president was elected for the first time in over a hundred years. Something akin to democracy may be rising out of tragedy in that country, but why does it have to come to that? Mass starvation drove out the military government in Indonesia in 1997, but does it take a disaster to come to that? Why is it that the officials of so many countries (some elected and some not) feel more beholden to the World Bank and corporations like Bechtel than they do to their own people?

A final and closely related rule in the Washington Consensus list that we will mention here is the deregulation of trade and finance. We've spoken of both of these in some detail already, but they are clear indicators of the overall belief system of the presently worshiped model of globalization and of where people of faith might stand in contrast. On the one hand, those who promote neoliberal, free trade globalization argue that deregulation, like the other rules in the "consensus" package, is not only good for business, but will eventually be good for the poor as well. On the other, some of them have also admitted that the benefits to the poor must necessarily lag fairly far behind the benefits to the rich, sometimes decades behind, sometimes generations. Poverty alleviation is often referred to as a "lagging indicator" for the economic health of a country. In essence they say that "one of these days, the poor will (hopefully) begin to realize some of the benefits that we presently are giving almost exclusively to the rich." They wouldn't put it quite that starkly, but listen closely to the nightly business reports on your local media and you will often recognize this general meaning behind their technical, sterile, objective-sounding words.

To this, religious progressives could make two arguments. First, this is something like an "economic eschatology." That is, it argues that the condition of the present is suffering, but when the "kingdom" finally arrives all people will eventually be fed. Even journalist Thomas Friedman, one of the sunniest proponents of the wonders of economic globalization, acknowledges that in its early stages it can cause disruptions and dislocations.[41] But he argues for holding the line and not making changes in the theory because eventually — some day — the destructive tide will turn and begin to lift all boats. However, as followers of the one who fed the multitudes and had compassion on the helpless, or the one who freed slaves from bondage in Egypt, how can we in good conscience support the intentional creation of misery between now and then? Even if it could be proven that overfeeding the wealthy would eventually feed the poor as well, how can we look in comfort at what globalization does to the poor now while waiting for the benefits to trickle down? Joseph Stiglitz has made the interesting observation that many of these policies actually cause damage for a longer period of time than globalism's supporters acknowledge. For example, when a country slashes public spending for education (in order, say, to save money to pay on its external debt), it may take from two to three generations to build back an educated citizenry. That's not something easily accounted for in the short term but can mean long-term damage to the health and future of the country.

The second response is that there is ample evidence that this claim—that the poor will eventually receive benefits—simply isn't true. And it is to the evidence of that truth that we now turn.

So What Really Happened?

Admittedly our choice of examples to illustrate the rules of globalization is somewhat biased, but when compared with the drumbeat of praise for globalization from its supporters, our examples from a different perspective seem almost tame.[42] But is there something close to an objective measurement of the results of the last thirty years of the golden age of globalization? A study that uses mainstream, consensually accepted numbers without hyperbole and exaggeration? Perhaps a helpful place to start is the series of evaluations put out over a number of years by the Center for Economic and Policy Research (CEPR). They analyze reports from the World Bank and International Monetary Fund on the growth and decline in economic and social indicators among nations who followed the "Washington Consensus," "neoliberal," "structural adjustment" policies. They carefully weigh each category in terms of country size, time span, and the item measured, and they consistently come up with a fairly unbiased look at the success or failure of countries that have subjected themselves to the rules of the present model of economic globalization. Economic growth or decline is not, of course, the only valid measurement of poverty reduction, but it does help give us a fairly clear handle on whether standards of living in various societies have risen or fallen during the period of time measured.[43]

We should say in advance that the authors are progressives and do begin with a suspicion about many of the claims about the joys of globalization, but the numbers they crunch are from establishment sources and are not manipulated. Their bias is more in the fact that they report these numbers at all (something seldom done in Congress or the media) than in any distortion or fabrication of them.

Here's what they found. First they discovered that, contrary to glowing reports in the press, economic growth around the world was actually much better *before* the present golden age of globalization (which began roughly in 1982) than it was during. Instead of this being an era of great growth, fueled by international economic integration, it has been a time of economic slowdown in some regions of the world, and actual decline in others. The authors tested the impact of increased deregulation on the incomes of poor people and found that, while globalization almost always benefited trade, it seldom benefited the poor, who are the majority of the population in most developing countries. "Global deregulation of trade and capital markets," they wrote, "does hurt the poor [and] trade flows, in more regulated environments, may be good for growth and, by extension, for the poor in the long-run."[44] That is, trade itself isn't bad, but in order for it to trickle down to the poor, the government needs to have some say in the economic money flow to guarantee that benefits will come to the lower income brackets of society. Otherwise trade creates a two-tiered society of people who are fabulously rich and desperately poor.

Second, they found that "income inequality between and within countries" went up as countries deregulated their economies. "In 1980," they wrote, "median income in the richest 10 percent of countries was 77 times greater than in the poorest 10 percent; by 1999, that gap had grown to 122 times. Inequality has also increased *within* a vast majority of countries."[45] We, of course, have discovered the same thing in the United States as we have become an increasingly deregulated economy, so this isn't something that is unique to poor and developing countries.

Here are some other findings.[46] In Latin America and the Caribbean, the gross domestic product (GDP) grew by 75 percent per person from 1960 to 1980, but only 7 percent per person from 1980 to 2000. The GDP in sub-Saharan Africa grew by about 34 percent per person from 1960 to 1980, which wasn't wonderful, but from 1980 to 2000 it actually *fell* by about 15 percent.[47] The per-person output among all countries measured grew by an average of 83 percent from 1960 to 1980, but from 1980 to 2000 the average growth of output per person was 33 percent.

Even in those areas where growth actually went up, as in Southeast Asia, the countries tended to grow better *before* the rise of economic and corporate globalization than afterward. For example, Hong Kong grew at 6.9 percent in the 1980s, and only 5.6 percent in the 1990s. Korea grew 9.4 percent in the 1980s but 7.2 percent in the 1990s. Indonesia grew 7.6 percent in the 1980s, but 6.1 percent in the 1990s. And note that these numbers are through the first half of the 1990s, before the collapse of the East Asian economies in 1997. Since these measurements are before that crisis, the numbers should reflect at least *some* level of growth, but they don't. They all would have registered an absolute negative in growth had they been measured up to, say, the year 2000.[48]

For the entire set of low- and middle-income countries, per capita GDP growth was less than half of its average for the previous twenty years. Startlingly, had Mexico's economy continued growing at the rate it grew before subjecting itself to the IMF and its "rules," it would have nearly twice as much income per person today. Brazil would have more than twice its current per capita income.

One part of the economy that almost everyone assumed benefited from globalization is the so-called "informal sector," those people who scratch out a desperate living selling watches in the streets and T-shirts on the beach. It was thought that a rise in the demand for jobs would lower their numbers and help them transition into the "formal" economy. However, according to a 2009 study sponsored jointly by the World Trade Organization and the International Labor Organization, that seldom happens. Actually a rise in global economic integration seems to create both a rise in people in the informal sector and an unfortunate decline in the nation's overall productivity.[49] The reasons are fairly straightforward. When a country wants to create a large pool of cheap labor to enhance its exports, it lowers the supports (and raises the punishments) for rural farmers, driving many of them into the cities looking for factory work. However, that is an imprecise tool for producing a labor pool, and what usually happens is that the flood of new workers far outstrips the number of new jobs. For every, say, ten new bicycle factory jobs created, there might be twenty new rural people driven to the city looking for a job. That results in a large pool of people in the streets looking for, well, anything: jobs, drugs, crime, the "informal sector," etc. Plus, the study found, the newly created jobs tend to require a higher and higher skill level, not the kind of thing

**Figure 1. Life Expectancy at Birth (by age group)
(in countries closely following "Washington Consensus" policies)**

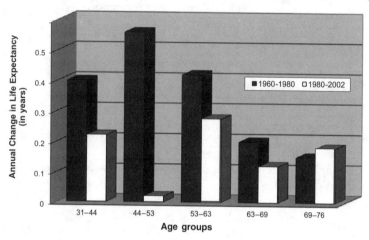

Source: World Bank World Development Indicators, Mark Weisbrot, Dean Baker, and David Rosnick, *The Scorecard on Development: 25 Years of Diminished Progress* (DESA Working Paper No. 31; ST/ESA/2006/DWP/31, September 2006), p. 3.

a poor worker just off the farm could immediately do. Therefore when so many of them came to the export centers looking for work, they found little. Some of these rural-to-urban "immigrants" set up their own shops and small factories producing goods roughly similar to those in the formal sector. However, the study found that because of difficulties in finding markets and suppliers, they generally remain poor, which keeps wages low and is a relative drag on the overall economy.[50]

How about social indicators? Unsurprisingly, CEPR notes that "with economic declines, there were also declines in life expectancy, infant and child mortality, literacy, and education...for the vast majority of low- and middle-income countries."[51] Even the level of human rights violations went up. Amnesty International has reported that there has been a measurable increase in human rights abuses in rapidly globalizing countries, because some governments use their domestic militaries to force poor farmers to give up historic farming practices and become cheap wage earners in the city, and others use force to quell the inevitable protests against these measures.[52] The struggle over water privatization in Cochabamba,

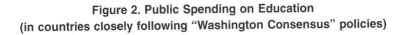

**Figure 2. Public Spending on Education
(in countries closely following "Washington Consensus" policies)**

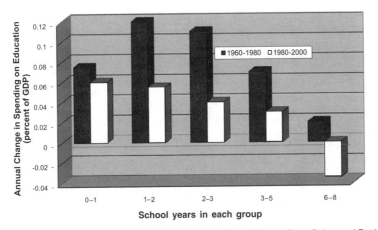

School years in each group

Source: World Bank World Development Indicators, Mark Weisbrot, Dean Baker, and David Rosnick, *The Scorecard on Development: 25 Years of Diminished Progress* (DESA Working Paper No. 31; ST/ESA/2006/DWP/31, September 2006), p. 10.

Bolivia, is a famous example.[53] The crackdown on public demonstrations over CAFTA (the Central American Free Trade Agreement) in Guatemala is another. On that occasion, protests against the agreement spread across the entire country, threatening the stability of the government. The president called out the army to quell the unrest, and two protestors were shot and killed.

Perhaps the most horrifying example was Chile. There, you may recall, on September 11, 1973, General Augusto Pinochet, with extensive U.S. CIA help,[54] overthrew a democratically elected (but leftist) government in a brutal, bloody coup. He immediately installed in positions of government dozens of economic engineers who had either been students of Milton Friedman, or who had graduated from an economics department that he had helped found at the Catholic University of Santiago. Over the next five years, following their advice (and that of Friedman himself, who visited the country in 1975 and advised the general), Chile's government rapidly pulled out of nearly every aspect of governing a country. It was economic shock treatment before the term came into vogue. Schools were closed, price supports were canceled, school lunch programs ended, government pensions were canceled, government assets were sold off. The market replaced the government as the central functioning, governing component of society. Within the first year, wages dropped by 40 percent, factories closed all over the country, and poverty rose to the highest level it had been in generations. Before the takeover and imposition of the harsh economic medicine, Chile's poverty level had been 9 percent and its unemployment was only 4.2 percent, both of which were lower than the United States. After the coup, both soared.[55] Before the coup, bread, milk, and bus fare took up 17 percent of the average worker's salary. After it, bread alone took up 74 percent. Immense, deep poverty and suffering became the norm for the country.[56]

In order to force the population to take the free market medicine, Chile's human rights abuses had to rise with its poverty, the kind of increases that Amnesty International has repeatedly documented in a number of countries. When a population resists, governments resort to force. Freedoms are taken away and people die. According to declassified CIA reports, in the early days of the coup roughly 13,500 civilians were imprisoned. Thousands were taken to two football stadiums in Santiago, where some were tortured in front of others to terrorize the rest into silence. Thousands more were executed outright at various places throughout the country, sometimes at the hands of the torturers, sometimes dropped from planes over the Pacific after being cut open to prevent their washing ashore later. Estimates are hard to come by but all told at least eighty thousand people were imprisoned without charges, and two hundred thousand fled the country.[57]

There are those who argue that examples like Chile prove that free market capitalism cannot function in a democratic society. In their hearts people want their governments to do certain things for them. They want protection from the raw-boned ravages of a free market, and they tend to vote for populist representatives who promise them protection (whether they follow through after elections is another issue). That argument may or may not be true, but there is ample evidence that this particular kind of free market — the one promoted by the IMF, the World Bank, the U.S. Treasury, and the various corporate-driven financial powers of the world — is very difficult to sell in a democracy. Amnesty's human rights studies show that. Their very careful, objective research illustrates repeatedly that with a rise in adherence to this economic model comes a

Figure 3. Average Annual Economic Growth by Country Income (in countries closely following "Washington Consensus" policies)

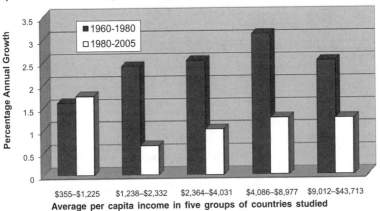

Source: Penn World Tables 6.1, April 2005, *IMF World Economic Outlook*. Mark Weisbrot, Dean Baker, and David Rosnick, *The Scorecard on Development: 25 Years of Diminished Progress* (DESA Working Paper No. 31; ST/ESA/2006/DWP/31, September 2006), p. 2.

rise in human rights abuses and that the two are inextricably linked. It is hard to have the one without the other.

Globalization's Theological Values

It is helpful for people of faith to note that Williamson's original "Washington Consensus" list was based on an underlying philosophy that was not — unless lobbied to be so — concerned with the issues that have been historically raised by churches, synagogues, and mosques, such as poverty, the environment, human rights, or even democracy. The three most important concerns of Jesus — poverty, health care, and food security — were nowhere to be found on Williamson's list. In later years he commented on the omission of poverty alleviation in particular, saying that he intentionally avoided any reference to it in his original list because such issues were simply not able to be discussed in the political culture of the Reagan administration. The list could not have represented a "consensus" of views had he attempted to include it.[58] Perhaps one of the things that people of faith need to add to their *own* list of activist goals for the twenty-first century is encouraging our nation's leaders to return hunger, poverty, human rights, and the environment to the top of our domestic and foreign policy agendas.

For many policy makers, however, globalization in general and the rules of the "consensus" in particular became so revered that they resembled a new religious faith. The principles of free markets, deregulation, privatization, and low tariffs, while secular in their implementation, were discussed and applied as though they were unassailable dogma, inspired by God, and received through divine revelation. Critics have described this slavish adherence to the principles of the consensus as "Market Fundamentalism," and the religious sound to that term is not accidental. It was first popularized by billionaire financier George Soros, who has become one of its harshest critics. He calls radical unfettered free trade the "dominant belief in our society today." It is a worshipful trust in, and loyalty to, the "magic of the marketplace" and is driven by a "human emptiness" that desires, but cannot be filled, by more and more goods and services. "Unsure of what they stand for," Soros says, "people increasingly rely on money as the criterion of value. ... The cult of success has replaced a belief in principles. Society has lost its anchor."[59]

This is a critique that many small-town country church preachers would feel comfortable making. Mainstream pastors have not always been adept at applying the Gospel to global realities, but greed and the worship of money have long been a staple in their sermon repertoire. Bill Moyers, on the PBS program *Now,* made the connection very clear when he described free market economics as "the ruling religion of America.... Its god is profit. Its heaven is the corporate board room. Its hell is regulation. Its Bible is the *Wall Street Journal.* Its choir of angels is the corporate media. You've got a religion in this country of free markets that is established in the political culture as well."[60] Management guru Peter Drucker adds that "it *idolizes* economics as the be-all and end-all of life."[61]

Drucker's description of this as "idolizing economics" is more appropriate than he realizes. Many official pronouncements from religious organizations have used the same terminology to describe our attitude toward globalization. A resolution in my own denomination's national gathering, known as a "General Synod," said outright that it was "a form of idolatry." The resolution noted that in the hearts of some of its adherents, modern economic globalization "has developed its own totalizing, systemic view of the world, with clear definitions of good and bad, articles of faith, rituals of worship, and standards for salvation."[62]

Understanding globalization as an "idol" is helpful because it lets us see it in a different light than usually portrayed by politicians and the media. When we usually think of idols, we define them narrowly as inanimate objects, fashioned by our own hands, that we imbue with the power of divinity. But that is only what they physically are. More important is how we relate to them, how we have faith in them and worship them. Something becomes an idol to us when we have faith in it as both trust and *loyalty,* and the second word is as important as the first. In our normal understanding of worship we think mainly of the *trust* aspect of worship. For those readers who are Protestants, faith as trust (going back to Martin Luther, who got it from the Apostle Paul) is a bedrock principle. In the words of theologian H. Richard Niebuhr, having faith means we put our trust and confidence in some center of value (which could be almost anything) that gives our lives a sense of meaning and purpose. Less obviously, however, our faith also draws out of us a deep sense of *loyalty* and fidelity to the values and the cause represented by that which we are worshiping, whether God or idol (or nation or group or holy book). We come before it first in trust, as something that gives our lives meaning and significance, but then we also become loyal to its cause and its values. When we trust and receive meaning from the one "God above all gods," then our loyalty is to God's cause of reconciling the alienated and healing the brokenness of the planet. But when our trust is in an economic system that preaches the values of self-interest, individual gain, and individual competition, then our loyalty is to a cause of self-interest and greed.

Niebuhr illustrated this by describing the faith of a nationalist. If you have faith in your country, have confidence in it, then your life is taken up into it. You feel larger and stronger and more meaningful because you are a member of something that is bigger, more important, and stronger than you are alone in your individual, otherwise insignificant, life. Conversely because of the sense of value and meaning that you receive from your faith in the nation, you therefore want to serve it. You are loyal to it. You are patriotic to it. You want to fight for it. In fact you may feel that you are more "moral" than your neighbors if you are more loyal, more patriotic than they are. If you become more extreme in your service to the state, you may feel that you are just being a more loyal servant of the state, you are just being a good American. But theologically you are also becoming more and more intertwined in worship of the state as an idol.[63]

Idolatry in this sense is not exclusively a religious term, but it describes the smallness or largeness of the objects of our faith. We all put our trust and loyalty in something, whether consciously sacred or secular. And we all have an inclination toward making the center of our trust and loyalty into something that is tangible, something that we can see, touch, understand, and attempt to manipulate. But the critical issue of idolatry is that the smaller we make that center, the more likely we are to exclude people from fellowship in our tent of worship. The larger it is, the more likely we are to have a bigger tent. The higher and wider it is, the more inclusive is our world and worship view. The smaller and more narrow it is, the more exclusive is our view.

Most of us in the developed world of the global north have been molded and formed by a worship of a very clear but very narrow economic idolatry that says that all questions of good and evil, right and wrong, justice and injustice can be answered in terms of money and income and the power and prestige that they produce. The more we give ourselves over to trusting the gods of finance and trade and derivatives to give our lives meaning, the more fiercely loyal we will become to the values they represent, and the more blind we will be to any alternatives to that "god." People who question the words or the application of the liturgy of finance are banished from the cathedral. In the United States, when someone suggests that the underpinnings of this religion might be a mathematical shell game / Ponzi scheme, they have been laughed at as though they were naïve or, worse, a sinner and apostate.

The last twenty to thirty years have been filled with occasions when economists and activists have questioned this reigning orthodoxy and were then denied advancements at universities, financial institutions, or government agencies. In the late 1990s, a World Bank study assessing the impact on the poor was suppressed for two years and then released in a rewritten, redacted form because the bank's overseers viewed it as too negative about the positive aspects of globalization. In the 1980s, as Williamson noted in his comment above about the absence of poverty alleviation in his list, establishment policy makers and economists were simply blinded from seeing issues of poverty and the poor because they contradicted their view of what economic globalization is supposed to be all about. In the decade leading up to the economic meltdown of 2008, many people attempted to warn us of the dangers of an unregulated, non-transparent, bloated, and broken banking system on Wall Street, but they were laughed at and sidelined by the financial brokers and their allies in the major media.

One example is Brooksley Born, the head of the Commodity Futures Trading Commission under President Clinton. In 1998 she began publicly to question the safety of derivatives, those loose, unregulated, deals made by "shadow (meaning unregulated) banks" that allow firms to borrow more and more money with less and less actual cash on hand. She believed that they were inherently unstable and might eventually create a bubble that could burst and take down the entire economy. Instead of being praised for her insight (which turned out to be correct) she was instead called into the offices of the Treasury department by Federal Reserve Chairman Alan Greenspan, Treasury Secretary Robert E. Rubin, and Securities and Exchange Commission Chairman Arthur Levitt Jr. There she was strongly and sternly told to back off. Derivatives, they said, were none of her business and out of her jurisdiction. Deregulation of the god of finance and unfettered freedom of self-interest and greed was the only way to bring in the Kingdom of heaven, they told her. Moreover, when greed and self-interest are allowed to run their course, they actually protect the overall society because nobody wants to get hurt or to anger their investors. When she attempted to take her concerns directly to Congress, she was steamrollered by the same three detractors and Congress refused to listen to her. President Clinton himself counseled her to end her crusade. As it turns out, of course, she was right, and they were blinded by their faith and loyalty to the ideology of Wall Street, the center of their value, the god of their worship. If you followed the news closely in the fall of 2008, you may recall that the buying and selling of derivatives was one of the central players in the financial collapse. It may be poor consolation, but in the summer of 2009, Born was awarded the John F. Kennedy Profile in Courage award for her ill-fated attempt to save the economy from itself.[64]

These stories exhibit a blind faith in the idol of Washington Consensus ideology: tax cuts, self-interest, and deregulation. Harvard economist Dani Rodrik has called the following of certain economic policies because we believe that they are true rather than because they can be proven to be true "faith-based economics." Joseph Stiglitz agrees. In his book *Globalization and Its Discontents*, he tells a story of a time back in 1997 when he heard that the IMF was planning on changing its charter to allow it to push poor countries into opening up their capital markets so that wealthy foreigners could buy and sell and gamble on the prices of their currency. He thought that that was a very scary and dangerous idea and he took it up with representatives of the IMF. He said to them, "Where is the evidence this is going to be good for developing countries? Why haven't you produced some research showing it was going to be good? They said: We don't need research; we know it's true. They didn't say it in precisely those words, but clearly they took it as religion."[65]

Rodrik noted another example of "faith-based economics" in terms of tax cuts comes from an interview with Kevin Hassett, economic advisor to John McCain. Toward the end of McCain's run for the presidency he began calling for more and more tax cuts as solutions to a wide variety of social ills. When Hassett was once pressed in an interview for evidence that lowering taxes helps the economy, he said, "What really happens is that the economy grows more vigorously when you lower tax rates. It is beyond the reach of economic science to explain precisely why that happens, but it does." The trouble is that it doesn't. Only a faith-based economic theology could make it seem so. In fact one of the (many) reasons why the economic stimulus package of early 2009 only modestly lifted the economy was that it was so weighted toward tax cuts, which have a very minor ability to influence commerce and create jobs. Rodrik commented on Hassett's words by saying that "you can be excused for thinking that the first of [Hassett's] statements is true, but only if you have an economically sound reason for it. But, as the second statement implies, there isn't one. I think it's time to stop referring to it as 'supply-side economics.' It is far more accurately described as 'faith-based economics,' and we should start calling it that."[66]

This sounds an awful lot like an old style of theological inquiry. In generations past theologians would begin with unprovable truths from revelation or natural law and then apply rigorous analysis to them to create great theological structures and dogmatic prescriptions — all of which were based on something that we *believe* to be true, but can't quite prove. For theologians, who of necessity struggle to make sense out of intangible, spiritual truths, this is inevitable. Economists unfortunately often do the same thing, except that they like to call their field a "science." They begin with abstract unprovable models drawn from commonly held assumptions about how the world works (which sound a lot like revelation or natural law), and then they develop elaborate economic theories and policies based on these models. Typically if an actual statistical test appears to falsify the theory behind the model, the test is rejected and the data is massaged and tweaked and the test redone until the results "prove" the theory. Why? Because economists believe the core tenets of their economic theory in much the same way that theologians believe the core tenets of their faith.

One of the few good things that could potentially come out of the present global economic crisis might be the realization (by people other than theologians and philosophers) of how much both Wall Street and Main Street had become so enthralled by the idols of self-interest and the god of finance that they put at risk the lives of millions of people around the globe to further their worship and their spiritual disciplines.

Finally, as an interesting aside, if you paid attention in your high school Philosophy 101 class, you may remember that Aristotle once famously spoke of the origins and purposes of money in ways that apply here. He said that humans acquire money for two reasons. The first and most "natural" reason is simply to gain the goods that we need for the "household" (the *oikonomiké*) or the larger "community" (the *polis*). The second and "unnatural" reason is to acquire wealth for its own sake (*chremastiké kapiliké*), as though money possession was an end in and of itself. In the first reason, money is a means to an important end. In the second it has a transcendent, almost god-like quality. The first, he said, is the "art of managing the household" and builds up the community. The second is competitive and ultimately destructive of the community. In the first, we acquire money because it is necessary for survival and for establishing the "Good Life," the moral life, the "virtuous" life. But in the second — which, by the way, emerged with the birth of regional and international trade — we create wealth for the sole purpose of creating wealth. For the first, we eventually hit a ceiling of how much we can acquire because our goal is a good life within the community. But with the second, there is no ceiling to what you can make because your goal is endless wealth acquisition through transactions. Aristotle had a particular disdain for what he called "money made from money" (*tokos ginetai nomisma ek nomismato*), by which he means investments, currency trading, and charging interest.[67]

There is, of course, a theological element in this. Making money for its own sake gives us a sense that we are larger and more than we actually are. It comes, Aristotle says, out of a desire for invincibility and immortality. It "puffs up," as the Apostle Paul might have added. In a subtle, unconscious way, we believe that we can become immortal — perhaps even divine — if we can acquire more life than was given us in birth. Through increasing wealth, we in effect believe that we are increasing life. However, says Aristotle, the by-product is that we eventually destroy the *polis,* the community that birthed us. When we put ourselves in competition with the rest of the planet, to be larger and wealthier than our neighbors, it invariably destroys the heart of community. Aristotle's antidote for this was education in ethics and more and better enforcement of regulations on finance.[68] Not bad suggestions, even today.

Conclusion

In spite of my sometimes critical words, I wouldn't actually argue that globalization is in itself a bad thing, and in any case it is probably an inevitable thing. What I do believe is that the philosophy and practice of our *particular* model of globalization disregards such values as the development of democracy, civil society, the equality of all human beings, and the protection of the environment. Globalization as we know it and practice it today is something like the shark in the 1970s Steven Spielberg movie *Jaws*. In it a mythical resort town called "Amityville" is terrorized by a deadly shark that is eating its way through the tourists. Richard Dreyfuss plays a young scientist who comes to town to help with the study and capture of the shark. In one scene he comments to the police chief that the shark they are hunting is not evil, but is just a "feeding machine." It will eat anything to keep itself alive, he says, anything in its path, with no thought about who is hurt or why. It bears no grudge. It seeks no favorites. It just eats. He bore no grudge against the shark. It was just doing what it does, which is to eat until it grows too big to function, and then it dies.

Globalization is like the shark. It does not have a conscience for either good or evil. It is a philosophy created solely for consumption. It too will eat anything in its path in order to continue to grow larger to benefit its creators. If it can make money by doing good, it will do good. If it can make money by doing harm, it will do harm. It isn't a moral decision, it's a business decision, a "feeding" decision. However, while it needs to eat to stay alive, it does not necessarily have to eat people or the environment to do so. Its grazing paths were not "destined before the foundation of the world" (1 Pet. 1:20). Communities of faith and conscience can — if they work hard and work together and learn the vagaries of the beast — redirect it toward health and growth and productivity for all. Or they can sit back and let the various elected and unelected officials of "Amityville" tell them that it is not really a problem, it is not really as bad as we think it is — and then watch as their community slowly is eaten away. With faith and courage and action we believe that another world is possible.

THREE

International Debt: Pat and Elaine

Debt is a new form of slavery as vicious as the slave trade.
— All-Africa Conference of Churches, 1999

The rich rule over the poor, and the borrower is slave of the lender.
— Proverbs 22:7

A few years ago I participated in a delegation sponsored by Church World Service to the poor Central American country of Honduras. We were there in part to help with some of the rebuilding efforts following Hurricane Mitch, but also in part to see some of the ongoing programs and projects that CWS was sponsoring in that country. At one point we traveled high up into the mountains, in the state of Intibucá, to visit a small community called Dominguez. One of our purposes there was to establish a library in the local school. CWS was in partnership with another fine nongovernmental organization called AlphaLit, which runs literacy programs all over the world. The arrangement was that CWS would donate the books and AlphaLit would organize literacy classes.

It was all a fine presentation and there were smiles all around, but when the festivities had ended one person in our group asked about the underlying issue of why we were even there. Why, she said, are we way up here setting up a library and literacy program in a school? Isn't this something, well, that schools do? Why isn't there a library here already? Why aren't there teachers teaching literacy here? Isn't this redundant? The answer from our host was revealing. Oh, he said, the government can't afford teachers. These schools were built years ago, during the big U.S. anticommunist building programs in Latin America, but we can only staff them with teachers for two or three months out of the year, sometimes fewer. Someone else then asked, Why doesn't the government have money for schools? His answer was equally revealing: Honduras, he said, has such an overwhelming and outstanding external debt that the annual payments on just the interest alone literally drained the country of the financial resources needed for what you and I would believe to be the most basic human services like education and health. Until finally receiving some debt relief from the Inter-American Development Bank in November of 2006, Honduras had been using more of its national income paying on its loans — many of which were a generation old — than it did on health care and education combined.

Here's another story. In the church I serve there is a wonderful family who moved here from Bolivia. A few years ago the father and his oldest son traveled back to their home to visit family and friends for a couple of months. When they returned, they regaled us with stories of how they rented a car and drove for days into the interior to visit cousins they hadn't seen in years. They told us hilarious and hair-raising tales of roads that had been overgrown by jungle or had deteriorated and crumbled down the edges of the mountains. They laughingly told how they had to get out and clear paths with machetes and shovels to get around boulders in order to continue. It made for great storytelling, but in the end someone asked the obvious question: Why doesn't the good government of Bolivia fix up its roads? Their answer was the same as that of our hosts in Honduras: Oh, the government doesn't have money for that kind of thing. It is too overwhelmed with paying back the loans it has had out for the past twenty-five years to be able to rebuild roads. Roads and highways are not nearly as important as paying banks for loans taken out by their grandparents over a generation ago.

These stories are telling in that they help me see in human terms the extent of the debt trap that afflicts so many countries in the global south. Countries like Honduras and Bolivia were far too poor to ever pay off their old debts, yet they could never develop economically until they had paid off their debts. It is a catch-22 that keeps countries like them impoverished forever unless something dramatic occurs that changes the rules and frees them from the crippling burden that has weighed them down for so many years. The hard facts of that reality were what brought such campaigns as the international Jubilee movement, Bono's "Debt and Trade in Africa," the

American Friends Service Committee's "Life over Debt" and many others into existence.

There are a variety of reasons why countries acquired those debts — some were their "fault" and some not — but the reality is that today they live not just under the burden of making punishing debt payments, but also under the strict and crippling "Washington Consensus" austerity programs of the International Monetary Fund (IMF) and other international financial institutions as pre-requirements for receiving financial "help." One of the goals of this chapter will be to make the connection between the debt crisis that began in the early 1980s and the development of our present hyper-globalized, hyper-economically integrated world. The debt crisis is one of the most important causes of the present surge in economic globalization, and it is one that is rarely discussed by analysts.

In many ways that crisis, and the strict repayment rules that followed it, did more to integrate poor country markets, economies, and cultures into the market fold of rich countries than any other single event in the past two hundred years. It's easy to overlook how dramatic this event was in the history of the planet because it seems like a simple banking transaction. A bank gives out a loan to a country and the country pays it back. It sounds fairly straightforward. But look at the scenario more closely. Let's say that the country of Bolivia wants to borrow a half a billion dollars from a consortium of banks in the United States to help pave and repair all of those inland roads that my friends had such a harrowing experience on when they went home. It's a worthy project. And a new road would be a good economic development project for the region. For example, potatoes have been a staple crop up in Bolivia's highlands for over a thousand years, and a good road up there would not only help my friends travel around, but would also get crops like potatoes and wheat down to the cities to be sold in markets. Let's say too that the money was spent wisely — not always the case, but grant it for this illustration. They hired contractors and workers and spent the money on good people doing good work, and at the end of the day they have a few more decent roads into the interior and everyone is happy. But now the government of Bolivia has to pay the money back. What does it pay with? Can they pay the Bank of America back with their local currency, the *boliviano*? Not likely. The bank may be full of nice people, but they loaned out dollars and want dollars back when repayment time comes.

So where does Bolivia get dollars? They can buy them (but that's a bit counterproductive) or they can borrow them (and then have the same problem one more time) or — as more often happened — they can start selling some of those potatoes and maybe some wheat and corn to the United States and then take their payment in dollars. And then they send those same dollars (more or less) back to the United States, to the banks, in repayment for the loans. So the more they borrowed from U.S. banks, the more they needed to produce something to sell to U.S. markets to get the dollars they then used to pay back the U.S. banks. In fact, the larger the debt became, the more intense was the need — the demand really — that Bolivia (and dozens of other developing countries) completely reorient their entire economy, from production for *internal* consumption to production for *external* consumption in foreign countries. Long before the "Washington Consensus," or "structural adjustment" programs were imposed on countries as ways of belt-tightening and loan repaying, a good many countries already were beginning to push their inward economies outward toward exports.

In Guatemala, for example, instead of growing corn (maize), which for centuries they grew themselves and consumed themselves, now it was more and more often forced to grow cotton, cardamom, hemp, flowers, sesame seeds, and winter vegetables for exports so that their government could get dollar currency to pay back to the United States on their foreign loans. The result is that for the first time in its entire history, Guatemala imports 20 percent of its corn for consumption from the United States.[1] Another reason for the decline in corn production, of course, was the flood of state-subsidized U.S. corn, which is cheaper than it costs local farmers to produce it. This was made worse following Guatemala's joining the Central American Free Trade Agreement.

The IMF functions like an international gatekeeper for all other global financial institutions. It puts pressure on poor and developing countries of the global south to make these cutbacks on expenditures so that they will be able to make debt payments. Over the past twenty-five years or so, in order to qualify for aid or limited debt cancelation, their governments have been forced to divert scarce dollars to pay off the old debts rather than spend them on health, education, or infrastructure. Kenya, for example, spends around 22 percent of its annual budget on servicing its debt, which is about the same as what it spends on health, roads, water, agriculture, transportation, and finance *combined*. Unsurprisingly, the human cost of shifting resources from health care and education to debt payments has been tremendous. A number of countries had improved in these areas during the 1960s and 1970s, but then saw them decline dramatically with the start of the debt crisis in the early 1980s. In the evaluation of globalization in our last chapter, we showed how a good many countries grew more slowly or actually declined during the last twenty-five years of globalization. The back story on that is that most of those poor countries entered the globalizing treadmill, because they had to produce ever more products for export in order to make payments on their growing debts.

It's hard to exaggerate how much difference this simple production change made in the lives, cultures, and economies of so many countries. In one generation the countries gutted centuries of production habits and became a piece of the international production-consumption process, and the effect that it had on their personalities and self-understandings as a race or people is profound. Not all, but a lot of the animosity of millions in the global south toward the wealthy countries of the global north is from the people in those countries who had to give up so much so that the business and trade interests of the north could be served so well.

Snapshots of the Extent of the Crisis

One good way to get a handle on the impact of the debt on poor countries around the world is to make a few comparisons of the amount of aid money going into them with the debt payment money coming out. Here's one example. In June 2007, over a span of one week, a number of organizations did some wonderful work in raising money to fight malaria in Africa. One was the Millennium Promise, which raised $2.7 million at a Manhattan fundraiser. Another was the drug company Novartis, which promised that same week to practically give away — by selling below market price — tens of millions of doses of its antimalaria drugs, the equivalent of $50 million. And the third was the Global Business Coalition on HIV/AIDS, Tuberculosis, and Malaria, which held a dinner and raised $2 million. Now, this is all good work, and it was a very impressive week for people of conscience. However, the fact is that just a handful of Africa's poorest countries send the same amount of money as was raised that week back to banks and other financial institutions as payments on their debts about every three days.[2]

Here's another example. Some years ago the UK's Comic Relief spent a full year doing concerts as fund raisers and raised £26 million for aid to Africa. That is also a lot of money, but in this case it was about equal to what Africa paid back to Europe in debt payments in just one day.[3] These comparisons are depressing, aren't they? Here is another example from Honduras, which I mentioned earlier. This is one of the poorest countries in Latin America, and it receives about $30 million in foreign aid from the United States each year. However, before its recent debt cancelation (for which we should all be pleased), it paid back to the United States, to banks, and "multilateral" (meaning international) financial institutions, more than that amount *every three weeks*. And these countries are not unique. The developing world on average spends about $1.30 on debt repayment for every $1 it receives in grants.[4]

What all of these stories tell us in real terms is that you can give money to Church World Service, World Vision, Habitat for Humanity, Heifer International, or any other reputable organization, and at the same time the United States can double or triple its aid to these countries, and still there is no way that they can dig their way out from underneath the crushing debts that are draining their futures away. One of the indigenous Mayan communities of Guatemala has an expression that says when you are walking backward, no matter how fast you go, you can never go forward.

Here are two final examples from Africa, which are typical of a number of other countries in the same situation. In the first, Zambia took out a number of loans in the 1970s and by the 1980s it had acquired around $3.26 billion in total external debt. Over the next decades it faithfully paid on its debt and cut back on its borrowing. However, by the time of an international debt cancelation conference in 2005, it announced that over those years it had paid a total of $4.5 billion and yet still owed $7.2 billion.[5] Second, Nigeria: In the mid-1980s Nigeria's total external debt amounted to $19 billion. Over the next twenty years it paid back about $35 billion, it borrowed only about $15 billion, and yet by the time of the conference in 2005 it still owed a whopping $36 billion! This same pattern has occurred in many other countries as well. In general, over the past three decades, the poorest countries of the world (more than sixty altogether), have owed about $540 billion, paid back about $550 billion (in both principal and interest), and yet still owe $523 billion.

The total external debt of Latin America tells a similar story. It was $60 billion in the mid-1970s. By 1980 it had grown to $204 billion, and by 1990 it was $433 billion. By the end of 1999, as interest continued to pile up, it reached $706 billion. All told, Latin American countries are paying first world countries (mainly the United States) $123 billion a year in debt service.[6] By 2008, even with a variety of very hopeful, positive cancelations, total Latin American debt had still grown to nearly $800 billion. Not a bad return on money, considering that the poor and developing countries of the world actually have paid off the principal of the debts years ago, so now all of the punishing, crippling payments are just icing on the cake.

One reason for this continued growth in debt comes from the fact that even in hard times a country still has to borrow from a line of credit for big projects and to stabilize its currency. Another is that some countries that are really strapped have actually been encouraged by financial advisors from the banks or the IMF to borrow even more new money to pay off the old money. Finally, a less obvious reason is the sinkhole of compounding interest. When a country can't pay on a loan, the interest still continues to grow. That interest is then added onto the principal, which creates an even larger debt bill, even if the country has cut back on its borrowing or in some instances has stopped borrowing altogether.

All of these examples of the size and extent of the debt are just numbers on a page until you see them connected to real people and real communities. It is estimated that around 7 million children die each year as a result of the debt crisis (in addition to wars, famine, underdevelopment, legacies of colonialism, etc.). Because indebted countries are so frequently required to cut subsidies for food, transportation, education, health, etc. (so that the governments can save money for repayment on their debts), poor children in those countries are harmed at alarming and unnecessary levels. Had the debt for the world's poorest countries been canceled back in 1997, when the international Jubilee movement first began, the money released for basic healthcare could have saved the lives of about 21 million children by the year 2000, the equivalent of 19,000 children a day.[7]

How Much Would It Cost?

It is often argued by bankers and government officials that the debts would be simply too expensive for wealthy countries to cancel. Moreover, we can assume that now that the entire globe has been wracked with a debt-related financial crisis, any call for cancelation of the debts of our poorer brothers and sisters will look even more impossible. So how much money are we talking about? Jubilee USA has estimated that there are around sixty to sixty-five countries that need total debt cancelation, with a total population of 1,037 million, and that together they shoulder a debt burden of $320 billion. The portion that the heavily indebted poor nations owe to the United States is about $6.8 billion. To put those numbers in perspective, here are a few comparisons:

- The total amount of the 1980s savings and loan bailout was $165 billion.[8]

- The total amount authorized by Congress in October 2008 for the first financial rescue package was $750 billion.

- According to research by economists Joseph Stiglitz and Linda Bilmes, the estimated total cost of the war in Iraq on the overall economy of the United States was $3 trillion in 2007. That translates into about $12 billion a day and about six times the amount needed to cancel all debts of all poor countries in the world.

Or, put another way:

- For a week's worth of the expense of the war in Iraq, we could create an interest-producing endowment that, under "normal" times of investment returns, could fund development in poor countries for the rest of eternity (well, more or less).

- In terms of individual human wealth, the amount needed to cancel all developing country debt is less than the net worth of the world's twenty-one richest individuals.

- Spread over twenty years, canceling the debts is one penny a day for each person in the developed world.

- And finally, following the recent Wall Street scandal, it seems only fair to make a few comparisons with bonuses paid out to the thieves who squandered money taken from our home loans on their gambling addiction to unproductive, shortsighted, and blatantly risky ventures. Goldman Sachs, for example, paid its chairman and chief executive officer, Lloyd Blankfein, $54 million. It paid co-presidents Gary Cohn and Jon Winkelried $53 million each, including cash bonuses of $26.7 million.[9] Their annual pay and benefit packages equal roughly what all sub-Saharan African countries pay on their debts *every three hours* in interest and capital repayments. Merrill Lynch, after its executives completely drove the business in the ditch and while it was losing money at around $27 million a minute, secretly decided to pay its top four executives $121 million each in bonuses; the next four got $62 million, and the next six received $66 million, for a total of $3.6 billion.[10] That's roughly the amount of money it would take to pay off all of the debts of Africa, Latin America, and everything my Uncle Al lost in horse racing that time back in 1967 in Ruidoso Downs, New Mexico (but that's another story).

A Personal Loan Analogy

In order to understand the extent of the problem, let's bring the story closer to home by putting it in personal terms. What would all of this look like if it happened to one person's individual budget?

Let's say a generation or two ago your grandfather took out some loans for an office complex he never got around to building from some unscrupulous bankers who never checked on how the construction was going, and then died old and happy on Marco Island drinking too many of those little drinks with umbrellas sticking out of them (alongside some of the bankers with whom he had become close friends). Starting the story of your financial problems back two generations makes sense, because the first loans of today's debt crisis were taken out in the 1970s, when most of the people who are paying them back today were only children (if born at all). In your story, your grandfather left you a will, which is nice, but instead of the personal fortune you expected, he bequeathed you his enormous debts and you were left with the absolute, binding, legal responsibility of paying them all back.

How do you do it? Imagine that your annual income is $50,000 (above average for a U.S. citizen), and your normal present monthly expenditures are about $4,200, which actually comes out a little over $50,000 per year (unfortunately it's not uncommon for Americans to go in the hole slightly every year, so you are at least normal). However, the debt payments on your "inheritance" are about $2,000 per month (about half the size of your monthly income), and the new payments go on top of your other normal living expenses. That means that your outgoing expenditures will go up by one third, and you will have to cut your normal monthly expenses nearly in half just to break even (which you weren't totally doing before).

So here's how you do it. The first and most important thing that you should know is that you are not allowed to file for bankruptcy. There is no bankruptcy in the international finance world, so in this analogy, you don't get that option. If you tried it, you would be banned from purchasing anything ever again from anyone outside of your own immediate family and household. Or if you tried to simply stop paying on the loans, you would be completely cut off from the rest of the outside community, and you would eventually starve. Imagine, for example, not being able to buy a car or a large appliance because you can't get a loan (nobody can get by without taking out a loan sometime) and you'll see how constricting that would be.

Now, to pay on the loans, first you would be told you must cut out all nonessentials (like computers, bed sheets, towels, TV, or more than one shirt), but of course that wouldn't be enough. Next would be cuts in the real essentials, like your health plan. You will have to get by without it. There are, as you know, millions of Americans who are forced to do this, and it's typically pretty scary. Next comes food. You don't need to eat healthy foods, and you probably don't need to have more than two meals per day. It will be difficult and painful, but you can make it. Much of the world gets by without three meals a day, so you have now joined them.

Then education: forget saving for your children's college tuition. In fact, forget sending them to school at all, because the private schools in your neighborhood are too expensive, and the IMF has forced your town to charge expensive user fees for public education as well. It's a part of its "aid" package to "help" your town raise money to pay on its own debts. So you no longer can afford any kind of education for your children, public or private. But that's okay. They shouldn't go to school anyway, because they need to go to work to earn money to pay back the debts. Next comes upkeep on your home. Don't even think about repairing the doors and windows, even though they need it, because you can't afford the carpenter, let alone the wood and nails. You can't even afford the tools to repair them yourself. So let the garage collapse and the porch sag; the banks need their money more than the house does. Forget too about heat and electricity. You can get along without it most of the year, and you need to save every penny to make the additional $2,000 per month in loan payments.

But even all of this is not enough. With all of these cuts, you are still only able to come up with an extra $1200 payment per month. To meet the level of payments demanded of you on your grandfather's debts, you still need at least another $800 per month. The only places to go for new cash are the government and private banks, which by the way are in cahoots with the local stores and constable who are enforcing these rules on you (and the constable probably defines his job as punishing you if you break the payback rules of your grandfather's loans).

So to pay your loans, these friendly "helpers" float you another loan, which once again you are not allowed to default on, with interest that rolls over into the principal and that therefore gradually increases the size of the total debt. Some years ago Honduras, the poorest country in Central America, was hit by a ferocious hurricane and nearly defaulted on all of its loans. To "help" them out the "Paris Club" (an organization of wealthy countries that coordinate loans together) agreed to allow Honduras to suspend payments for five years. Sounds good until you hear that they also allowed the interest ticker to keep on running during those five years. That meant that when Honduras — still battered and beaten and nearly crushed as a country — began making payments again, the loan balance was nearly a third higher than before. (Thanks for the help, guys, but next time I think I'll go it alone.) In your personal loan story, your lenders agree to give you this loan on the condition that you agree to cut back further in your expenditures on health, education, and infrastructure, and you agree to work where they tell you to work, produce what they tell you to produce, and spend what they tell you to spend, all so that you will have the money to send back to them in payments on your grandfather's debt (plus interest, of course).

With the "help" of the local banks and government "aid" agencies, you and your family are now starving, uneducated, in poor health, in a crumbling home, and you are borrowing money from one bank to pay off money owed to another bank, on loans that your grandfather took out to retire to an island. Welcome to the "Washington Consensus," the neoliberal, free market philosophy of a smoothly running global economic system. Now, to be fair, if you are able to survive the aid being given you (and your kids don't stage a revolt and take over the house and refuse to pay the debts), it is entirely possible that you will eventually be able to pay off the original debt and the subsequent debt, and eventually after you are dead your children could start seeing incomes that approached yours before this mess all began . . . but at what price? Do you think that your scarred, bruised children who saw you die of exhaustion and their childhoods ruined will look back on this experience and say the path forced on them for debt freedom was worth it? If the numerous stories of poor countries who suffered through the IMF medicine and then refused to ever again take their help is any indication, the answer is no.

This story is roughly analogous to what the developing world debt crisis is all about. It may be slightly exaggerated, but unfortunately not by much. If it sounds vaguely similar to the kinds of abuses of debts and loans that Amos and Nehemiah were complaining about in the Hebrew scriptures, you're right. There is much of the same mentality here as can be seen in the wealthy landowners of biblical times loaning money to their poor neighbors, jacking up the interest, and then forcing them into poverty and slavery to get it back. Some things never change, do they?

History of the Debt Crisis: How We Got from There to Here

The above is a parable, but it is a fairly accurate representation of the present crisis. The following is a more historical review of the same story.

In the 1960s the United States spent huge sums of money on the Vietnam War and paid for it by printing dollars instead of raising taxes. You may recall that the Bush administration did a similar thing in the early 2000s. It not only didn't raise taxes to fund the wars but actually cut them, creating much of the huge and intractable deficits that we have today. One of the things created by all of that new money flushing through the system, then as now, was that the economy actually experienced a temporary economic boom at home even while fighting a war abroad. However, as it goes with basic supply and demand economics, when you produce too much of one thing the value of each individual one of them goes down, and eventually the value of each dollar declined. We in America did not feel it immediately, but other countries (who did not have the benefit of our money-printing machines) felt the value of their dollars dropping everywhere.

Some countries back in the 1960s responded by coming together and creating cartels to help prop up the prices of their exports. The oil-producing countries were particularly hurt by the drop in the value of the dollar because their oil was purchased in dollars. As a response, in 1972 the finance ministers of the Organization of Petroleum Exporting Countries (OPEC) met together and announced increases in oil prices at breathtaking levels.

I don't want to make this overly complicated, but they actually raised the price of oil in two phases. First, they tied the price of oil to the price of gold. The significance of that was that in 1971 the United States had uncoupled the value of the dollar from the price of gold and allowed it to float up and down with the market. That was one of the reasons why the dollar's value had declined, starting all of this. Moreover, since the price of gold happened to be skyrocketing in value when the United States took that action, prices for Middle Eastern oil did the same.

The second action was ostensibly a reaction to the Yom Kippur War. The Arabic-speaking countries of OPEC announced that they would punish all of the countries who had supported Israel in that war with an oil embargo. They specifically targeted the United States because we have always been Israel's biggest ally and financial benefactor, but they also went after other wealthy gas-guzzling countries that sided with Israel in less dramatic ways. The United States still had access to oil from other sources, but — because it was now more scarce — it would be at a higher price. And since oil usage is global, when prices go up in one part of the world, they go up everywhere. So every oil-producing country made at least some money off of the increases, even if they had no hand in the embargo.

In the three months following the embargo announcement, the price of oil around the world quadrupled to nearly $12 per barrel (a high price in those days). Over the next year and a half, the price of Saudi light crude oil soared from $2 per barrel to over $13 per barrel. The price then leveled off for a few years to just under $15 per barrel until 1979, the next time they raised prices. Then, from 1979 to 1981 crude oil prices more than doubled again to $35 per barrel. The price at the pump rose from 38 cents per gallon in 1973 to 55 cents in 1974 and from about 55 cents in 1979 to nearly a dollar in 1982. Those prices sound meager by today's standards, but relative to other prices at the time, it was a shock. The 1973 increase was 210 percent. The 1979–80 increase was 135 percent.

If you are of a "certain age" (as they say), you will recall what the price shocks did to the American economy back in those days. Suddenly there were long lines at gas pumps all over the country and the Nixon/Ford administrations called for gas rationing. The way it worked was that if you had an even number on your license tag (including "vanity" plates), you could buy gas on even-numbered days of the month, and if you had an odd-numbered license tag you could buy it on the odd-numbered days. I was a divinity student at Vanderbilt University in the early 1970s, and I served a little weekend student church about a hundred miles away in Marion, Kentucky. My pre-oil-shock agenda was that I would drive up to Marion on Saturdays, visit a few people, spend the night, preach the next morning, have fried chicken for lunch with a church family, and then drive home again. But with gas rationing, that got much more complicated. On those Saturdays that fell on even numbers, I would fill up my even-numbered-tagged car and make the drive, but the next day one of the church parishioners would have to fill up my car with a big gas tank he had filled up the day before and saved for me, so that I could make the drive home. On those Saturdays that fell on odd numbered days, I would borrow the car of a young woman I was dating who had an odd-numbered tag. What was nice about that was that her car got better gas mileage, so I could drive all the way up and back again on one tank of gas. That was the complicated way that we all survived the oil crises of the 1970s.

This arrangement made the OPEC countries more money than they had ever seen before (somewhere in the neighborhood of 400 hexa-quadra-trazillion dollars...and change). They made so much money that they were not able to spend it or store it inside their respective countries. There is a story (perhaps apocryphal, but still telling) that Saudi Arabia, during those days, made so much money that they literally could not store it in their central bank. The checks just took up too much space. So much so that they had to build a special banking warehouse just to stack the paper that came into their country.

It is beyond the scope of this book, but interesting to note in passing, that the explosion of wealth was not always a good thing for the oil-producing countries either. A rapid increase in wealth can have a negative impact on a country. Today more than half of the OPEC countries are poorer than they were back during the oil boom of the 1970s. The problem is sometimes called the "Norway Curse," named after the time when Norway discovered oil in the North Sea. That was seen as a good thing at the time, but it eventually caused its economy to slide downward. That seems counterintuitive, but what happened was that the increase in exports of oil drove up the value of its national currency, which then made its manufactured and agricultural exports go up in price relative to similar products in other countries and which then made the country less competitive. (This is complicated, but when the value of a country's money is low, it costs less for people in other countries to buy its products; when it is high, it costs more for them to buy the same products.) So while oil exports went up, all other exports went down, and eventually Norway's overall economy slumped. Norway is an advanced country and eventually pulled itself back up, but many less developed countries, with unstable institutions and weaker leadership, have been badly damaged by this syndrome. Nigeria, for example, was an early beneficiary of the oil production boom of the early 1970s, but at the same time saw its agricultural exports drop from 11.2 percent of GDP (gross domestic product) in 1968 to 2.8 percent in 1972. That is a serious collapse, from which the country has yet to recover.

New money also often brings corruption and waste. In Nigeria, tens of thousands of entrepreneurs flocked to Lagos and printed up business cards with "Contractor" on them to get a piece of the oil-rich pie. It became the world's largest importer of champagne, with gold bathtubs being not far behind. It is estimated that in the 1970s one-eighth of the world's merchant fleet was waiting offshore to unload imports, usually of luxury items. In 1975 politicians ordered 20 million tons of cement, enough to build an entire city. They paid for it out of government funds at hugely inflated prices and then received the difference between the inflated and actual price as kickbacks. When questions were raised, the buildings containing government records mysteriously burned to the ground.[11]

Sometimes wars and internal disruptions can come from oil wealth that many see as easy money. A prominent example of this today is, of course, Iraq, where Sunni and Shiite militias battle each other for rights to the only lucrative export the country still has. But rebel movements in Nigeria, Algeria, Thailand, the Niger Delta, Colombia, and Sudan finance themselves in part by stealing oil from government or private pipelines. Colombia has the interesting distinction of having both the right-wing paramilitaries and the left-wing FARC tapping pipelines, or offering "protection" for a price, to finance their respective movements.[12]

The place where all of this touches on the debt crisis was that the OPEC countries solved their abundance-of-money "problem" by investing their newly acquired "petrodollars" in the banks of wealthy countries. That created another problem, however, because, while the banks suddenly had more money than they had ever conceived possible, the United States and northern Europe were going through a recession (caused in part by the inflationary spending of the 1960s) and had few people wanting to borrow the money. When a country is in a recession, people don't buy as many things. Developers don't build shopping malls because people aren't going to shop in them, and they don't build housing developments because people aren't going to buy them. The banks were in the dilemma of having an enormous amount of money to loan out but few people who wanted to borrow it.

At about this time, the people in the banks began to realize that something radically new needed to be done with this incredible stock of money, just begging to be loaned out for interest and profit. So for the first time in the history of banking, someone — we don't know who first thought of it — came to the novel conclusion that banks did not have to loan just to individuals or corporations, but they could actually loan directly to sovereign governments as well. And the first piece of the present debt crisis puzzle fell into place.

There actually had been scattered instances of banks loaning to countries before that time, but nothing on the scale of what eventually evolved. In the midst of this recession, which was depressing commerce in wealthy countries and driving poor countries to desperation, literally hundreds of banks in wealthy countries, flush with petrodollars, launched programs that shoveled money out the door at an amazing rate to poor countries starved for cash.

I gave a talk in a church just north of Boston some years ago about the origins of the international external debt crisis. I walked through the factors that brought the banks to this point of pushing loans on poor countries, the impact those loans had on the countries later on, and what we should do about it. I think the talk was fairly well received. Following the talk a retired banker, who had been active in arranging some of those very loans back in the 1970s, came up to me and said, "You didn't get it right." I wasn't sure what he meant. "You didn't say enough about the pushing. We pushed and cajoled and did everything we could to force those countries to take loans." That got my attention. "We got raises," he said, "not because the loans were any good, but just because of the number and size of them. It was a crazy time. We were making loans we knew were no good, but we did it anyway. It was a crazy time."

His experience has been mirrored by leaders of the countries receiving the loans. One minister of finance from a Latin American country told an interviewer that whenever he would go to international conferences, he would be accosted by U.S. bankers offering loans. "They wouldn't leave me alone," he said. "If you're trying to balance your budget, it's very tempting to borrow money instead of raising taxes to put off the agony."[13] Eventually he caved in and accepted a huge loan that his country never really needed and that his people thirty years later are probably still paying on.

Countries that needed loans got money. Countries that might need loans later on got money. Countries that didn't need loans at all got money. It didn't really matter to the banks. Some countries took the loans because they were poor, the oil price shocks were crippling their economies, and they needed a loan just to get by. These were sometimes called "consumption loans," taken out simply to pay the bills. During the 1960s, for example, the United States had dramatically increased its aid to Latin America as a way of buying favor in the wake of the rise of Fidel Castro. But during the 1970s our fear of Cuba subsided, and with it came a decline in interest in giving foreign aid. Poor countries that were expecting our aid and reeling over oil prices began to take out huge loans. Another enticement for taking a commercial bank loan was that it came with fewer strings attached. When a government, such as the United States, gave a loan, it usually had a specific development-related purpose, such as a dam or rural electrification, and numerous "Buy American" strings. But when a bank offered money it was usually a block loan, often described as "for general purposes," to be spent in any way the country pleased. A functioning democracy like Costa Rica could spend it on road improvements, or a dictator like Congo/Zaire's Mobutu Sese Seko could spend it on weapons to be used on his own people, and the banks would seldom care.[14]

In Nigeria, in 1975, right in the middle of the champagne, gold bathtubs, and cement over-purchase scandal, First Chicago Bank and Trust arranged a $1.4 billion loan to the Nigerian government for mostly "undesignated" purposes. The money was ostensibly to pay back the government for the rampant embezzlement at the root of the scandal, but mainly it just continued it. Did anyone check this loan out to see if Nigeria would be a viable recipient of this kind of money? Or did they just not care?

Other countries took out loans simply because the deals were impossible to pass up, often at below market rates. For a while loans were actually being offered at negative real interest rates, meaning that at the end of the payment period the country would have paid back less than the amount borrowed. The theory of development pushed by the banks and their co-conspirators in the World Bank, the IMF, and various governments, was that an increase in indebtedness would eventually create an increase in exports, which would create an increase in income, which would create an increase in standards of living. Borrow the money, spend it (wisely, one hoped) on economic development projects, and within ten years you will not only pay back the loans, but you will have developed so much economically that you would be considered a first world country. It was called "the doctrine of debt as the path towards accelerated development."[15] Or occasionally by its critics as the "Snake Oil" theory of development. One doesn't have to think too hard to understand why.[16]

In the swirl and flood of big money, banks often competed with one another to make big loans and often joined with other banks to get a piece of their action. In 1979 Bank of America was attempting to arrange a loan to a Latin American country. The loan was already large, over $1 billion, but it got larger when others heard about the project and joined in. Bank of America couldn't finance the entire amount itself, so it planned to put up $350 million, and then sell off the rest. But the size (not the quality) of the loan was so popular that in the end Bank of America had to put up only $100 million, and other banks added an additional $2.4 billion to the loan — two and a half times more than the country had requested or needed. It was like a Christmas tree with everyone adding its own ornament.[17]

These stories have three things in common. First, it didn't matter whether a country asked for a loan, wanted a loan, needed a loan, or asked for it out of greed, graft, or corruption. In the end the loans would be granted anyway with no oversight or due diligence. There is a story, for example, of one bank loan officer who read an article about Costa Rica in *Time* magazine and called up the government to offer it a loan.[18] Second, and we will say more about this below, in 1982 a confluence of rising interest rates and collapsing income from exports caught up all countries, not just those with moral, ethical, functioning, democratic governments. The good, the bad, and the ugly all went down when the credit crisis hit, sweeping everybody up (or actually down) in its wake. Third, no matter who was at fault, at the end of the story it is always the poor people within the poor countries who have to bear the worst brunt of the clean up. This is another parallel with the present financial mess that began on Wall Street. The people at the top who are most responsible for the disaster still have high-paying jobs, while many of the people at the bottom who were caught up in the money shell game lost their homes, their jobs, and their livelihoods and are often living with family or in neighboring homeless shelters.

Similarly, with few exceptions, the wealthy bankers in the United States and Europe, and the wealthy presidents and finance ministers of the poor and developing countries have all retired — still wealthy — in pleasant homes with pleasant surroundings. But those who are paying for the debacle are the children and grandchildren in the borrowing countries who have now seen support for their education, health care, sanitation, and infrastructure crumble in order to save money to make loan payments. Whenever someone says today, as people do often say, "Well, I believe in personal responsibility; I believe if they take out a loan they ought to pay it back," tell them, well, yes, I agree, and let's go to that banker who pushed the loans to get a promotion and who has now retired to a $10 million home in the Port Royal neighborhood of Naples, Florida, or the dictator who pocketed the loan and who has now retired on one of his seven yachts off the Cayman Islands, and let's see which one of them we can get to pay up. But let's not go to the kids at that abandoned school back in Dominguez, Honduras, where we were opening that library, and tell them that in order to pay off the debt that the banker and the dictator arranged thirty years ago, their school will have to be closed. It's not only a bad line of logic, it's also immoral.

The Day the Music Died

In 1982 this dance of pushing and pulling loans came to a quick and painful end. It began with the U.S. Federal Reserve raising interest rates dramatically in order to help slow down the "stagflation" that had gripped the economy during the late 1970s. ("Stagflation" was the term coined in the 1970s for the condition of inflation and stagnation at the same time.) The action worked, but it also threw the U.S. economy into a deep recession. What that meant for poor indebted countries was (1) because of the recession, the United States (and Europe) bought fewer of their goods; and (2) because of the rise in interest rates, the amount of their loan payments doubled.

That caused a "perfect storm" of a disaster to hit the poor and developing countries of the global south. They spiraled downward into an impossible debt trap. Their ability to pay on the loans went down at the same time that the amount they needed to pay on them went up. Earnings from their exports dropped by 28 percent in 1981 and 1982, while the interest rates on their commercial bank loans rose from an average of 0.5 percent to an average of 13.1 percent, with some soaring as high as 27 percent![19] That is unpayable by any definition — except perhaps that of the bankers who made the original loans. If there had been an international mechanism for bankruptcy (and as we learned above, there wasn't), this would have been the time that it kicked in. The indebted countries spiraled steadily downward and backward. Some — most particularly, Mexico and some of the larger developing countries — received major bailouts. Some of the rest received heavily conditioned loans from the multilateral lending institutions, like the World Bank and the IMF, about which we will have more to say soon. And many are today poorer and less economically developed than they were before the crisis struck thirty years ago.

Attempts to Address the Crisis

So this was the story of how the more than sixty poor and developing countries of the global south came to be tied to the crippling debts that have pulled them down, driven their people deeper into poverty, and damaged their prospects for a better future. But it only brings the story up to about the mid-1980s. From that time to the present there have been a number of attempts to "fix" their problems. A few of those plans have met with some success, some have just perpetuated the status quo, and some have made the situation worse. We'll take a look now at the most prominent of those plans, and then at the end of the chapter we'll share a few words on some of the ways you can get involved to work for a healthier, more ethically responsible international financial system.

As we've noted, there are many similarities between the debt disaster of 1982 and the bursting of the housing loan bubble in 2007 and 2008. In both instances aggressive agents pushed loans onto borrowers who could ill afford them at variable rates of interest. In both, some of the borrowers were poor and desperate and took the loans to get ahead, whereas others were unscrupulous and took the loans to make a killing. But in the end, the explosion of the two bubbles took everyone down together.

The responses to the two crises had similarities as well. In both, the first inclination of the rescuers was to help the lenders and not the borrowers. The first money spent on the housing loan crisis was directed, not at the poor families who were in default and now living in their in-laws' garage, but at the wealthy financial institutions that made the unwise — occasionally immoral and illegal — loans. The first plan of Treasury Secretary Henry Paulson was to buy up the huge loan packages that were on the secondary market, and thus help protect the incomes of the banks. That was essentially the same direction taken by the IMF and the World Bank in the early 1980s when they bought up the bad loans from the commercial banks. However, in Paulson's case, he eventually changed that course because he realized how fundamentally "globalized" those loans had become and that buying them individually would be impossible. Instead he bought stock in the financial institutions themselves. In the earlier crisis, the loans to developing countries were usually still held by their originators, so the plan of buying them up to rescue the banks went forward. The IMF and the

World Bank (using taxpayer money) bailed out dozens of (mainly U.S.) banks by purchasing billions of dollars' worth of their most shaky and discounted loans. But it's important to point out that in both of the crises the rescuers made it clear that their first priority was helping those who had made the terrible loans, not those who (occasionally under pressure) had taken them. It's interesting (though fruitless) to ponder where our recession might be today if the Bush bailout money had gone to the places where the crisis started — homeowners who couldn't make their mortgage payments — instead of where the crisis landed — the bankers who saw their gambling money dry up. It was like trying to stop a leaky faucet by throwing sponges on the floor, but doing nothing about the leak itself.

This bias in the 2008 bailout money was not lost on the people at the Jubilee USA network, the organization most dedicated to ending developing country debts. At the height of the debate over how to spend Congress' $700 billion package, they were at a meeting of the IMF/World Bank encouraging them to "act with the same urgency in tackling the food crisis and global poverty crisis as they have the banking crisis." Neil Watkins, national coordinator of Jubilee USA Network, put the matter bluntly: for the IMF to tell a country like Haiti (which had just experienced four hurricanes, a food crisis, and a tragic school collapse) that their debt cancelation was going to be put off one more time, was "like Hank Paulson telling Wall Street he will get back to them sometime next year." "As we've seen this month," he said, "when Wall Street bankers are affected, they get fast tracked for debt relief. But the people of Haiti don't seem to matter very much in Washington."[20]

It's interesting to note that after Haiti's horrific earthquake of January 2010, the IMF offered Haiti $102 million in new reconstruction money. However, it was in the form of a loan, not a grant, further perpetuating its ongoing, damaging debt problems. Haiti owes various banks and countries over a billion dollars, and until this most recent tragedy it paid out around $20 million a year, which is roughly equal to the foreign aid that the United States gave Haiti each year. When the IMF announced its new loan, Jubilee, Oxfam, the ONE campaign, Jewish World Service, and many others campaigned to get the IMF to offer the money as a grant instead of a loan, but the IMF refused. Presumably it believed that the poorest

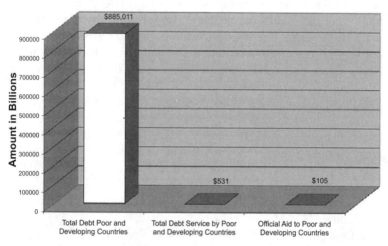

Figure 4. Aid and Debt Flows in 2008

Source: World Development Indicators database, September 2009, *www.worldbank.org.*

country in the hemisphere, and now the most devastated, somehow had the productive capacity to pay it back, someday, somehow.

The "Baker Plan"

The first "solutions" to the debt crisis were standard banking solutions, based on the misconception that the problem was a temporary liquidity problem. They tried rollovers, refinancing (taking out new debt to pay on old debt), rescheduling, and renegotiation. In 1985 the Reagan administration's secretary of the treasury James Baker launched a plan (called the "Baker Plan"), which packaged all of these ideas together along with some new ones, such as opportunities to consolidate or diversify the loans, or even to buy them back at a lower rate. One interesting idea was "Debt for Equity Swaps," whereby a country swaps part of its productive capacity in exchange for the cancelation of some portion of its debts. For example, Chile agreed to give away its national pension and social security program to a bank in Chicago in exchange for alleviation of some of its debt load. It worked, but it was a major psychic crisis to lose an entity so central to Chilean national identity. But even with these new programs, the Baker Plan had little real effect on the debt crisis because it continued the false assumption that countries actually were wealthy enough to pay back the old loans, which they clearly were not. The real underlying issue was that the countries did not (and do not) have the financial infrastructure to pay their own bills, pay for their grandfather's loans, and pay what it takes to grow their economies all at the same time. Treating them as though they could meant relegating them to perpetual, eternal poverty.

The "Brady Plan"

By 1989, a general consensus was emerging that this was more than a simple balance of payments issue and couldn't be addressed by the normal tricks of rollover, rescheduling, etc. Those procedures simply shuffled the money around and didn't address the problem. That year, Treasury Secretary Nicholas Brady launched the "Brady Plan." There are two parts to it that are good to remember. The first was a call for an across-the-board reduction in the debt owed by some of the largest of the developing countries (Mexico, Argentina, and so on) and for the IMF and the World Bank to guarantee the repayment of the rest. In exchange, the countries would have to implement some of the draconian economic policies that would later be called "Structural Adjustment" policies and that would still later fall under the heading of the "Washington Consensus."

The countries agreed to these policies, which almost invariably impoverished millions of people, but they had little choice. The IMF has an incredible amount of power and influence within the financial world and turning them down would mean being cut off from almost any other credit, ever again. If you say no to the IMF, you may never again see a dime cross your borders in aid or loans or investment. Also, it didn't hurt in the negotiations that the leaders of the poor countries were actually very wealthy themselves. If the stringent, belt-tightening policies begun with the Brady Plan and followed up with IMF structural adjustment programs caused mass hunger and poverty in their countries, the leaders would by and large be immune from it. Many of them kept their own money outside of their host country anyway and would not be harmed when the inevitable crash came.

The second important part to the Brady Plan was a repackaging of many of the old loans into bonds, which would then be sold on the secondary market, much like equity stock. These were called "Brady Bonds" and to protect the investor they were partially underwritten by the U.S. Treasury. These proved a very popular investment, and by the mid-1990s about $170 billion worth of these bonds were selling in the market. By 2000, that number had risen to over $2.5 trillion. The rise of the secondary market is an entire subject unto itself, with pension funds, mutual funds, hedge funds, and insurance companies all leaping into it with ever more complex financial instruments and derivatives, all finally collapsing in 2008 at the same time. But it's interesting to note that Brady Bonds played an important role in getting that movement started. Their partial U.S. backing made them very safe for investors to experiment with, and they were created at just the time when the United States was relaxing its requirements, accountability, transparency, and regulations as to who could get into the market to buy and sell. They were so well received that by the mid-1990s some developing countries began issuing bonds on their own to raise capital because they knew they would be bought up at low interest. Until the recent global financial crisis, bonds accounted for about 60 percent of developing country debt, compared with only 13 percent in 1980.[21]

The Rise of the Multilaterals

In spite of the importance of all of these responses to the debt crisis — the rollovers and restructures, the Baker Plan, the Brady Plan, and other similar measures — by far the most crucial element was the role played by the IMF and, by extension, the World Bank and other regional development banks (because the other banks typically followed the IMF's lead).

The IMF, as noted in chapter 2, was originally established in 1944, along with the World Bank, with the responsibility for stabilizing the global economy. Whereas the World Bank was to give long-term loans for development (originally Europe and Japan, but later poor countries in the global south), the IMF was mainly to give short-term bridge loans to countries caught in a balance of payments gap. But that began to change with the oil price shocks of the 1970s and especially with the debt-related financial meltdowns of the 1980s. With the arrivals of the administrations of Margaret Thatcher in the UK and Ronald Reagan in the United

States, the economic policies of the IMF began to swing dramatically to the right. In fact, James Baker even threatened to cut off funding to the IMF at one time if it didn't change more rapidly to adopt economic policies more amenable to U.S. political priorities.[22] So instead of loaning to help a country get by temporarily until it could balance its accounts, the IMF began loaning money conditioned on extensive internal structural adjustment changes in the recipient countries. And in addition to making these new loans, it also (along with the other multilaterals) began buying up distressed loans owned by the commercial banks.

By the end of the 1980s, the multilateral lending agencies owned 80 percent of all of the developing country loans. They began forcing the countries to adhere to the policies that we have described here variously as "Structural Adjustment," "Washington Consensus," "Friedmanism," "Thatcherism," "Reaganomics," and "Neo-liberal." Among other things, the countries were to deregulate labor markets (making it harder to unionize); devalue currency (making it easier for foreigners to invest, but harder for poor people to buy food); cut public expenditures on the poor, public sector jobs, and price supports for farmers; lower barriers to imports; end protections of local industries against foreign ownership and investment; sell off prized state industries; raise prices for basic commodities and basic services for the poor, and so on. They all look good in terms of balancing the public checkbook, but they were terrible in terms of their impact on poor people.

To be fair, some of the items on their lists could be considered sound policies for a healthy economy, even by those who care about poor and hungry people. Getting inflation under control, for example, keeps prices down for everyone, including the poor. And generally speaking, there is nothing wrong with getting a country not to spend more than it takes in. But applying these principles every time in every country in every situation, without correct sequencing or social protections, created tremendous hardships, and the IMF seldom seemed sensitive to that. It didn't take into consideration that there would be real people with families with hopes and aspirations for their futures who would be impoverished or homeless or uprooted by some of these policies. Sometimes, if the underlying circumstances were sound and a safety net was in place, the policies helped. Sometimes they did very little. But in many countries, when conditions were not right, when the safety nets were not in place, and when the financial institutions were not strong, the results were devastating and millions of people dropped into poverty, became immigrants, or even died. During the time that poor and developing countries were under the control of the IMF (and the institutions that followed their lead), per capita income consistently went down, poverty went up, and inequality widened.

Statistics are notoriously difficult to follow in these matters, but here are a few fairly clear ones. A few years ago the United Nations Conference on Trade and Development (UNCTAD) studied the journeys of the forty-eight least developed countries under the guidance of the IMF's "Structural Adjustment Facility," which it officially launched in 1986. The UNCTAD study found that on average the gross domestic product per person was going down slightly, by 1.4 percent, in the three years before they initiated IMF policies; it leveled off for the first three years that they were in practice; and then they declined again after that by about 1.1 percent. If taken by itself, that part of the story could allow one to say that at least the countries didn't get any worse under IMF control — except for two things. First, the fact that GDP flattened out during those years actually meant that their country lost ground, because if income stays flat but inflation goes up, you actually wind up being poorer in the end. Second, the UNCTAD report also found that "under the time of IMF guidance, their indebtedness actually became worse. It grew to unsustainable levels."[23] So their incomes flattened out (and personal wealth declined) in real terms, while their loan payment demands went up. After a few years of increases in debt accumulation, they will have to once again tighten their belts to pay off the new loans.

Some regions of the world fared worse than others. Between 1980 and 2000 (the years when the IMF's structural adjustment programs were most in effect), the incomes of the poorest 20 percent of countries in southern Africa fell by 2 percent a year. But during the twenty years *before* the 1980s, their economies *grew* by 2.3 percent per year. Admittedly, national income is not always the best measure of the health of a country — distribution of wealth within the country is often a better indicator — but clearly even the most progressive, just government cannot distribute income well if the national income is declining every year. And that was what happened for most countries under IMF regulations and conditions in the past twenty-five years. Interestingly, as we noted in chapter 2 on the broad picture of globalization, the countries that had the highest rate of economic growth during this period (for example, China, India, and South Korea) were also the ones that devised their own paths for growth and ignored IMF prescriptions.[24]

These countries are often held up as poster children of the philosophy of free market growth, while in truth they starkly rejected many of the basic "Washington Consensus" principles of the free market. China, for example, created a two-track structure in which an international market system operates on top of its domestic state-ordered system. That allowed it to liberalize its foreign trade, but still use government policies internally to direct and distribute the incoming wealth to a larger portion of its population. Until the recent global financial crisis, this idea, that a government should have a hand in distributing national income to lift up the incomes of the poor and tamp down the incomes of the wealthy, has been an absolute anathema in Washington and in IMF rules. But since the crisis, most developed Western nations have become far more interested in following China's course.

This idea of redistribution within the country is one of the central pieces missing in the global advice and management of country economies. It is considered a good thing to throw open the doors of a country and invite in a free flow of trade and finance, but what if the income from that open door policy stays only in the hands of a small minority of upper-class elites?

A useful comparison for this point is Colombia and Brazil, two strong economies in South America. Both have shown similar high rates of economic growth over the past twenty years. But in Brazil, the percentage of people in the country living in poverty is actually going down, while in Colombia it is going up. Why? It isn't related to their belief in "free trade" or their openness to international markets, because in that they are very similar. What is different is that in Brazil there are a large number of government-driven mechanisms that intentionally help the lower and middle classes (job supports, housing, food subsidies, health care, etc.) and in Colombia there are very few of these. In fact, in the last decade a good number of them have been cut to save money.[25] It isn't their leaders' openness to globalization that is at issue here; it is their openness to caring about the well-being of their people.

Joseph Stiglitz, in his book *Globalization and Its Discontents*, describes how the IMF's "one size fits all" approach failed again and again, in part because it failed to understand local situations and local cultures. At one point he tells the story of the IMF putting extreme pressure on Uganda in the 1990s to place fees on education as a way of raising money to be applied to payments on its debts. According to their statistical studies, gathered globally, the IMF determined that raising school fees had little impact on school enrollment and if applied nationwide could raise a considerable amount of money. However, Uganda's president Museveni balked. He knew that for much of sub-Saharan Africa simply finding food to survive was a daily trial and that most families felt forced to forgo education (especially for girls) for jobs. So in a rare instance of a country standing up to a powerful international financial institution, he ignored their advice and abolished all school fees and threw open education for everyone. Within two years school enrollment soared. Ironically, almost every economist on the planet understands that one of the key elements in turning a country around is education for its young people. Those at the IMF, however, have consistently supported policies like these, which produce short-term financial gain but also function to keep a poor country poor.[26]

Interestingly, the UNCTAD study cited above concluded its work by questioning the science used by the IMF to determine its economic policies. It said, "the efficacy of the economic reforms, on which so many lives and livelihoods now hang is, and must remain, an act of faith."[27] I agree.

STRUCTURAL ADJUSTMENT PROGRAMS

Much has been said about the structural adjustment policies of the IMF and its partner institutions. Here is a summary of the most important of those. If this list sounds similar to our earlier list of the basic principles of the "Washington Consensus," it's not an accident. Both evolved at roughly the same time from roughly the same people holding roughly the same ideologies.[28]

1. Public Sector Layoffs

Most poor countries have huge federal staffs. In many ways, it was their best jobs program. However, the public sector is often bloated, so understandably the IMF says cut it down. The problem, as with so many of the

IMF's prescriptions, is that it tends to demand the changes immediately without jobs programs or an economic safety net to catch those who are fired.

2. Privatization of State-Owned Enterprises

Water, telephone, electricity, health care, education, national forests, etc. Everything is sold off. And, because most poor countries do not have enough wealthy people within their borders to buy these public corporations, the majority are either sold to foreigners or sold at fire-sale prices for huge losses. The old Soviet Union is the worst example. During its transition to capitalism, a small number of insiders bought the entire Soviet industrial sector for cents on the dollar. They became billionaires and impoverished the country in the process.

3. Spending Cuts in Basic Social Services

These include education, health care, and other social programs. The philosophy, again, is that anything that does not enhance the ability to balance the budget and make payments on the loans should be cut. But in the end, the future health and well-being of the country is often undermined. An illustration is Honduras. Honduras is one of the poorest countries in this hemisphere and in the years leading up to 2007 (when it received some debt relief) it had been working to qualify for the IMF/World Bank debt relief program called the "Highly Indebted Poor Country Initiative" (HIPC). However, according to the initiative, indebted countries can receive relief only if they agree to the restraints we've stated here, including cuts in education. However, much of the physical and social infrastructure was disintegrating, and the future of education was in jeopardy. So in 2001 the Honduran legislature voted to increase teachers' salaries over three years. It was a leap, but teachers' salaries were so low that even the increase kept them below the Central American average. The IMF responded by informing Honduras that because of that legislation — voted on by democratically elected representatives — the country's debt relief would be postponed indefinitely. So the government of Honduras caved in and rescinded the law. The teachers did get a raise, but it was less than half of what was projected, putting Honduras once again dead last in teachers' salaries for the region. What Honduras saw as an education crisis that was destroying the future of its young people, the IMF termed "fiscal slippage" which they could — and did — change.

4. Abolition of Price Controls on Basic Foodstuffs

Frequently poor countries subsidize basic goods like bread or cooking oil. But typically the IMF demands that these subsidies are cut (to save money for the loans, etc.). While, again, saving money makes sense in general, it is the poorest of the poor who suffer, and in many countries food riots have broken out when the subsidies were cut.

5. Wage Freezes and Labor Suppression

The lower the local wage, the more appealing the country is for foreign investment and the building of foreign-owned companies. Mexico, for example, was forced to lower its minimum wage as one of the conditions for signing NAFTA. Also strongly encouraged is legislation that weakens unions, or encourages state-sponsored unions, which would be more apt to go along with wage-lowering proposals.

6. Devaluation of Local Currencies

If a country's currency is forced down in value, it encourages foreign investment and purchases because goods and services become cheaper relative to the investor's currency. However, it also means that the local people have to spend more of it to get the same products. It in effect makes the local population slightly poorer.

7. Export-Oriented Production

Developing countries are heavily encouraged to make a historic switch from producing for domestic consumption to producing for foreign consumption. Factories that once made products for local sales now refocus on products for exports; farmers who once grew agricultural goods for domestic needs now grow cash crops for exports. Millions of farmers and indigenous people lose their land to large farming conglomerates growing the new crops. The result is that a good many countries are no longer food-sufficient and now depend on imported foods that they once grew themselves. Mexico, after NAFTA, began a steady shift away from growing corn—a staple foodstuff for over five hundred years. Today it imports more from the United States than it produces itself. The fragility of that became clear recently when U.S. production of corn began to be siphoned off the food market for the production of ethanol, causing prices in Mexico to leap upward.

The Highly Indebted
Poor Country Initiative (HIPC)

Beginning around 1995 the tide of global public opinion on the debt crisis appeared to turn. That year the G8 (an annual gathering of a group of the world's eight wealthiest countries) met in Halifax, Nova Scotia. At that meeting, following intense lobbying by people of faith and conscience around the world, the leaders for the first time agreed that nothing short of outright cancelation would ever get at the root of the problem. They sent that message to the World Bank and the IMF, and James Wolfensohn, then president of the World Bank, took it seriously. He asked his staff to put together a proposal for complete cancelation of all debts for about fifty countries with no conditions, and they did that.

At the same time however, Stanley Fisher, deputy managing director of the IMF, designed his own plan, one that had no debt relief, more loans, and more conditions. For the next few months disputes over these two very different proposals caused near war to break out between the two organizations until Lawrence Summers, deputy secretary of the U.S. Treasury (now head of President Obama's National Economic Council) told the two of them to quit fighting, get together, and work something out. In 1996 they finally did that but the plan that emerged, called the Highly Indebted Poor Country initiative (HIPC), was almost entirely what Fisher and the IMF had first wanted. It demanded six years of the brutal structural adjustment programs to qualify, it calculated eligibility based on value of exports and not on a country's poverty or ability to pay (Haiti, for example, the poorest country in our hemisphere, was left off the list), it made overly optimistic assumptions about most countries' ability to pay, it picked a wildly impossible number out of the air for what it called a "sustainable" amount of debt (40 percent of a country's income from exports), and it was very slow.

As an aside, later in chapter 7 we will talk about the great Jubilee laws of Leviticus, chapter 25, which were an early attempt to address the disparities of poverty, debt, and slavery by turning back the clock to a time reminiscent of the Garden of Eden. It was a utopian dream in its day, and in fact was never allowed to happen. One interesting early discussion of the rules and guidelines for Jubilee debt cancelation is found in *The Antiquities of the Jews,* by the ancient first-century historian Flavius Josephus. Josephus was

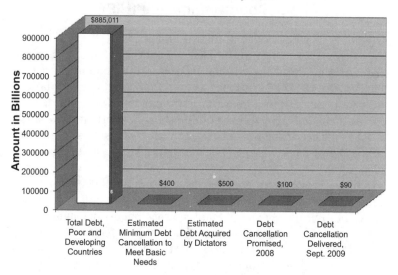

Figure 5. Poor Country Debt

Source: World Development Indicators database, September 2009, *www.worldbank.org;*
Unfinished Business: Ten Years of Drop the Debt, www.jubileedebtcampaign.org.uk.

a member of the highly educated, wealthy classes, and the guidelines he lists were written by people representative of that class. In
his discussion, he describes them ponderously and in excruciating
detail, going line by line, rule by rule, until in the end one finally
wonders whether the actual point of the guidelines was to guarantee that no one would ever receive any debt relief. Today it's also
hard to read his tedious, complicated description of what was probably the first HIPC plan, without coming to the same conclusion.
It makes one wonder if today's number crunchers in the IMF are
not the intellectual descendants of the attorneys and accountants of
Josephus.[29]

After a few years it became clear that the HIPC initiative was
simply too stringent and cumbersome to work, and it had to be
revised. Also, by the end of the 1990s the international grassroots
antidebt campaign had grown increasingly active and influential,
and it was beginning to put measurable pressure on their host governments to do something more. Jubilee chapters were popping up
in country after country, and though it was an issue that attracted
broad support, it was unusual in that it was driven almost entirely

by people of faith; in the United States it was mainly Catholics and mainline Protestants, but it also had a good smattering of progressive evangelicals. They took as their theme the biblical image of the Jubilee, which decreed the freeing of slaves and canceling of debts, but in addition many also felt *spiritually* connected to the cause because for generations their churches had been sending missionaries and (more recently) antihunger money to many of these same desperate countries. The fact that whole regions that they thought they had been helping were now sliding backward into even deeper poverty because of a financial system over which they had little control tugged at their religious heartstrings and challenged them to action.

A tipping point came in 1998 at the G8 meeting in Birmingham, England. Seventy thousand activists came to the event from all continents and walks of life to demand that the wealthy countries act on the ongoing misery that had befallen the poor countries. They had with them a petition signed by 1.4 million people from all over the world. Young and old, wealthy and poor, religious and secular walked arm in arm and called for a shared vision of a world more just and humane. Then in 1999, at the April World Bank/IMF meeting in Washington, and again in the June G8 meeting in Cologne, Germany, tens of thousands more marched and the petition was again lifted up. This time the number of signatories had grown to 17 million. By the time the completed petition was finally handed over to UN Secretary General Kofi Annan later that year, it had reached 24 million signatures and had broken two Guinness world records, one for the largest petition ever organized and the other for the most internationally compiled. The press surprisingly covered the meetings, the march, and the petition. President Bill Clinton (coming late to the issue) threw his support behind debt relief. And an "enhanced" version of HIPC was announced by the G8 members, promising "faster, deeper, broader" debt relief.[30]

It was an exciting and hopeful proposal. The number of countries on the list to receive relief was to be expanded, the bar they needed to reach cancelation was lowered, the six-year qualification period was shortened, poverty reduction was now to be a central goal and not just balance of payments, $100 billion was set aside for immediate relief, and civil society would be consulted in constructing each country's debt cancelation and poverty reduction program. Plus, the United States, Canada, France, Germany, Japan, Italy, and

Britain all promised to cancel 100 percent of the bilateral debt owed
to them by poor countries. It wasn't every thing that the antidebt
campaigners wanted, but it came close enough that, to the naïve
eye, the era of global economic justice seemed discernable on the
horizon.

I was present at the World Bank / IMF gathering in Washington,
D.C., in 1999, and the air was truly electric. There was a sense
that something finally was going to be done to end one of the truly
crushing, but invisible, social evils of our time. There were speeches,
there were workshops, there were marches, there were rallies. At
the end of it all we locked arms and wrapped ourselves around the
reflecting pool in front of the U.S. Capitol to symbolize the great
chain of debt that surrounds so many countries of the world. "Break
the Chain of Debt," we all chanted. A young iron worker from La
Paz, Bolivia, was standing next to me, giddy with enthusiasm. His
neighborhood, his family, and his union had all collected money to
get him there. He had a little sister who had dropped out of school
(as had he earlier) so that she could work and feed the family. And
now he was going to go home with a life-changing story. It was an
exciting time, a hopeful time. We all believed that *kairos* time was
happening, but, in the end, not much changed.

As it happened, some of the countries that pledged cancelation
of their individual bilateral debt did follow through, but others did
not. On average, their cancelation brought down the debt load by
about 25 percent, which is an improvement. However, most of the
affected countries were only able to pay on about 75 percent of
their debts at that time anyway. So in reality, the country to country
cancelation brought their official debt payments down to what they
were presently able to pay, so in the end it didn't change much.

The IMF, for its part, continued blocking debt relief with ever
more requirements and rules. By the mid-2000s, only ten countries
were close to qualifying (out of forty-one on the HIPC list and more
than sixty on Jubilee USA's list). In the new and improved HIPC the
IMF was supposed to produce "Poverty Reduction Strategy Papers"
with input from each indebted country, but a number of independent analyses showed that the papers were empty or ineffective.
The UK-based World Development Movement looked at four of the
new poverty strategies and found they were almost identical to the
earlier nonpoverty alleviation strategies. The major difference was

the change of the name from "Structural Adjustment" to "Poverty Reduction."[31] But otherwise they were the same. Also each of those papers was supposed to be designed with input from civil society, but in a great many instances that never happened. One report from the Catholic Episcopal Pastoral Social Commission of Bolivia said that the supposed "civil society" organizations invited to planning sessions were actually representatives of banking consortiums and low-level government bureaucrats — not really the teachers, workers, and farmers envisioned in the plan. In Nicaragua the strategy paper for that country was not even translated into Spanish — how could civil society offer input if they couldn't read it?[32] And the Josephus-style, anti-Jubilee hurdles created by IMF continued to be immense. Tanzania, for example, had to prepare three thousand reports for its debt reduction program in the year 2003 alone, and host over a hundred delegations from IMF and World Bank officials checking up on their progress, the costs of which were deducted from the money they were eventually to receive in debt relief.

All in all, the new plans seemed to be the old plans. They were built on the same ideology of antigovernment, procorporation, deregulation, privatization, and trickle down policies as the earlier ones. There seemed to have been the same drive to increase the national income, with no awareness of the need to distribute it equitably within the country; no awareness of how cutting schools can impact a country's education; no awareness of how cutting health care can impact a country's ultimate health.

There is, however, one more recent event that has in fact produced fragile but measurable results, and that shows that diligent and indefatigable work by people of faith and conscience working together can in fact save lives and ease hardships. There are still an enormous number of problems and pitfalls along the way, but from this event has come a definite promise of hope. It was the G8 meeting at Gleneagles, Scotland, in 2005. That year it was being chaired by British prime minister Tony Blair, who had been strongly committed to finally doing something significant on global poverty and the debt issue. In fact, there were rumors that one of the reasons that he had allowed the United States to talk him into going to war in Iraq was because he wanted to win over President George W. Bush for his international humanitarian causes, causes that the president by and large was not otherwise interested in. When the conference took place, once again the streets were filled with throngs of people demanding quicker, deeper debt relief. But, contrary to so many other gatherings, this one appears at the date of this writing to have finally produced more positive than negative results.

On the positive side, the Gleneagles meeting appears to have been a watershed for the international organizations working for social good. Over 250,000 people from all over the globe came to the event, with concerts, rallies, sharing, and networking among the people and groups. Out of this meeting evolved the "Make Poverty History" campaign in the UK and the "One" campaign in the United States, which took up the debt crisis issue as part of a larger global economic justice campaign, which also included demands for trade justice and more and better aid. Scores of celebrities (in part at the behest of musicians Bob Geldof and Bono) were in attendance at the parallel "Live 8" concert and subsequently made debt, trade, and aid the focus of their humanitarian work. The world is not well, but it will be a better place in the future in part because of the interconnectedness and common bond forged at this one gathering.

And it was important in terms of financial pledges from the G8 representatives. The plan they drafted would wipe out most of the debt owed to the multilateral institutions for all of the countries that had completed the HIPC process, as opposed to the partial relief offered in previous plans. And the plan pledged $50 billion for actual cancelation immediately. On the downside, the G8 leaders were only willing to extend the relief to a potential forty-one countries, still far short of what the Jubilee organizations had hoped for. And some of the institutions involved offset the cost of their debt relief by reducing future aid allocations. Nevertheless, for those forty-one countries, it was still relief, and the agreement did tacitly recognize the inadequacy of the "debt sustainability" language that had been used up to then.

The initiative has since become known as the Multilateral Debt Relief Initiative (MDRI). Through it twenty-three countries have received 100 percent cancelation of their debts, the majority of them in Africa. And there are another twenty countries that could be eligible later. Even though it still doesn't rise up to the level called for by debt campaigners, it nonetheless means (when the amounts of previously canceled debts are added in) that eligible nations will be saving about $2 billion in debt payments each year.

That may not seem too much compared to the astronomical amounts the Bush and Obama administrations spent on bailouts and stimulus in the United States, but for desperately poor countries it will be life saving. Tanzania has used some of the funds from its debt relief to increase primary school enrollment by 50 percent. Ghana used some of its money to rebuild dilapidated highways to distant rural farming communities so as to improve agricultural marketing and to resource schools and health clinics. Benin invested its new money in health and education and funded small-holder projects in agriculture. So while there is still much to be done and there is still too much bureaucratic stonewalling (for example, the IMF dragged its feet for far too long before granting relief to countries like Liberia and storm-ravaged Haiti, and the Inter-American Development Bank at first refused to participate in the MDRI), nonetheless there is much to be grateful for.[33]

The job is not over. There are still many important campaigns in the Jubilee struggle. One would be working for full inclusion of all countries still saddled with damaging, punishing levels of debt. Some countries like Lesotho, which is desperately poor and devastated by HIV/AIDS, are to date still not included on the list. One way to address that is by passing the "Jubilee Act" in Congress, which calls for the United States to work toward complete multilateral cancelation of all debts for sixty-seven countries with none of the harsh structural adjustment conditions tied to it. It passed in the House in April 2008, but by the time it was introduced in the Senate, distraction from the presidential campaign slowed its movement and it was never brought to the floor for a vote. It was introduced once again in December 2009, but once again other issues took precedence, and it was never voted out of committee to the floor.

Another issue is the campaign, recently spearheaded by the government of Norway, to cancel "odious" and illegitimate debts. In general these are debts taken out by dictators and military governments antidemocratically and against the needs and wishes of their people and therefore should not be paid back. This concept has a personal resonance for a country like Liberia, which is today paying off loans taken out by the brutal regimes of Samuel Doe and Charles Taylor, who borrowed money to buy weapons and then used them on the very people who are now stuck with the bill. The concept is controversial and has been applied only sparingly throughout history. The United States applied the principle in 1898 when it invaded Cuba and then claimed that Spain should pay off all of the debts Cuba incurred while a Spanish colony. More recently, after it invaded Iraq, the United States argued that the new democratic government did not have to pay off the "odious" debts of the dictator Saddam Hussein. But in other instances, such as Nigeria or Rwanda, where the United States did not have a personal stake in the outcome, it has been silent.

Over the years antidebt campaigners have expanded the concepts of illegitimate and odious debt beyond debts incurred by dictators to debts that were made immorally. The Jubilee USA Network, for example, has argued that debt should be considered illegitimate if (1) the creditors made the loans irresponsibly (recall the comment of my banker friend, who said his bank gave out bonuses to loan officers "not because the loans were any good, but just because of the sheer number and size of them"), (2) a wealthy country gave out loans for political, not developmental, reasons (for example, when the Reagan administration loaned billions to the countries surrounding Nicaragua in the 1980s to give the impression that their capitalist economies were booming and Nicaragua's was declining); and (3) creditors continued to give loans even when they knew that corrupt governments were siphoning off the money (for example, the World Bank continued to give millions in loans to the Congo's Mobutu Sese Seko, long after it was clear that he was pocketing the money and using it to oppress his people).[34]

Yet another still pressing issue is ending the so called "vulture funds," a type of investment fund that buys up devalued poor country debt on the secondary market and then sues in a U.S. or UK court for full price. Many poor and developing countries that have been sued for total loan amounts decide to give in and make payments because the fight in court would take more money than would the increase in payments. In 2007, Zambia lost its case in court and was forced to pay $15 million to Donegal International, which had originally paid only $3 million for the debt. These people move and live at a special level of evil and their practices should be ended by the concerted legislative action of all countries involved.[35]

But in spite of all of these challenges ahead, there is no denying that hard work of people of faith and conscience all over the world has made the level of crisis in the countries stricken with debt lower today than it was just a few years ago. People can make a difference. And you are one of those people. You can make a difference. This issue, like no other since the civil rights era of the 1960s, is an example of how people of faith have stepped forward and made an impact on the direction, visibility, and outcome of a campaign to make the world a better place. In this campaign, like few others, every dollar that is freed up by the United States, the World Bank, the IMF, the Inter-American Development Bank, or any other, is a dollar that saves a life, builds a road, or sends a child to school. When you wonder if all those people signing post-cards to the U.S. Treasury, or making phone calls to senators and representatives actually did any good, think of the children in the little school up in the mountains of Honduras who might be get-ting an education now because of their country's debt cancelation. They don't know how it happened, but I am certain that their little community is a better place for all of those efforts.

PAT AND ELAINE
AND A FAITHFUL PROMISE

Here is a story about how two people with no experience and no political connections can work together to change U.S. policy and save lives. The two are Pat Pelham and Elaine Van Cleave, two soccer moms from Birm-ingham, Alabama. Pat and Elaine go to First Presbyterian of Birmingham, and one day, back in the late 1990s, they were attending a Bible study together and learned that millions of mothers around the world just like them often cannot feed their children. This pained them deeply, and they decided to do something. Knowing that our government has an important role to play in ending hunger they invited all of the big politicians from Alabama to a dinner and presentation about antihunger issues. They invited the governor, their congressman, their senators, etc. The turnout was small, but their congressman, Rep. Spencer Bachus, and his wife did attend and they had a chance to get to know him.

Meanwhile, in 1998, activists in Britain were launching the "Jubilee" campaign, which was designed to convince governments and inter-national financial institutions to cancel the debts of poor countries. Here in the United States, a number of U.S. religious groups, including Bread for the World, the Christian hunger advocacy organization, were working to draft debt-cancelation legislation to be introduced to our Congress. The next year, in 1999, Rep. Bachus was named chair of the subcommittee in Congress that would hear the legislation. Bachus is very conservative, and no one held out much hope for the bill coming out of his committee.

Not long after that, however, David Beckmann, the president of Bread for the World, heard about Pat and Elaine's big political dinner, and he telephoned Pat and told her about the legislative initiative. He invited the two of them to come to Washington and arrange to meet (again) with Rep. Bachus.

They came, but they felt incompetent and completely inexperienced. They had no experience talking with congressmen, no background in international finance, and — as they put it — no experience with debt beyond their own credit cards. What they *did* have with them were personal stories, sincerity, a deep faith, and four hundred letters about debt relief signed by members of a local church.

They arrived the day before the meeting, and the Bread staff briefed them intensively about all the policy matters. When they arrived at Rep. Bachus's office they were met by the congressman himself and half a dozen of his aides, all in dark business suits. Mr. Bachus opened the meeting by saying, "Pretend I don't know anything about debt relief. Why should I care?" Intimidated by the setting and this opening challenge, everything they had tried to learn in the cram sessions went out of their heads. There was silence in the room.

Finally, Elaine spoke from her heart, where her journey had started. She explained that she was a mother of three small children, and that it would break her heart if she were not able to feed them and send them to school. She said she understood that debt relief would mean that many mothers in the developing world would be able to feed and educate their children. She said to Rep. Bachus, "You could do something about this." At that, the stern formal meeting opened up with lots of discussion, which concluded with Rep. Bachus saying that he thought he could support debt relief. The six dark suits behind him were shaking their heads "No," but Bachus did go on to be a champion of the legislation. And as a result of the debt relief campaign 20 million more children in sub-Saharan Africa — more than half the entire population of California — are in school now than there were in the year 2000.

Pat and Elaine and other Bread for the World people in Birmingham didn't stop with one meeting. They organized more community events —

now to celebrate the leadership of Bachus on this issue. They convinced the local newspaper to write about it. They recruited other churches in Birmingham to get their members to write letters to Congress. In so doing they were creating and building political will in their district for the issue. In the end, when President Clinton signed the legislation that funded the U.S. role in debt relief for poor countries, David Beckmann was invited to be present, and President Clinton gave Spencer Bachus credit for playing a crucial role in winning approval from Congress. For his part, Beckmann gave credit to Pat Pelham, and Elaine Van Cleave.[36]

FOUR

NAFTA:
Why Does Nikolas Dance?

I voted against CAFTA, never supported NAFTA, and will not support NAFTA-style trade agreements in the future. NAFTA's shortcomings were evident when signed and we must now amend the agreement to fix them. While NAFTA gave broad rights to investors, it paid only lip service to the rights of labor and the importance of environmental protection.
— Candidate Barack Obama, February 28, 2008[1]

In late January 2008, I was in Chiapas, Mexico, with a group of people studying the impact of globalization on farmers. Chiapas is one of Mexico's most resource-rich states, and also its poorest. So along with Witness for Peace, Equal Exchange, and my own organization, Jubilee Justice, we were looking into the connections between globalization, justice, and, of course, greed.[2]

It was an interesting time to be there because if you were watching the news very closely at the time, you knew that Mexico was that very week exploding in protests and demonstrations over the fifteenth anniversary of the start of the "North American Free Trade Agreement," or NAFTA. More than two hundred thousand people, mainly farmers, were demonstrating in the central square in Mexico City, called the Zócalo. On their way they had driven trucks in long caravans at five miles an hour, bringing traffic to the city to a halt. One aging truck was burned as a symbol of their anger. In Veracruz, a hundred thousand people marched in the streets. Nearly as many were in Acapulco and Oaxaca. Thousands more formed a human chain along the border at Ciudad Juárez blocking entry into El Paso, Texas, carrying a banner that read *Sin maíz no hay país* (Without corn there is no country). Even in the smaller cities thousands of protesters lined the streets, shutting down traffic and commerce. One local newspaper announced, "Head-on struggle against NAFTA explodes." What was going on?

It turns out that these were scenes of Mexico battling for the soul of its economy. Farmers, trade unionists, educators, students, community organizers, and pastors, priests, and nuns had all taken to the streets in an intense struggle (in vain it turns out) to convince their government to reconsider its commitment to NAFTA, which the vast majority of Mexicans (and large majorities in the United States and Canada) saw as offering them a painful, damaging failure. On January 1, the last tariffs were removed on imported corn, beans, sugar, and milk, ending the rocky transition to a radical free market economic model governing the relations between Mexico, Canada, and the United States, and farmers and urban poor people were terrified as to what might happen to them next.

Interestingly, little of this was covered in the U.S. press. This was especially because this was in the middle of the presidential primary season and both Democratic presidential candidates had supported changing NAFTA, along with the majority of U.S. and Canadian citizens. Even Prime Minister Stephen Harper of Canada said there were things in it he wanted changed. So with all of that, it is at least odd that the mainstream media in the United States only barely noticed that hundreds of thousands of people in neighboring Mexico were in a desperate standoff to end it or change it.

While all of this was going on, I was staying for a few days up in a small community named La Ceiba, just south of the border with Tabasco in the home of Nikolas and Anna Chocul, who were introduced to me simply as the "old ones," and indeed they did look old. They were about five feet tall, with wizened faces and seemingly frail on their feet. Their home had essentially two rooms, one for cooking, and one for sleeping. One light bulb in each, no floors in either, and a common latrine a few hundred yards away. Nikolas spoke haltingly in Spanish (his native language was Tzeltal), but eventually I learned that in spite of their age and health he and his wife still had to go up the mountain each day to pick the coffee cherries. He had four children altogether, three boys, one daughter, and an undetermined number of grandchildren. I saw the fleeting face of his daughter occasionally through the door in the cooking room, but where were the sons? *El Norte,* he said. They had all gone north. One was in California on a farm. One was doing some kind of construction work. The third was still trying to get in. His daughter was living with them because her husband too, had gone to *El Norte*. He and his wife had expected to receive remittances from the sons, but so far little had been sent home.

Nikolas's life and circumstances overwhelmed me. Coming from my nice, air conditioned, floored home, I couldn't imagine his hard, unrelenting life. But I tried not to act like the patronizing rich guy, and I asked him about his family. I showed him pictures of my grandchildren, and he smiled.

Later that evening we went to the town church for community worship, a common meal, numerous speeches and presentations, and then a party. We pushed all the chairs to the sides of the room and the community brought out instruments and played for us. And when the music came up, there at the front of the sanctuary I saw Nikolas, larger than life, and he was dancing!

I was stunned. He was halting on occasion, not always in time to the music, but there he was, along with others — in fact dozens of others — dancing, and dancing as though his life was, well, wonderful and full of joy. From my soft, North American consciousness, I couldn't imagine how he could do such a thing. If I were in his shoes I'd be in incalculable grief. I turned to a young woman named Gladys, who was a consultant for the local co-op that Nikolas's community sells its coffee to, and I shared my amazement. She laughed at me with a sound of real merriment, but I could tell that she was wondering how I could ask such a thing. "You don't know much about us, do you?" she said.

Background

There's no clear, direct line of cause and effect between Nikolas dancing and the protests of NAFTA, but there does seem to be an emotional one, perhaps even a theological one. In its fifteen years of existence, the North American Free Trade Agreement had created some staggering winners and we hear about those often in the mainstream media. But it also created staggering losers and Nikolas and his family and community were among the worst of those.

To understand the depth of what so many people were protesting that week we need to step back twenty years and look again at the debt- and trade-related crises of the 1980s and see how the pain and fear in those events drove successive Mexican governments to accept an agreement that was ultimately destructive to many of its poorest citizens, especially farmers. In many ways NAFTA was sold as a way out of the weight of external debt that had plagued Mexico (and much of the developing world) since August 1982.

Mexico was not always buried under unpayable debts. For the first fifteen years following the Second World War, Latin America in general took in very few foreign loans of any kind and most of those were from its own domestic banks. That changed somewhat when Fidel Castro took over Cuba in 1959 and the United States lavished the region with loans and grants to keep it from viewing Cuba as an attractive alternative model of development, but these were modest by today's standards.

The big increase took place during the early 1970s when private banks in wealthy countries (mainly the United States, Europe, and Japan) received billions of "petrodollars" from OPEC countries and then loaned them out with abandon to poor and developing countries. You may remember from the chapter on debt that this was the decade when many third world countries were forced to shift from production for themselves to production for exports in order to make payments on the loans.

Mexico's story, however, has a slightly different twist. For a while it was not as affected as other countries by the need to increase exports to earn money for loan payments, because in the mid-1970s it discovered significant oil reserves of its own. That gave it a temporary windfall, which lasted until 1982, when it was hit by a worldwide drop in oil prices. So there was a period of time when it could have used its windfall to develop its agricultural sector or if it wanted to expand its income-producing exports, it could have created support programs to help its farmers in the transition, but it did neither. Instead it used its oil revenues to make its existing loan payments and then borrowed more money (the recycled petrodollars) from the banks. In the end, therefore, instead of helping the development of the country, Mexico's growing oil income only put off recognition of its dire financial reality until it was too late, and when the reckoning finally came it was a disaster.

The balancing act lasted for about a decade until the beginning of the 1980s. At that time three things happened at almost the same time. First, the price of petroleum fell, taking with it Mexico's debt-paying cash cow. Second, the United States entered a deep recession and dramatically decreased the amount of commodities it could buy from Mexico. And third, in part because of the recession in the United States, the interest on the loans it had taken out during the 1970s skyrocketed. It was a painful confluence of forces, some of Mexico's making and some beyond its control. Mexico effectively went "bankrupt" (though as we have noted before, one of the nice things about this system for lenders was that there was no international mechanism that allowed countries to actually declare "bankruptcy").

Dozens of other developing countries had also gotten deep in debt, but Mexico was the first to fall, and it was the largest. In September of 1982, it declared to the world that it was immediately ceasing payments on all of its external debts and the announcement shocked the international financial community. The potential of a meltdown of such a large country with so much outstanding debt terrified markets around the world, igniting talk of a global panic and transcontinental recessions. Within weeks, the IMF called an emergency meeting of countries, banks, and multilateral financial institutions, and together they forged an $8 billion bailout package of new loans, extensions, and restructures that postponed the collapse. However, Mexico had an underlying financial instability that could not be addressed by loans or tweaks. It simply was not sufficiently industrialized to produce the massive exports necessary to earn enough dollars to make payments on the loans. It didn't have the economic infrastructure to produce enough "stuff" to sell to make enough money to keep up with the loans. Looking back it is hard to believe that the financial wizards involved in the bailout did not see how fragile their package actually was. There was certainly no obvious way that the loans could ever be paid back, given the structure of the existing global economic system and given Mexico's rural, farm-based, low-income population. But somehow, at the time, the crisis was dealt with as though it was a mere short-term balance of payments issue that could be "fixed" soon with just a few bridge loans, reschedules, and rollovers.

Unsurprisingly, within a year Mexico was in trouble again and was signing a second bailout arrangement — this time back with the commercial banks — to borrow an additional $7 billion in order to stretch out the rescue package and guarantee interest payments just a little bit further.[3] But in reality without a comprehensive debt cancelation program, Mexico would still be saddled with loan payments as far into the future as anyone could see. Today, even after

Mexico's payments have been lowered and extended and rescheduled again and again (and some repackaged and sold as "Brady Bonds" on the secondary market), they still hover around $180 billion and will continue to be a drag on the life and health of the country for generations.

That may, in fact, have been the result that the IMF and the other financial powers were trying to achieve. According to the free market ideology behind most of the prescriptions given in crises like this, Plato's "highest good" for humanity is no longer happiness, but a neoliberal market system and a shrunken national government. As we noted earlier, Milton Friedman, the patron saint of modern free market theory, believed that governments should consist of little more than the military and fire departments, and nothing can shrink a government more than unpayable debts. They force the government to sell off its basic functions to the private sector, which according to the theory always runs things better than the government. Some critics, therefore, have accused the IMF and others of intentionally giving the governments of various countries the kind of financial advice that ultimately (and intentionally) destroys the state's ability to govern.

In Mexico, when the debt crisis hit, its interest payments rose from 19 percent of total government expenditures in 1982 to 57 percent in 1988. At the same time its capital expenditures (the money it spends on itself) fell from 19.3 percent down to a nearly comatose 4.4 percent. This incredible shrinking government forced the slashing of things such as state credit, government-subsidized agricultural inputs, price supports, state marketing boards, and extension services.[4] The state telephone company was sold (with technical assistance for the sale coming from the World Bank), and rates rose from 16 pesos per minute to 115 pesos per minute (the World Bank prophesied that rates would eventually come down with the competition, but that has yet to happen).

All of this forced a complete rethinking of the role and size and meaning of government. No one would argue that before this time Mexico's government was lean and efficient. It was in fact bloated and inefficient. But the cuts were so fast and so deep that they constituted a second crisis within the debt crisis. The state was in a panic and the people within the country suffered terribly.

Four years later Mexico hit yet another financial crisis, and this one drove it directly into negotiations for NAFTA. The initial cause was a second plunge in global oil prices that occurred in 1986. Once again Mexico announced that it would be unable to make payments on its loans. This time, included with the now predictable bailout package,[5] were new free market demands that would later become known as "structural adjustment programs" (SAPs) and a new trade deal that would later become NAFTA.

One interesting and shortsighted demand was for all government employees to have their wages indexed for steady increases to keep down inflation, while real inflation was nearly doubling. This one action moved hundreds of thousands of federal employees and their families into poverty. The minimum wage was also indexed to rise at a steady (and unnatural) rate, creating a growing gap between incomes and food costs. From December 1987 to May 1994, the minimum wage increased by 136 percent, while the cost of a basic basket of consumer goods rose by 371 percent, a gap of nearly 30 percent.[6] This package of prescriptions was sold to Mexico as something that would not only help the country pay off its loans, but would also eventually create wealth that would be beyond its wildest imagination. When the plan was presented, Mexico was weak and fragile and in shock. How could it refuse?

The double economic crashes that came so close together in the 1980s left Mexico reeling and dizzy and at the same time perfectly poised to accept new structural adjustment requirements and a NAFTA "trade" deal that were biased toward the northern countries and had inequality at their heart. Journalist Naomi Klein has labeled this kind of intervention, "disaster capitalism" because it occurs most often whenever there is a disaster (natural as well as economic) and the population feels temporarily stunned, powerless, and pliable to outside suggestion. When that happens the economic doctors of the far right rush in with financial "aid" conditioned on the acceptance of radical free market policies like privatization of water, education, electricity, and health care — policies that drive some people into extreme poverty and some into extreme wealth. When people have experienced a major hurricane or a revolution or — in Mexico's case — two successive back-to-back economic catastrophes, they are willing to reach for anything, even if it seems unwise in retrospect. Mexico's acceptance of the terms of NAFTA appears to be a good example of "disaster capitalism" in practice. After suffering two economic shocks in three years, the populace of Mexico was hurting, not only economically, but psychically, and was ready to acquiesce to any medicine that promised to stabilize their fracturing, fragmenting country. Their eager acceptance of this economic shock therapy was also aided by two successive presidents who were in complete agreement with the harsh policies, Miguel de la Madrid (1982–88), who began the NAFTA negotiations, and Carlos Salinas de Gortari (1988–94), who completed them and signed the agreement in 1993. According to Noreena Hertz, author of *The Debt Threat: How Debt Is Destroying the Developing World,*[7] it didn't hurt that both presidents were so wealthy that they knew that a failure with NAFTA would not hurt them no matter how bad it might be for their country. Both were willing partners in the agreement that even some of its supporters now say has failed Mexico.

Back in 1988, just as the new structural adjustment package was being signed and negotiations for NAFTA were beginning, I was living with a family in Cuernavaca, while taking an "immersion" Spanish course in a local "gringo" education center. One day one of our instructors named Eduardo drove a number of us out to a party in a small neighboring town named San Miguel Tlaixpan to give us a taste of *la realidad de México.* By that he meant cock fighting and sangrias, which he lovingly referred to as Sangria de Cristo (if you're Catholic and know Spanish you'll get the joke). On the way home we got totally lost and wandered aimlessly through the back roads of Mexico for about an hour (perhaps due to the sangrias?). But the good news was that our detour gave us a chance to have a good conversation and get better acquainted. Among the interesting facts that I learned about Eduardo that night was that he was actually a trained economist and had once worked for the Mexican Finance Ministry. But following the economic crisis of 1986, he was laid off and now was back home in Cuernavaca living with his parents and teaching Spanish to gringos.

I asked him how he was making out during the difficult times. Not well, he said, but he was getting by. Of more concern to him, however, was the future. Mexico was growing too dependent upon the United States, he said, too many strings tied to the ideas and economics of the north. To describe our relationship, he used an interesting metaphor that I've never forgotten. He said that Mexico (and much of Latin America) relates to the United States like those tiny insects that live in the hair of a huge water buffalo. They live off its scraps and organic material and waste, and they are dependent upon these for their very livelihoods. Most of the time they get by, but that dependency has its downside. If the buffalo makes a mistake or gets ill the insects are hit by it three times harder. If the buffalo runs blindly into a fire, for example, the buffalo may get burned, but the insects die. If the buffalo falls into the water, the insects drown.

"How will all of this affect you in the future?" I asked him.

"I don't know," he said. "I'll be fine. When money comes back into Mexico, I'll move back to the Federal District and get back my job. But," he pointed with his thumb back over his shoulder at the town we were leaving, "I am afraid for all of the people in places like that. I am afraid that someday America will make a wrong turn and all of them will be burned up in the fire."

So What Is NAFTA?

Specifically, NAFTA is the acronym for the North American Free Trade Agreement. It is a three-country trade agreement between Canada, the United States, and Mexico. It was roughly patterned after an earlier trade agreement made between the United States and Canada, though in practice it is much different because of the increased number of provisions and demands and because of the great disparities between the culture and economy of Mexico and those of the United States or Canada. Negotiations on the treaty began in 1986, following, as we have noted, two financial crises that had left Mexico weakened and vulnerable, and as a result it agreed to many things, some of which were ultimately not in its best interests. Negotiations began just after the second of those crises, during the U.S. administration of Ronald Reagan. It was officially signed by George H. W. Bush and then finally passed through Congress by President Bill Clinton in 1993. When it was initiated, in January of 1994, North America became the largest free trade zone in the world.

From the beginning there was tremendous opposition to the agreement in all three countries. Protests followed by violent reprisals broke out in Mexico as tens of thousands of farmers took to the streets in opposition. In the United States, opposition to it came from worried small farmers, progressive economists, social justice organizations, churches, synagogues, human rights organizations, environmental groups, and labor unions (all of whom the press referred to oddly as "special interest groups") and third party candidate, Ross Perot. You may recall that he famously coined the expression, "the great sucking sound" to describe the noise he prophesied would be heard when millions of U.S. jobs were sucked down over the border into Mexico.

Many analysts believe that it would never have passed had then-candidate Bill Clinton not taken it up in his 1992 presidential campaign as a way of attracting Republican votes. Then when in office he felt compelled to make it a legislative priority, and certainly there is little in it that resembles traditional Democratic Party trade policies. Faced with enormous opposition from both Democrats and some Republicans in Congress, he pushed his Mexican and Canadian counterparts to add two additional "side agreements," one on labor rights and the other on the environment to make it more palatable to his constituents. (They had to be added as "side" agreements because the Bush administration had signed the treaty under the "fast track" authority, so no amendments or changes were allowed to be made to the core treaty.)

The fact that the original agreement made no reference to protecting the planet or workers says much about the philosophies of those who put it together. They evidently did not see such concerns as part of their job description. This is reminiscent of the observation made by John Williamson (author of the famous article on the "consensus" of establishment Washington economists) that he left out any reference to poverty alleviation in his list because in the 1980s poverty was not something policy makers were interested in.

The Side Agreements

Under the two agreements added by the Clinton administration, the three countries would agree to establish a variety of commissions and subcommissions to study and deal with labor and environmental issues. On paper, the commissions would have the power to levy fines against any of the three governments that failed to impose its own preexisting laws. These provisions have received praise because for the first time the well-being of humans and the environment were put into a major treaty on trade, which would then have the potential of setting a precedent for future agreements. However, in practice both supporters and opponents have acknowledged that the side agreements have had little actual impact, partly because the commissions are poorly funded with little enforcement power and partly because the commissioners themselves have often seemed to have little interest in exercising what enforcement powers they did have. For example, the side agreement on the environment established the Commission for Environmental Cooperation (CEC) as an environmental watchdog. One of its good features was that citizens could call for investigations into allegations of a country's failure to enforce its own environmental laws. Theoretically citizens and environmental groups could hold companies in each country accountable for obeying the law. However, in practice the CEC has seldom done that. According to a 2006 study by the Department of Environmental Sciences at the University of California, Riverside, the CEC never really had a chance. It was too poorly funded and too narrowly focused to achieve its goals, it lacked a leadership that wanted to push to expand its operations, and it faced a strong trade community that fought it with money and influence to keep it from achieving its goals. According to the report the CEC was reduced to minimal technical studies and actions and little real action.[8]

The side agreement on labor has fared no better. It established the North American Agreement on Labor Cooperation (NAALC) to monitor and work on labor protections, and it too has had little impact in the cases brought under it so far. On the plus side, trade unionists in Mexico, the United States, and Canada have been able to use the provisions to spotlight and uncover labor-rights abuses. However, few of those reports of abuses have ever been resolved. Ten years after NAFTA was created, an article in the pro-NAFTA *Wall Street Journal* made this scathing assessment: "Not a single worker was ever reinstated, not a single employer was ever sanctioned, no union was ever recognized" by the commission.[9] In Mexico, workers' efforts to organize independently or to protest bad working conditions have often been blocked by a coordinated effort of businesses, the government-sanctioned union (Confederation of Mexican Workers), and the government itself. Labor laws often go unenforced, and sometimes overt repression is used against workers to keep them from organizing or filing grievances.

Lifting Trade Barriers

Although there were hundreds of provisions in the agreement, the most publicly discussed and debated were those concerning the eliminations of tariffs, quotas, and other barriers to exports and imports between the three countries. These items were to be phased out gradually and were finally eliminated on January 1, 2008 (just before the protests that I had witnessed while visiting Chiapas).

For the postwar decades before NAFTA, each of our three countries had established tariffs to make foreign imports more expensive and also subsidies to make domestic producers stronger. Governments used these tools as ways of protecting local farmers and local industries. With NAFTA both tariffs and subsidies were to be phased out in stages, with the hope that eventually producers from one country could compete with producers in another on what was called a "level playing field." One problem, of course, was that with Mexico joining the other two, the playing field was no longer level. Giant U.S. corporations such as Cargill, Archer Daniels Midland, and Monsanto were allowed to compete with small labor-intensive factories and farms in Mexico, totally overwhelming them with their economies of scale. As it turned out, the best way that a Mexican factory was able to compete evenly with one inside the United States was when the factory was actually U.S.-owned and operated — an arrangement that occurred frequently.

Another problem was that the lowering of subsidies and tariffs was not done at a uniform time and degree by all three countries. Perhaps if these measures had been implemented equally across all borders, the theory that free and equal competition would foster more efficient production and greater increases in incomes would have been true, or at least it would have had a better testing. But under the provisions of NAFTA, each nation had a different phase-out plan for subsidies and tariffs and a different list of products that could be protected.[10] And even within that framework, all three countries violated NAFTA provisions when it benefited them. For example, agriculture in the United States is one of the most subsidized sectors in the world, and countries like Mexico (and others) have suffered because of it. It was a painful blow to Mexican farmers, who were forced to have their subsidies cut while those in the United States continued unencumbered. Exports of highly subsidized corn produced under highly mechanized conditions from the United States soared in the early NAFTA years, growing at a rate of 9.4 percent a year, and causing, by the mid-2000s, a 45 percent decrease in the corn prices that farmers received for their crop. By 2007, agricultural exports to Mexico were at $12.7 billion, which was over 40 percent of its food needs.[11] Farmers like my friend Nikolas and his family up in the mountains of southern Mexico were literally going hungry while monopolistic processing companies in the cities kept consumer prices from barely dipping at all.

Mexican farmers were being undersold in their own local markets. Each year, small-plot Mexican farmers found that they were spending more on growing their crops than what they could eventually sell them for, and then they had to borrow money to make ends meet, often then falling deep into debt poverty. It is a downward cycle that has driven tens of thousands off their land and into the cities or over the border into the United States looking for work. It's not precise, but interesting for comparison to point out, that on average every hour Mexico imports $1.5 million worth of food from the United States, and in that same one-hour period, thirty farmers migrate to the United States. For millions of people in Mexico, migration is not just for self-improvement and a way of realizing the "American Dream"; it's also a strategy for survival itself.[12]

A few years ago I was touring a market in San Cristóbal de las Casas, comparing prices of produce there with prices for similar produce here in the United States. I met one former farmer in his mid-forties named Alberto Gonzales (no relation to the former attorney general), who was now tending a farm stand for his uncle, with whom he was now living. We exchanged pleasantries and photos of our children and then I asked him how it was going for him as a farmer. He confessed to me that until not too long ago he had considered himself to be a successful farmer with ten acres of land where he grew tomatoes and onions and employed a dozen people. But now it was all gone. His family moved in with his uncle, and he lives off his generosity and the small remittances sent back home to him from his oldest son, who had migrated to San Diego. He said that the reality of his situation was that he could now buy produce more cheaply in the local market than he could have once grown it on his own land. "For those people with the big farms and the big tractors, those who know the big people, NAFTA has been very good. But for the rest of us, those of us who worked hard, but were not already rich, it was a war, a bloody war. And we lost it."

And Along Came China

NAFTA was not the only factor that put a negative economic pressure on small farmers like Alberto. Another was the simple growth in the number of young people looking for work. Ironically in the 1960s, the United States had funded hundreds of rural health clinics throughout Latin America as a way of lifting their standard of living (and making Cuba look less appealing by comparison). An unexpected result was an increase in the number of children who survived childbirth and who, by the 1990s, were reaching adulthood and looking for jobs.

A second factor was the chronic indifference of successive Mexican governments to the plight of rural areas. One of the government's frequent promises has been for aid to retrain or relocate those who have been harmed by trade policies such as those of NAFTA, but little has ever come of it. In fact, in the years since NAFTA was enacted, the government all but terminated its rural assistance programs (critics suggest it was a way of insuring a steady stream of poor, hungry people into the cities to work in the U.S.-owned assembly plants). There were, for example, clauses written into NAFTA that, if implemented, would have safeguarded at least some of the vulnerable farm products for fourteen years, but they were never invoked.

A third factor was yet another savage financial crisis, which hit Mexico in 1994. A presidential candidate was assassinated, President Salinas devalued the peso, and nervous investors pulled their money out of stocks and securities in a crash. It was a panic eerily like the U.S. bank collapse in 2008. Money dried up, unemployment soared, and trade with the United States plummeted. The United States quickly arranged a $20 billion loan package to Mexico (tied, of course, to even more free market, "Washington consensus" policies) to keep it from collapsing and to keep it from taking other countries down with it, but the country suffered terribly during the crisis.[13]

However, the most important non–NAFTA-related factor negatively affecting Mexico's economy was (and remains) emerging Asian countries, especially China. China has the highest population in the world, but until the late 1990s it was relatively insulated from the global economy. During that decade it lobbied mightily to have the West forgive or forget its brutal, oppressive, and antidemocratic ways and allow it to become a member of the World Trade Organization (WTO), because that would give it access to lucrative trade deals in the global market.

In 1999 China was finally allowed in and soon became a major international player. The country represented a whole new productive region, with ten times more poor and hungry workers than Mexico had. And, conforming to standard market logic, the entrance of China as a competitive option meant that for most U.S.-based corporations there soon began to be less and less incentive to stay in Mexico, and more and more incentive to move east. Aside from a few products that needed close proximity to the United States in terms of shipping times (one week for Mexico vs. three weeks for China), Mexico had much less to offer than China. By the year 2003, China was exporting more to the United States than Mexico — $152 billion compared to $138 billion — for the first time in history. A late 2009 study by the Carnegie Endowment found that 82 percent of Mexico's exports of "high technology" goods, representing 40 percent of total exports, were threatened by Chinese competition.[14]

Even before the entrance of China into the global market, the size of Mexico's new NAFTA-driven export economy was exaggerated. That is because so many of the workers in the *maquiladoras* — those (mainly U.S.-owned) assembly plants that line Mexico's border with the United States — were people who had been displaced from farms in other regions of the country. In fact, many critics have suspected that the reason for the near-total neglect of the rural areas by so many Mexican governments was a clear decision to drive more people off the farms and into manufacturing. *Maquiladoras* had been in existence in small numbers for decades, but after NAFTA they surged. If anything related to NAFTA ever provided a veneer of success, it was the huge leap in their numbers after 1994. However, the numbers were misleading. In the year 2000, at the height of NAFTA's impact on employment, the *maquiladoras* were employing about 1 million people. That's a lot, but in that same year the population of the farming region declined by nearly 800,000 people. Those were mainly people who had lost everything — homes, farms, livelihoods — and moved to the cities hungry and penniless looking for work. So the net gain in jobs in the *maquiladoras* was in actuality only around 200,000. Nice, but not stunning. And the social, emotional, and financial costs of such a high level of human displacement should call into question whether the new employment "gains" were worth it.[15] All told, agricultural jobs declined in Mexico from 8.1 million in the early 1990s to 5.8 million in the second quarter of 2008, a loss of more than 2.3 million jobs.[16]

However, beginning in 2000, China fast became Ross Perot's "great sucking sound" for Mexican jobs, and the *maquiladoras* began to shut down. By 2002 more than a hundred of them had been shuttered, and 600,000 people lost their jobs, almost entirely due to the impact of China as a new global exporter. By 2007, before the present crisis, the number of *maquiladoras* factory jobs had declined to barely more than they were in 1994, before NAFTA had taken effect. The number of non-*maquiladora* jobs was *lower* than before NAFTA. The only two sectors that actually grew after the onslaught of Chinese competition were service jobs (counter help, clerks, and so on) and "informal" jobs (selling Chiclets and watches on the beach). And, of course, with the beginning of NAFTA there has also been a steady growth in the number of displaced farmers migrating to the United States looking for jobs, inflaming ethnic tensions and political opportunism within our own country.[17]

Most of us who watch the economies of the United States and Mexico closely were concerned back in 1994 that, with the signing of NAFTA and with Mexican salaries being one-tenth of what they were in the United States, companies would move rapidly and permanently to Mexico. Little did we know at the time that China would soon be doing to Mexico's jobs what Mexico had done to ours. China's workforce is larger and poorer than Mexico's, and the country has far fewer regulations regarding product safety, treatment of workers, or the environment than has Mexico. Plus it has a policy of undervaluing its currency, which makes its products cheaper for U.S. consumers. So in 1999 it opened its doors for business and the sucking sound began. From 2000 to 2007, manufacturing in Mexico declined by 10 percent, and China rose from being our seventh largest trading partner to our second. By 2002, for the first time since the NAFTA experiment began, foreign investment coming into Mexico fell: from $14 billion to $10 billion.[18] Both these trends have continued to the present. As economic journalist William Greider once put it, in globalization's "race to the bottom," China has become the "new bottom."[19]

Once again, Mexico's own government could have done a number of things to help its workers meet the Chinese competition. It could have built a stronger infrastructure, for example, or it could have built more ports and highways to facilitate trade. It could have passed laws protecting workers, or creating severance pay for times that they were out of work, or created training for new work when old jobs died out—but it did none of these. It chose instead to follow a Milton Friedman, "Chicago School," hands off, laissez-faire, free market ideology, and the poorest sectors of its society are still suffering because of it today.

The movement of industry from Mexico to China is not directly related to NAFTA, but it is directly related to the philosophical center of free market theology, that the central purpose of human existence is not for the pursuit of happiness or service to others, but for economic transaction and profit for the already wealthy. The central goal of the market system, as we have said, is not to intentionally cause harm to anyone (as liberals often seem to suggest) but simply to make a profit by any means. The market is constantly on the prowl for people who can work at lower and lower wages, because labor is the largest piece in the production chain. If it can find them by moving from the northern U.S. industrial belt to the "New South," it will do it. If it can find them by dipping over the border into Mexico to the *maquiladora* zones, it will do it. If it can find them by moving to China's central textile producing region, it will do that. Or, if it can find cheap, desperate-for-work employees in Indonesia, Thailand, or the Philippines, with even fewer environmental, health, or safety regulations, it will leave China in a heart beat and move there.

The market, as we noted in chapter 2, is the shark in the movie *Jaws*. It is a feeding machine that just does what it does, with no sense of conscience or reflection on the morality of its behavior. Insofar as the market reflects moral behavior at all it is because people of faith and conscience have lobbied, cajoled, badgered, and pushed it to do so. There is nothing in the heart of capitalism that indigenously produces a conscience. We can push, for example, for our national leaders to sign a "free trade" agreement with Colombia only when it improves its dismal human rights record (toward teachers, unions, community organizers, and pastors), and if we are successful they might do it. Or we can push them to push Mexico to live up to the side agreements on labor and the environment that were critical to the passage of NAFTA, and if we are successful, they might do it. But those are the only ways that the market and its allies will exhibit a concern for the needs of others. It's not that the market is evil. It's that the market doesn't care. Its job is to make money, not save the planet or promote human rights. The "shark" always does what it does. It isn't possible for people of faith and conscience to ever completely or totally remove it from the water or create in it a change of appetite. But it is possible for us to direct it and position it in ways that are more humane and less damaging. Governments, of course, will always claim that that is what they are already doing (when was the last time a politician said that he or she was supporting a free trade agreement so that it could destroy family farms in poor countries?). But it is up to people of civil society to make sure that when they say that they are also telling the truth.[20]

Investor Protection Provisions

But trade is not the only part of NAFTA that has come under scrutiny and questioning. In fact, some of its critics dislike it so much that they will put the words "free trade" in quotes, or question the use of the words "free trade" at all, because the concepts of "freedom" or "trade" constitute a relatively minor portion of the agreement. Of the over nine hundred pages of rules and provisions, the majority deal with the changing of — or overriding of — domestic laws within each of the three countries. According to economist Joseph Stiglitz, these provisions give an inordinate number of rights and privileges to business, rights that are in effect taken away from individuals, provisions that he believes "potentially weakened democracy throughout North America."[21]

One of the most contentious of those new rules was the so-called "Chapter 11" provision, which allows a corporation from one country to sue one of the other two countries in special tribunals if it believes that a law or judicial decision will adversely affect its potential profits. The tribunal is closed and nontransparent, and it has the authority to override laws passed by the legislative bodies of the three countries. If a company is successful, it will receive compensation directly from the federal government. Over the years of its enforcement, the NAFTA tribunal has heard suits attacking environmental, health, and safety regulations, and worker rights. By the year 2008, over $14 billion in claims had been filed. One of

Figure 6. Growth in Mexican Manufacturing vs. Agriculture

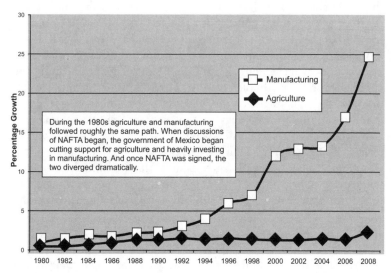

Source: *OECD.StatExtracts.org.*

the things seldom noticed about the NAFTA tribunal system is that only companies (and their host countries) can file a complaint. That is, if a corporation feels that its future profits will be harmed by this or that labor law or environmental protection law, the tribunal will hear them. But if my friend Nikolas and his local Tzeltal community in southern Mexico feel like they have been economically damaged because their corn crop has been unfairly undercut by subsidized U.S. corn, they are not allowed to use the tribunal. It was created for businesses, not people. Because the tribunals are only to protect businesses, the implication is that regulations of all kinds, good and bad, should be ultimately reduced or ended.

One of the most famous examples of this was back in the 1990s in a suit brought by a Delaware company named Metalclad against the country of Mexico. Metalclad had purchased a Mexican firm, Coterin, which was attempting to build a hazardous waste land-fill outside the Mexican community of Guadalcazar, in the state of San Luis Potosí. Metalclad had received the required federal construction permits, but at the last minute construction was blocked because of protests over the dangers of the toxic wastes in the facility, and eventually the entire project was voted down by the city council. Soon after, in 1997 the governor of San Luis Potosí, issued a decree establishing a protected natural area that included the landfill site, which effectively prevented any landfills from operating there. In response, Metalclad sued the country of Mexico itself, under the Chapter 11 provision of NAFTA. Metalclad argued that the town made a decision that denied it an opportunity to make a profit and that the national government of Mexico was responsible because the acts of the town officials were under its governance.

Specifically, it cited Chapter 11, section 1105, which required "fair and equitable treatment" of investments, and section 1110, which prohibited a local government from "expropriating invest-ments without due compensation." It argued that Guadalcazar had violated these chapters by denying the company the right to build the toxic waste site. The dispute went to NAFTA's three-person dispute arbitration panel, and the panel found in favor of Metal-clad. The panel said that the democratically elected municipality of Guadalcazar (and by extension the government of Mexico) did not have the authority to ban construction of the waste dump that could have made a profit for the Delaware company, and that the government was required to pay Metalclad $15.6 million in future damages.

Unlike Mexico and Canada, the United States has been fortunate in that most of the NAFTA tribunals have found in favor of the United States and against foreign corporations, but even so, it still gives one pause that courts and elected legislatures can be poten-tially overruled by unelected panels in closed-door discussions. Here is another example. In the late 1970s, a large Canadian develop-ment firm named Mondev International of Ontario entered into an agreement with the city of Boston to build a number of shopping malls and hotels. In 1986 they completed the first project, a hotel complex called Lafayette Place. However, construction took several years, and by the time Mondev was ready to purchase and build on a second parcel of land owned by the city, the value of Boston real estate had gone up and the city asked for more money. Mondev refused and took the city to court. It lost the case when it went before the Massachusetts Superior Court, and then in effect it lost again when the U.S. Supreme Court decided not to hear the case. In almost any other circumstances that would have been the end of it. However, in 1999 Mondev appealed to the NAFTA tribunal, which, according to the treaty that our two governments voted on and signed, is an even higher authority than the U.S. Supreme Court.[22] Mondev argued that "failure to obtain damages through the U.S. judicial system amounts to discriminatory expropriation without compensation."[23] As it happened, the NAFTA tribunal wound up siding with Massachusetts and agreed that the state did not have to lower the asking price for the parcels of land to be sold to Mondev. But it still raised concerns because this case actually had little or nothing to do with international trade. It was simply an attempt by a corporation in one country to circumvent the court system of another country. While the NAFTA tribunal agreed with Massachusetts, it nonetheless accepted Mondev's logic when it agreed to hear the case. The fact that Mondev lost should not diminish the fact that an international tribunal saw itself as having final jurisdiction over democratically elected officials in the city of Boston. More than half of the cases brought to the NAFTA tribunal are not over issues of trade or tariffs, but over labor and the environment. Georgetown law professor John D. Echeverria has called this "the biggest threat to United States judicial independence that no one has heard of and even fewer people understand."[24] At least one of the NAFTA panel judges has openly expressed reservations about it. Abner Mikva, a former chief judge of the federal appeals court in Washington and a former congressman, said that "if Congress had known that there was anything like this in NAFTA, they would never have voted for it."[25]

The Case for Changing NAFTA

During the presidential primaries, candidates Barack Obama and Hillary Clinton both campaigned against NAFTA, as it now stands, pledging to change it if elected. During the February 26, 2008, debate Obama told the late Tim Russert, "I think we should use the hammer of a potential opt-out as leverage to ensure that we actually get labor and environmental standards that are enforced." This resonated strongly in the old industrial states like Ohio and Pennsylvania, where thousands of jobs had been lost to Mexico following NAFTA's passage (and less strongly in other parts of the country where it has had a smaller effect). Then, shortly after Obama was inaugurated, several organizations of faith and conscience began campaigns to put pressure on Congress and the new administration to follow through on that pledge, and almost immediately there was a push back. Some (mainly conservative and probusiness commentators and organizations) argued that opening it up again would be opening a Pandora's box of demands and wishes, all of which they suspected would be bad for business. (Canada would want us to quit suing it over its soft wood-pricing schedule; Mexico would want us to stop dumping below-cost corn on its market, etc.). Also, a few respected progressive economists, including Robert Reich and Paul Krugman, have argued that we should instead emphasize other issues that make more of a difference. And finally, many progressives simply didn't spend time on the issue because they felt powerless to do much about it. It is too huge and too complex, and organizations that lobby against it are small and poorly funded. At one level, they were right. Without a major campaign, with international support, most important issues of this magnitude are determined by forces beyond the influence of local citizens' action groups. The campaign against a Free Trade Area of the Americas (FTAA) was huge a few years ago, but it finally died because South American leaders were growing tired of U.S. meddling and IMF incompetence, and not because of letter-writing campaigns in the United States.

Nevertheless, a case can be made for people of faith and conscience being concerned about, and being involved in, the struggle to adapt the treaty even with these considerations. First, the argument that we should not be too concerned about it because it actually affects our jobs and wages very little is probably accurate but essentially irrelevant. In the United States and Canada overall job loss and wage suppression (where workers take pay cuts out of fear of job loss) have affected us not nearly as much they have affected Mexico — 1 to 2 percent for the U.S. work force and 10 to 15 percent for Mexico's. And the jobs we have lost to Mexico pale in comparison to jobs lost to Asia, especially China.

However, it is irrelevant if we are truly people of a global God. If we see ourselves as brothers and sisters in a global family of spirit and holiness, then the difference between the suffering of Mexican families in Oaxaca and suffering families in Detroit should not be a concern to us. Too often people who are otherwise deeply compassionate will narrow the focus of their compassion to only those people of their own country, ethnic group, or social class. The God that creates life and gives it meaning does not make that distinction.

Second, even if it is true, as many assert, that the basic structure of free trade is so embedded in the trade and life of our three countries that we can never go back — the toothpaste can never be put back into the tube — nevertheless, reenvisioning the basic principles and practices of NAFTA could set an important precedent for future treaties. Even without rewriting its core chapters, a new administration could put teeth into its two side agreements on labor and the environment; it could establish a continental development fund to help build the economic infrastructure of Mexico (much like Europe did with the EU); it could correct the secretive tribunal system that presently has the authority to override laws passed by democratically elected representatives. All of these changes would not radically alter the integrated economies that we have created since the advent of NAFTA, but they could create an important and positive model for future agreements negotiated under a progressive U.S. president.

Finally, a North America–wide, values-based conversation about reenvisioning NAFTA would be a good project to undertake, even if it fails. The variety of flaws that are in NAFTA touch on many of the deeply held spiritual concerns that people of faith have given their time and efforts to for many years. The fact that the debt crisis of the 1980s drove Mexico into the brutal "bailout with strings" programs of the IMF must touch the hearts of church people who worked so hard with Jubilee USA in canceling international debt. The fact that union organizers are often banned from *maquiladoras*, their leaders beaten, their cars destroyed must pull at the hearts of the many Christians and Jews who worked so hard on civil rights in this country for so long. The fact that the drive toward more and unchecked, unregulated industrialization in the *maquiladora* zone is destroying rivers and streams and fish and animal life at an alarming rate must enrage evangelical Christians who have recently been drawn to the ministry of saving our planet.

There are so many ways that so many people can see the campaign to reenvision NAFTA as an expression of their faith, that even if the campaign fails it could potentially raise our consciousness and be a model for the next generations to follow through on.

However, none of this can happen unless our trust in and loyalty to a global, universal God brings us to a sense of unity and oneness with other fellow strugglers in all three countries. Too often the struggle in Canada has been to keep the flattening, dumbing down U.S. culture out of their country. The struggle in the United States

**Figure 7. Growth and Decline in Mexican
Gross Domestic Product (GDP)**

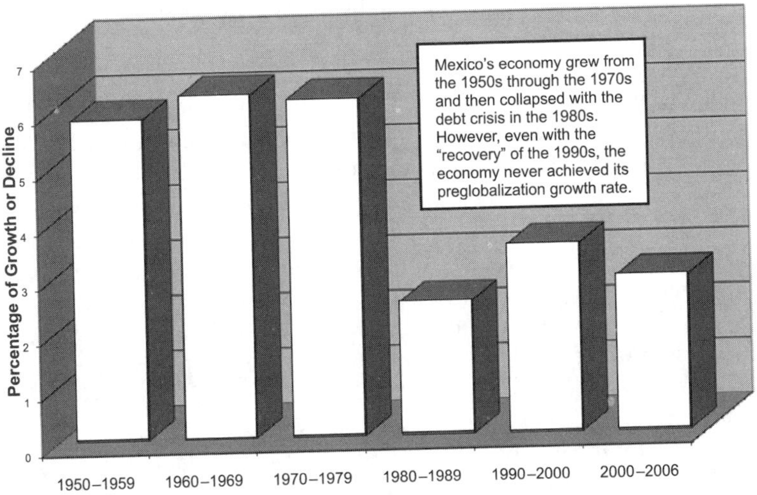

Source: *Mexico: Economic Growth, Exports, and Industrial Performance after NAFTA,*
UN Economic Development Unit, 2005, 22.

has been to keep from losing jobs to Mexico. The struggle in Mexico has been against imperialism and imposition of foreign domination. But the truth is, justice and equality know no boundaries. We could have accomplished much, much more had we worked together rather than in our separate zones. This is not a call for a merging of our three countries (as the Right suspects is in progress already) but a call to people of faith and conscience in all three countries to recognize common cause in justice. It wasn't just rich citizens in the United States who came down hard on poor people in Mexico. Rich people in the United States are no friend to the poor in the United States either. And rich people in Mexico oppress poor people in Mexico. This is not a regional or ethnic issue.

A few years ago Mexican farmers held a nationwide protest against NAFTA, even storming the doors of the Mexican Congress. However, dedicated opponents of NAFTA in the United States by and large watched in silence from afar, and the protests failed. What would have happened had U.S. and Canadian farmers, activists, progressive politicians, Christians, Jews, Muslims, environmentalists all joined in protests and letter writing to the Mexican president and Congress in solidarity with the farmers' struggle. History might have been made. As it was, we stayed in our own countries and did not support the struggles of our brothers and sisters south of us. That was wrong.

Back in Chiapas in 2008, after our dinner, presentations, and dancing, I walked up the hill toward the small home of Nikolas with several others, including Gladys, the co-op consultant, and I said again how amazed I was that people in this small, desperately poor town were able to dance and play and party and sing. Nikolas had also entertained us by playing his guitar with several others for over an hour. She gave me that look again, of patience, but real merriment. "I think the difference is . . . " She was trying in faltering English, but she didn't know the words. "I think what you do not understand. . . . " And then she finished in Spanish: *No bailamos por lo que ahora sabemos; bailamos por lo que pueda ser.* "We don't dance because of what we know now," she was saying. "We dance because of what can be." That may be the first time that I've really understood the deeper, spiritual meaning of hope.

FIVE

Immigration:
Jasmine and Daniel

The so-called "illegals" are so not because they wish to defy the law, but because the law does not provide them with any channels to regularize their status in our country — which needs their labor: they are not breaking the law, the law is breaking them. — Most Reverend Thomas Wenski,
Bishop of Orlando, Florida

Few subjects are more directly linked to globalization than migration — families disrupted from lifelong homes and communities and driven to urban centers or across borders looking for work or food. It happens all over the world. Great Britain is in turmoil attempting to assimilate millions of new "irregulars" (their term for the "undocumented") that have come recently, mainly from their former colonies.[1] France and Germany are struggling with violent backlashes against Muslim immigrants by skinheads and white supremacy groups. Australia has just passed harsh laws seeking to slow the tide coming from Pakistan, Afghanistan, and Sri Lanka. And Spain, whose southernmost town of Ceuta is the gateway into northern Africa, is building walls and detention centers and doubling its military force to keep out immigrants from Morocco, Algeria, Libya, and as far south as Sudan. All over the world poverty — exacerbated by the economic polarization that comes with free-market policies — is forcing people to move just to stay alive.

The Human Face of Migration

But the country I know the most about is Mexico, so I'll start there. Also, Mexico deserves special attention because it arguably sends a higher percentage of its population beyond its borders looking for work than any other country in the world. It is second only to India (a country three times larger) in the amount of money its foreign working citizens send home to their families. In the mid-2000s, this averaged $24 billion a year and was the country's third largest source of income after oil and illegal drugs.[2]

And I can't speak about Mexico and immigration without telling the story of Daniel Hernández and Jasmine Díaz-Pérez, two young people whose families I met a few years ago while I was visiting in their home in Chiapas, Mexico. Chiapas used to come up infrequently in immigration conversations because it was too rural and too far south to send many people all the way up into the United States. That's all changed now. Since the early 1990s, Chiapas and its neighboring state, Oaxaca, have become the fastest growing "sending" states in the country. In fact, in the years following the implementation of NAFTA (passed, as you may recall, as a tool to help stem the tide of immigration), immigration to the United States has nearly doubled, with much of that coming from these southern states of Mexico.

Daniel and Jasmine would have been about seventeen or eighteen when I was there. They had spent their entire lives in a little village high in the mountains about two hours north of the capital, Tuxtla Gutiérrez, and they had just become engaged. Their parents were wonderful, hardworking people, whose families had lived and loved and struggled in those mountains, growing corn and beans and coffee for generations. However, many of the global economic forces we have talked about in previous chapters hit them hard in the 1980s and 1990s and changed their lives forever. With each economic hit, the countryside around them would empty out more of its young people. Great swaths of rural Mexico were — and still are — becoming littered with abandoned ghost towns. In many, only the elderly and those too weak to travel were left behind.

Some went to the beaches to sell T-shirts and Chiclets to tourists. Some moved to the ghettos surrounding major cities to sell themselves as day laborers. More often, they would go to the U.S.-owned assembly plants along the border with the United States, the *maquiladoras,* or go further north across the border and become undocumented, illegal, and hated immigrants.

Jasmine's community had finally gotten to that level. Living conditions had declined terribly, and many in her family and community decided that they too had to go north. Hopefully the men —

Figure 8. Remittances to Mexico by Economic Migrants

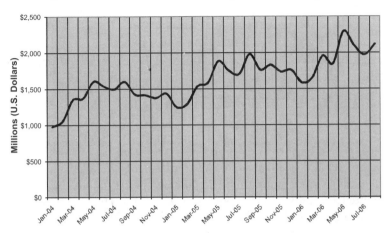

Source: Bank of Mexico (*http://www.banxico.org.mx*)

and it was usually men — would find work and then send remittances home to the others in the family. That was the plan, at any rate, but their options were terrible at best. Typically, if groups like theirs got in, and if they did find work, they would rent a cheap room together in a motel, take turns sleeping and working, eat as little as possible, and then send money back home. It was an awful way to live and it was dangerous just getting there; but if they made it in, one day's work picking vegetables in southern California or mowing lawns for a landscaper in Tulsa — even at below minimum wage, even with no benefits — could feed a family of six in Chiapas for a week.

Economic Causes of Migration

They would live hidden in the shadows in a country that schizophrenically both reviles them and needs them. Increasingly during the last years of the Bush administration and early years of the Obama administration, they lived under the constant fear of an Immigration and Customs Enforcement raid, followed by incarceration or deportation or both. In March of 2009, the Pew Hispanic Center released a study showing that Hispanics were incarcerated in our federal prisons in unbelievable numbers, but with only a small percentage being charged with anything that you and I would consider a crime. The vast majority (81 percent) were there not because of robbery, theft, murder, or rape, but because they came into our country and were caught holding down a job.[3]

When people in the United States discuss immigration, they by and large address it by focusing their debates on what to do about immigrants once they are in the country. Liberals typically talk of bringing aid to migrants who have been caught along the border and crafting a fair route to citizenship for the 12 million undocumented immigrants presently in the country. The opinion of labor groups had until recently been divided between the old established AFL-CIO and its breakaway rival the "Change to Win Coalition." The older union supported the guest worker program because it limited the number of people allowed in the country, while the younger union argued that it amounted to institutionalized slavery and put a downward pressure on wages and working conditions for nonimmigrant workers. In April 2009, the two came together and proposed a national commission that would manage future immigration. The commission would set the numbers of foreign workers to be admitted each year based on demand in American labor markets.[4] Conservatives on the other hand are generally divided between those in the working class who think (wrongly it turns out[5]) of immigrants as a serious threat to their jobs, and those in the business class who think of immigrants as cheap, unprotected labor to work the farms, pick tomatoes, and clean the motel rooms. One group wants to treat them humanely, another wants to treat them inhumanely, and the third simply wants to get some work out of them.

But less often people ask the deeper, more complicated question: Why are they coming here at all? What drives people, rooted for centuries in their own history and place, to feel compelled to leave everything they have ever known and travel thousands of miles to a strange land in the first place, and in ever larger numbers? Just saying "they want our jobs" or "they want to better themselves" doesn't really get at the root issues. Millions of young people are leaving their homes and risking their lives for the journey to *el Norte*.

On the one hand, one could argue that migration to the United States has evolved over the last generation as a social movement with a momentum all its own, with millions of young Mexican

"You don't exist"

"If I kill a dog, I will get in trouble. If I kill you, I won't get in any trouble. No one knows you are here. You don't exist."

These were threats made by a human trafficker to Flor, a thirty-seven-year-old survivor of modern American slavery, who came to the United States to earn money after losing a child to starvation in Mexico. She was forced to work seventeen to nineteen hours a day for no pay in a sewing sweatshop. "People feel if you come in illegally, anything that happens to you is your fault," said Lisette Arsuaga, with the Los Angeles–based Coalition to Abolish Slavery & Trafficking. "Slavery is not an immigration issue. It's a civil rights issue. There's no justification for making someone a slave."

— *Kansas City Star,* December 12, 2009[6]

males seeing the journey as a new rite of passage. But on the other hand, the real engine of growth behind migration is economics, with several specific — possibly intentional — policies of both the United States and Mexico that are forcing migration to take place. Two that directly touched the lives of Jasmine and her family were the collapse of coffee prices and the influx of cheap U.S. corn. In our next chapter we will discuss the coffee crisis more fully, so here we will say only briefly that it occurred in the 1990s after the United States pulled out of the International Coffee Agreement. The United States had supported the agreement until then because it regulated world production and consumption and maintained a baseline income for poor coffee farmers. When the United States — the largest consuming country in the world — pulled out, the agreement fell apart and more and more countries increased their coffee production until soon nobody was making any money. Production went up while demand stayed flat, and the result was an economic disaster for farmers like those in Chiapas and elsewhere. Coffee has always been a delicate crop to make money on without regulation, because its prices change rapidly on the world market while it is cultivated very slowly by the farmer. For example, in 1997 Brazil suffered a frost, which lowered its coffee production and temporarily raised prices on the world commodity exchange. Unfortunately, hundreds of thousands of farmers all over the world thought the hard times were over and began planting more trees. But a good coffee tree takes around five years of cultivation to produce the first cherry; and by the time the first of their beans were ready to be sold, the prices had already fallen back down to "normal." Their new harvests glutted the market, driving coffee prices down even further. It was a catastrophe caused by the conflict between short-term pricing and long-term growing. And the result was one more contribution to the massive population flows out of the rural areas of dozens of countries and into the cities or neighboring countries. From about 1990 to 2002 world prices dropped nearly 70 percent, which means in human terms that tens of millions of poor farmers lost their farms and their homes. In Mexico, it also meant that hundreds of thousands of them began migrating north.

The second major problem, the influx of cheap U.S. corn, was a direct result of NAFTA. Among other things, NAFTA forced an end to the subsidies that Mexico gave its farmers and to the tariffs it used to prevent U.S. corn and other commodities from flooding their market. After both were canceled, the doors were opened to highly subsidized, highly mechanically produced U.S. corn; and it came into the country in record amounts, devastating Mexican small-plot farmers. According to the provisions of NAFTA, the United States was also required to lower its subsidies to its own farmers, to make the playing field more level between U.S., Canadian, and Mexican farmers. But more than fifteen years later, the United States has still failed to do so. Instead, government subsidies to U.S. commodity producers have actually gone up over the years, and today U.S. corn pours into Mexico at prices 25 percent less than it costs them to grow it, and far less than any small crop farmer in Mexico can match.[7] During a particularly hard five years, between 1999 and 2004, the prices paid to Mexican corn farmers fell more than 50 percent, while the price of tortillas to Mexican consumers actually rose 380 percent.[8] As Mexican economist Miguel Picard has put it, Mexican farmers are not competing with U.S. farmers; they are competing with subsidies paid by the U.S. *taxpayers*.[9]

In theory, the U.S. government gives subsidies to farmers for commodities like corn, wheat, cotton, rice, and soybeans to help boost our exports. They arise from the problem that the United States has too many farms producing too much grain and we can't sell it domestically at U.S. prices. Therefore, our official government policy is that we help farmers export it so that they can make a living, and we do it by subsidizing their production. However, critics have noted that the bulk of the subsidies go to a small number of large corporate farming interests, like Cargill and Archer Daniels Midland, who because of their size ("economy of scale," as it is often called), already have a huge economic advantage. So subsidies are just the icing on the cake. Two-thirds of all U.S. farmers receive no commodity payments at all and of those who do — the wealthiest, largest, top 10 percent — receive two-thirds of the money.[10] It is also probably no coincidence that the large agribusiness corporations can afford major contributions to members of Congress, while most small farmers survive by working at part-time jobs on the side. And the 2010 Supreme Court decision allowing corporations even more freedom to influence elections and policy will probably not change that.

This strong belief in God's preferential option for the wealthy is not unique to the United States or even this hemisphere; it is the dominant theological ideology of the wealthy classes of every country on the planet. Our wealthy, well-educated trade representatives often get together at international conferences in opulent surroundings, where they work out smooth, efficient trade policies, and then go home without speaking to a single small farmer from Iowa or *campesino* from Guatemala. It isn't that they hate poor people or intentionally want to "crush the face of the poor into their poverty" (at least not most of them); it's just that conditions of the poor and struggling seldom come up unless they are standing outside the gates with pitchforks and sabers demanding some small say in the proceedings.

In 2007, a number of organizations of faith and conscience, most notably the Christian citizens' movement Bread for the World, mounted a tremendous effort to finally make changes in some of the subsidy policies. Thousands of members nationwide met in church basements and parish halls writing letters and making phone calls. They visited their representatives and tried their hands — usually for the first time — at actual old-fashioned "lobbying." Their proposals seemed to most to be quite modest. They asked that Congress make a general overall cut in commodity subsidy payments and subsidies to giant corporations, and then to redirect some of the money saved into the enhancement of domestic nutrition programs like WIC, food stamps, and food banks. It seemed only fair and just, and the kind of changes that a moral country that cared for its weakest citizens ought to support.

However, they were met by heavy, expensive, and professional lobbying from the other side, combined with an unfortunate lack of understanding in the United States of farm policies and subsidies. Most people did, and still do, believe that a U.S. subsidy for a crop helps our poor struggling farmers. Very, very few people understand just how few and how wealthy are the people who actually receive the subsidies. Together these things conspired to make most of the proposals fail. Nutrition programs received some help, which was good, but the distorted subsidy policies stayed basically intact.[11]

Given all of this, it's not surprising that NAFTA, which was sold as a way of decreasing immigration, wound up actually contributing to it. In the decade from 1994 (when it was first initiated) to 2004, Mexican migration to the United States nearly doubled. Mexico today has one of the largest human migratory outflows in the world. Estimates of Mexicans entering the United States every year range from four hundred thousand to six hundred thousand people.[12] According to the Mexican government's own reports, unfair competition with U.S. commodities is a major contributor to its losing nearly 30 percent of its farm jobs since the trade pact went into effect. In addition, since 1982 (the start of the first "Washington Consensus," neoliberal, free-market policy imposed on Mexico by the IMF) Mexico has cut its help and aid to farmers by more than 70 percent. All told, that translated into millions of farmers and millions more of their dependents fleeing their fields. It created a massive conversion of farmers to migrants and migrants into cheap labor in the United States.

Often when discussing U.S. subsidies, people will ask why the government of Mexico didn't just fight back as a number of other countries have. Brazil, for example, filed an "antidumping" complaint against the United States at the World Trade Organization for its subsidies of cotton, and it won. The WTO ruled that U.S. subsidies distorted world cotton markets and harmed cotton-exporting countries like Brazil.[13] Mexico could have done at least something similar to protect its own citizens, but it didn't. In actual fact, the Mexican government's policies toward its farmers were even harsher than the provisions of NAFTA required. They had, for example, the option of phasing out tariffs on U.S. corn and other commodities gradually, over fifteen years, which if done well could have at least given farmers time to transition to new crops. Instead, the year after signing NAFTA, Mexico began removing its tariffs on U.S. commodities. It cut its own subsidies and price supports for farmers and even dismantled the agency whose job it was to stabilize corn prices within the country. The result was that its small farmers received a deep and painful pounding from the onslaught of cheap U.S. corn while its consumers received a wide upswing in the prices they paid in the market.

Why did they do that? Why did the government of Mexico not only *not* act to protect some of the most vulnerable sectors of its own economy, but also *did* act in ways that seemed designed to intentionally harm them? Why would they do that?

The long answer to that question is very complicated and arcane. So before we get to it, the short answer is that there exists in Mexico very powerful commercial corn and tortilla interests for whom the arrival of foreign corn at rock-bottom prices was a gold mine. When a corporation in one country sells corn, or flour made from corn, or tortillas made from corn, or a variety of other corn products, it is not at all a bad thing if a neighboring country sells its basic raw material at a fire-sale price. It can, in fact, become a huge windfall.

The main beneficiary of this kind of arrangement in Mexico is Roberto Gonzalez Barrera, the very politically connected and powerful head of the world's largest corn processing empire, called "Gruma" (acronym for Grupo Maseca, S.A.). Gonzalez Barrera's father founded the company in 1949 to produce processed rehydrated corn flour and mechanically prepared corn tortillas. But its income was undistinguished until 1989 when Carlos Salinas, an old family friend, became the president of Mexico. That event changed corn production and eating habits in Mexico profoundly.

Mexican corn production and consumption before that time was based on a complicated system that kept tortillas cheap while keeping farmers and *tortillarías* (tortilla manufacturers) in business. A federal corn agency called Conasupo would buy up corn from farmers at a subsidized price and then sell it to the *tortillarías* at a lower price. Then, to make sure they passed the bargain price on to consumers, the agency put a price cap on how much the tortilla makers could sell the tortillas for. It wasn't perfect, but everyone made a little money and nobody went broke.

One of the things Salinas did when he became president was to make his brother the head of Conasupo. Under the new leadership the agency froze the amount of corn that would be sold to the tortilla makers and said that orders beyond that would be filled only by mechanized, mass-produced corn flour, not the traditional hand-produced (and more flavorful) corn *masa*. It may be a coincidence, but at that time there were only two major producers of corn flour. One was Miconsa, a poorly run government enterprise, and the other was called Maseca, which happened to be owned by Gruma. Next, the government phased out the program of supplying the tortilla millers with inexpensive corn altogether and instead encouraged them to buy Gruma's Maseca corn flour. If the millers refused and paid a higher price to get better corn, the Ministry of Commerce wouldn't let them pass on their higher price to consumers. The millers were trapped. They were forced to buy inferior-tasting corn flour, made by the president's friend, which their consumers did not want, or buy the higher priced, but better-tasting, corn *masa* and be forced to sell it at a lower price. All told, between 1993 and 1995, these measures caused seven thousand Mexican tortilla-making shops to close.[14]

Interestingly, one of the few millers of tortillas that did *not* go out of business in those days was Grupo Industrial Maseca, or Gimsa, which was yet another subsidiary of Gruma. Through its parent company, Gruma, Gimsa cut a deal with the Ministry of Commerce that allowed corn millers to get paid the difference between the market price for its corn flour and the capped price as a "rebate." The rebate was theoretically for all millers of corn flour, but by that time most of the competition had gone out of business. The only flour-making alternative to Gimsa of any size was the government company, Miconsa, which was later sold off, giving Gimsa a near-monopoly in the market. This "rebate" amounted to roughly 35 percent of Gimsa's revenue in 1992, or 1.93 billion pesos ($492.6 million). It grew to 43 percent of Gimsa's revenue in 1994. Today Gruma and its various subsidiaries control 77 percent of the corn flour market in Mexico, for a total global operation of over $1.1 billion.

All of this is complicated and dense-sounding, but the most important "take away" point is that with every twist and turn of government policy, Gruma or one of its subsidiaries made a killing. And at the same time that these policies were taking place,

Figure 9. Growth Rate of Migration, Mexico to the United States, Various Years

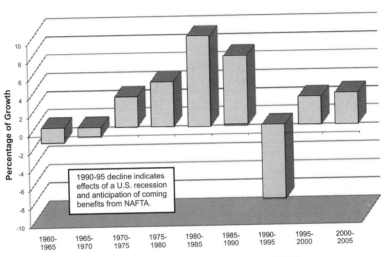

Source: United Nations Population Division, "World Migrant Stock, 2005."

NAFTA was being signed and was voted into law. So at one and the same time the government was signing an agreement to lift tariffs on cheap foreign corn and creating policies to channel it into the hands of the world's largest corn products producer. Subsidized U.S. corn began to flow into the Mexican market and an age-old era of Mexican production of its own corn effectively came to an end.

The lifting of the tariffs was a gift to Gruma because it supplied them with cheap corn, from which they made their cheap tortillas, and with which they wiped out tens of thousands of local corn farmers and tortilla producers, who had been their competitors. That in turn forced consumers to turn to Gonzalez Barrera's products as the few remaining corn flour and tortilla alternatives. In less than one decade his competition had disappeared and his costs had plummeted. It was a perfect storm of benefits for Gonzalez Barrera's bland-tasting manufactured flour and tortillas.

The Gruma company had yet another windfall in the early 2000s, which once again brought misery to Mexico's poorest populations. It was when the United States was temporarily experimenting with ethanol as an oil substitute that required huge amounts of corn and that drove up corn prices for the first time in a decade. Perhaps unsurprisingly, Gruma is also integrally linked with the Archer Daniels Midland company, which is a major recipient of U.S. corn subsidies and a major contributor to U.S. politicians. In 1996, ADM bought 22 percent of Gruma. Today its chief operating officer and its vice president for planning and business development both sit on Gruma's board. ADM mills Gruma's wheat flour products in both Mexico and the United States, which ADM then sells under the brand name of "Mission Foods." Therefore, when the demand for corn for biofuels caused the price for corn products to shoot up, it not only forced hungry Mexicans to switch to wheat products but it also became one more gold mine for Gruma and its U.S. partners. They were poised to win either way the market went, and they did.[15]

Jasmine and Daniel

None of these secret deals and entanglements were in any way clear to Jasmine and Daniel and their families when they made the awful decision that they would have to leave to find work. All they knew was that nothing was producing a profit at home and to stay was to starve. Eventually the family got together a few thousand dollars — a lot by rural Chiapas standards — and six volunteers, all good workers, all young men, and all willing to make the journey to the United States. The problem with the plan was that Daniel was one of those young men chosen to go, and he and Jasmine had just gotten engaged. They said they just couldn't stand being apart from each other, and they begged to be kept together. Maybe they both could find jobs; maybe they could afford a place together. Maybe they could finally get married. So young as she was, the family finally agreed. They added Jasmine to the group, and then they all left.

They walked down the mountain from their high, remote community and made their way on foot up the west coast of Mexico. There is another more common method they could have tried. There is a freight train that runs from southern Chiapas up to the Mexico-Texas border, a four-to-five-day trip. It is illegal to ride on the train and extremely dangerous. It has been dubbed *el tren de la muerte,* "The Death Train," because of the number of people who have fallen off and been crushed under its wheels. In spite of its dangers, every year, tens of thousands of economic refugees, mainly from Central America, take their chances on it, and hundreds of them never make it to the end. Those who do, and survive the journey, speak of migrants being thrown into trees, decapitated by power lines, sucked under the wheels, limbs severed. *Se los comió el tren,* their companions would say, "The train ate them up."[16]

However, for Jasmine and her companions, to gain access to the train would have meant walking due south for nearly two days to the little town of Arriaga, where the train starts out, and where jumpers can get on, and that would have been time lost from the ultimate journey north. So instead they walked. They walked north along the spine of the westward side of the Sierra Madre Mountains, occasionally taking a bus, sometimes hitchhiking, but mainly walking for almost three weeks. Then, exhausted and nearly broke, they stopped at the town of Altar, Mexico, about sixty miles south of the U.S. border, where they hired a man named Bolívar Cerbando Morales-Gálvez to be their *coyote*. *Coyotes* are those often unsavory, often unscrupulous people who work along the Mexican/U.S. border dealing in human lives. For a fee they will smuggle people like Jasmine and Daniel and their family across the line and into the new world. Whether the families succeed or fail, the *coyote* still gets paid. Typically, they don't really care which way it comes out.

There are actually several routes into the United States from Altar. The safest is around through the town of Sasabe, because there is less sand and more shade and the journey is not as harsh. Another route is shorter, but straight north through the brutal heat and terrain of the Sonoran Desert. Jasmine and her family didn't have the twelve to fifteen hundred dollars left that a coyote usually charges people, so he took what they had, and then led them up through the Sonoran.

But it didn't work out. They were too weak, the journey had been too long, and the heat was too punishing. After three days they couldn't go any further. Some wanted to go back, but by that time they had gone too far and couldn't return. They begged Morales-Gálvez to call for help, but he refused. He claimed that his T-Mobile satellite desert phone couldn't get reception in the desert. No one believed him. Finally, about a hundred miles southwest of Tucson on the Tohono O'odham Indian Reservation, most of them collapsed. They couldn't go any farther and Morales-Gálvez, who still had his own water and food, abandoned them. Three of Jasmine's uncles, who still had some strength left, continued walking on ahead to search for help. At a small town called Papago Farms they ran across Border Patrol agents canvassing the area. They turned themselves in and then led the agents back to their friends.

When they got back to the others, they found all of them in critical condition, near death from exposure and dehydration. Two recovered fairly quickly. Two more were in intensive care for several days. Some took more care. But young Jasmine never made it. She died en route in the ambulance. They tried to resuscitate her at the hospital, but she was already gone. Daniel survived, but no one knows where he is. They say he ran screaming from the hospital when he got the news, and there's no word on what happened to him or where he is. He never made it back home. He never contacted anyone about getting a job. He simply disappeared.

Victims of the System

I don't pretend to know how to wade through the complex immigration laws in America. I don't know how to craft a balance between the sometimes legitimate immigration concerns of a state like Arizona and the over-reaching responses they have made to them. I can't begin to understand all of the legal, economic, and historical issues that will resolve the unhappy place where we are today.

But what I *do* know is that people like Jasmine Díaz and Daniel Hernández are not our enemies. They didn't come here to hurt us or take our jobs or soak up our tax dollars. Their story is not just about *immigration* reform, whereby people who work hard, play by the rules, and want to make a living and raise their families can have an opportunity to do so; it's also about *trade* reform that would prevent ordinary people from being driven from their land and their homes and their families, to become sweatshop workers or international sources of remittances. Jasmine and Daniel tried to come here because they were hungry, because they were desperate, and because they loved each other.

And I know that little Jasmine died for our sins.

She died so that we could continue to worship a market system that destroys people and cripples families far away so that we can live well here at home — a system that forces prices down so that we can drink cheap coffee and forces immigration up so that our farmers and industries can have cheap labor. And I know that when they finally brought the *coyote* to court, in addition to whatever the judge did to him for abandoning all of them to suffer in the Sonoran Desert, at the end of the day, you and I and all of our families are co-conspirators in his crime.

SIX

Coffee:
Victor and Hugo

The Coffee industry is one of feast or famine, but, for the small producers, it is usually famine. — *The Coffee Book*[1]

Why It Matters

Since so many congregations and religious groups have heard about and become involved in the international coffee crisis and the fair trade movement, we would be remiss if we didn't say a few words about how the story of coffee fits into the global picture of trade and faith.

For several years I used to travel each summer to Guatemala with a big red-haired farmer in my congregation named Hugo. He sponsored children through a well-intentioned but sometimes naïve Christian sponsorship organization, and because I lived in Guatemala back in the 1980s, he took me along to guide him around and translate for him. One of his sponsored kids is named Elvia, and she lives high up in the mountains in the Chiquimula province, just north of the border with Honduras. The first time we went to see her, she lived in a one-room home literally on a wide spot next to the road with her parents, three siblings and their families and their children, and two neighbor children. Elvia's older brothers and families lived with them because no one had the income to live out on their own, and the neighbor kids lived with them because their parents died in a car accident and Elvia's family just took them in.

Their home was just one large room with a dirt floor not much larger than the size of many North American kitchens. After our first visit, they got a little money from World Vision, the evangelical development agency, and they built another room onto their home but it was still no larger than a small one-person apartment in the

United States. They are the poster family for the overused term, the "poorest of the poor." And her father, Victor, was a coffee farmer.

Coffee is a huge portion of Guatemala's economy. According to a recent study, it accounts for 12 percent of Guatemala's GNP and generates 30 to 35 percent of its foreign exchange. More than 12 percent of Guatemala's economically active population works in the industry, including 90 to 95 percent of child labor. However, only 20 percent of the coffee workforce depends primarily on the coffee industry for their livelihood. Most of the rest are either migrant workers who come down from the Central Highlands to work two to four months during the coffee harvest, or they are like Victor, a year-round resident who survives by working his own farm in the off season.[2]

Our first visit was all sweetness and light. Victor took off work to be home and greet us. Hugo gave out toys and clothes to all the children. Everyone seemed glad to see us. We noticed, however, that a new baby, born to Elvia's older sister, looked frail and thin. She had a light greenish tint to her skin and never smiled. "Bad water," our guide told us. "And not enough protein. There's no fresh water here and they don't have a healthy diet of foods."

While we were there I talked to Victor about his work. He said he worked for two plantation owners and split his time working for both of them. He gestured to one of the farms far off across the valley and up another mountain. I was amazed. "How far is that?" I asked. He laughed and shook his head. He didn't know, but I could tell it had to be a good three- to four-hour walk. "Where is the other farm?" I asked. He gestured in the other direction, equally far away. Another long walk. "You do this every day?" I asked. He laughed again. Of course he did. Why was I so foolish as to ask?

It is often noted that coffee is the most frequently traded commodity in the world after oil. It is handled by half a billion people and consumed by more people than drive cars or own televisions. In recent years it has become a cash cow phenomenon for specialty shops like Starbucks and even caffeine drive-by shops like Dunkin Donuts (which recently quietly surpassed Starbucks in price for an average cup).

In the early 1990s, however, prices paid to local coffee farmers turned steadily downward and are now at what Oxfam UK estimates to be a one-hundred-year low.[3] There isn't any way that

you can put a pretty face on that. It is a catastrophe by any measurement. On the one hand, for consumers in the United States this
has meant little. The price of coffee never even kept up with inflation. However, for coffee growers it has been a growing, terrifying
nightmare.

The next year, Hugo and I returned to Guatemala and again
trekked up the mountain to see Elvia and her family. During the
year Hugo had arranged to send crates of chickens to the family.
"For protein," he had said. "Half are 'layers' and half are 'fryers.'
So they can eat some and get eggs from the others."

When we arrived, however, we found that all the chickens had
died. A disease had come through. The children had all gotten sick.
The animals had all died. The little baby was still ill. Though her
mother was cradling her in her arms and singing silently, the baby
stared vacantly into the distance and never smiled. Her hair was
thin and yellow.

I asked Victor what had happened. He said he didn't know. A
development organization had given them medicine, and they took
it but it was gone and the baby is still very sick. "Can you afford
any on your own?" I asked.

"No," he said. "We don't have money for the medicines. Last
year the foreman paid me less than he paid me the year before. And
again this year less than last."

"Why is that?"

He shook his head. "Each year I work harder. I cover more
plants. I pick more beans. This year I joined with the group for
the washing and removing of the skin of the beans. But each year
my money gets less."

"What will you do?" I asked.

He smiled, but he did not laugh. "I will work harder."

What Happened to Coffee?

Victor was not wrong about his declining pay. Wages for coffee
farmers have been declining almost every year since the early 1990s.
They are on a slight uptick now, due to a decline in the harvest in
Brazil, but nobody believes that it will last. According to Oscar
Guevara, mayor of the town of Chiquimula, in the year 2004, "the
owners of the coffee plantations were paying 25 *quetzales* ($6.00)

per day, but now the people are earning between 10 and 15 *quetzales* ($2.50 to $4.00) per day, which was not enough for one person to survive on, let alone their children."[4]

The World Bank estimates that anywhere between 30 million and 60 million coffee farmers around the world lost their livelihoods because of this crisis. Major areas of the world that were once rich in coffee wealth are now in tatters. In Colombia, once famous for its deep rich coffees and Juan Valdez commercials, coffee has fallen to fourth on its list of exports, and the coffee federation that produced the commercials is bankrupt. In Ethiopia, the historic birthplace of coffee, coffee has shrunk from 70 percent of its exports earnings to 30 percent.[5]

Meanwhile, the "collateral" damage is enormous. When people can no longer live off coffee growing, they are forced to make painful decisions. Some flee to the cities and work in sweatshops so that you and I can buy ten-dollar dress shirts in big box stores. Some flee to the United States or Europe to find a better life, often being met by an increasingly hostile populace, or dying in boats or deserts along the way. Remember the twenty-four Mexicans found suffocated in a boxcar in Iowa a few years ago? Roughly twenty of them were out-of-work coffee farmers. Or the fourteen who died of dehydration in the 115-degree heat trying to cross the Sonoran Desert into Arizona? They were from Veracruz, Mexico, and were all coffee farmers. Anywhere from three to four hundred people die crossing the desert each year, and about half are coffee farmers.

Others manage to stay on their lands by growing illegal crops. In Colombia it's coca and poppies, the plants from which cocaine and heroin are derived. In Ethiopia and Kenya, it's *khat,* an amphetamine-type drug that is illegal in the United States and many European countries but popular among young people. In addition to a high it also can lead to hallucinations, emaciation, impotence, and cancer. But it pays about $9 a bushel while coffee runs at about $.01. If your family was hungry, what would you do?[6]

Still others have beaten their plowshares into swords and declared war on their governments. In Chiapas, Mexico, the Zapatista rebels evolved in large part as a protest against the state-sponsored reduction in prices paid to coffee farmers. In Africa, the collapse of coffee production pushed Rwandan coffee farmers into desperation, increased social tension and was one factor behind the ethnic Hutu massacres of a half-million Tutsis. And in Colombia the ranks of the left-wing rebels and right-wing paramilitaries swelled as more and more coffee farmers lost their incomes. Both groups have learned to cash in on coca growing — which was fueled by the decline in coffee prices — by in effect placing a "tax" on cocaine production, and as a result have become the highest paid rebel movements in the world.

Add to these unfortunate consequences the loss of revenue to countries where coffee income has been critical. In Ethiopia, where growing *khat* is now on the rise, the drop in coffee prices has cost the country $1.12 billion in lost export revenue in just the past five years alone. Put in more human terms, that amount of money could have built 1,250 health centers or 2,000 primary schools. There is, of course, no guarantee that all of the lost income would have been spent on the poor, but one can guarantee that now none of it will be. The crisis has also set back much of the progress achieved by debt activists in recent years. Ethiopia, for example, spent years in draconian belt tightening to qualify for cancelation of $58 million of its debt payments in 2001. Yet during that same period it lost almost twice that amount from the decline in coffee revenues.[7]

On the way home after our second trip Hugo anguished over how to do more to help his sponsored children. "Next year I'll send more money," he said. "Next year I'll set up a trust, so that whatever happens to me they'll always be helped." Hugo looked as strong as a bear, but his hips and thigh were slowly being eaten up with cancer, and he knew that one day he would no longer be able to make the long journey up into Chiquimula to see the kids. I tried to walk him through what I knew about the vagaries of the global economy and its effects on people like Victor and his family, about chronic and intentional overproduction that forced too much coffee onto the market and forced down prices paid to farmers. And campaigns to get the United States and Europe to support price stabilization plans, and new business models like "fair trade." But in the end he said he didn't know anything about any of that. That was just politics, he said, and he didn't get involved with politics.

Why Did It Happen?

The causes of the coffee crisis are many and complex, and most have more to do with human sin than standard economic trade theory. From the 1960s through the 1980s there was an international coffee agreement that kept coffee prices at a relatively stable price, and most farmers, while poor, at least made a living. The United States supported the agreement because it kept poor people in Latin America from getting hungry enough to consider Cuba a role model and start overthrowing their oppressive governments. But after the fall of the Soviet Union, we changed policy and pulled out of the agreement, effectively killing it. Almost overnight hundreds of new producers jumped into the market seeking a larger piece of the pie, and prices paid to local farmers plummeted. The way Oxfam UK puts it, we moved from a "managed" system to a "flooded" system, and people like Victor and his family paid the price.[8]

More subtly, the policies of wealthy countries, and the international financial institutions that they control, seemed almost intentionally designed to keep production high and prices low. During the 1990s, the IMF and other regional banks made hundreds of loans to countries to develop coffee plantations. However, with each new farm producing more and more coffee, there was less and less profit to go around, and the farmers got increasingly poorer. In fact, over roughly the same period of time coffee drinking in the United States actually declined slightly, which further drove down profits for producers.

To make matters worse, in the early 1990s the IMF arranged huge loans by regional banks to help bring Vietnam into the world coffee market. And they came in with a vengeance. In less than a decade Vietnam moved from being a small, insignificant producer to number two (after Brazil). That made the growing glut on the global market swell even larger, and soon no small farmers, not even those in Vietnam, were making money. By 2000, the Vietnamese government was burning hundreds of thousands of hectares of coffee trees to help drive prices back up, but by then the damage had been done. In addition to overproduction driving down prices, Vietnam also suffered internally. During the 1990s, over four hundred thousand people rushed to the Dak Lak province, the largest growing region, to plant coffee, known during the boom as the "dollar tree." Hundreds of thousands of hectares of ancestral forests were cut down and the land intensively irrigated, leading to soil erosion and serious water shortages. Natural rivers ran dry and underground water levels dropped. When drought struck in 1998, two hundred reservoirs dried up and water supplies were drained. During the drought it was estimated that 90 percent of families in Dak Lak did not have access to sufficient water.[9]

Many transnational coffee corporations are so large that they literally set national economic policy for some developing countries. They invest heavily in the development of coffee plantations in places like Laos and Thailand, which creates an overproduction of coffee. And as we've noted, overproduction means lower profits for individual farmers and higher profits for corporations. In chapter 2 we told the story of how Nestlé threatened Mexico with moving its purchasing contract to the emerging coffee regions of Vietnam. In response, Vietnam excitedly doubled its planting of coffee trees (clear-cutting forests and draining wetlands to do so), but in the end Mexico cut its prices to keep the account and Nestlé stayed with them. Mexican farmers lost because they were paid even less for their coffee beans than before. Vietnam lost because they produced tens of thousands of pounds of new coffee beans that nobody would purchase, and Nestlé made a fortune. Speaking from the perspective of the logic of globalization and free trade, Nestlé described the transaction in its 2000 annual report by saying, "trading profits increased . . . and margins improved thanks to favorable commodity prices."[10]

Another very clear way that rules are weighted against the poor is in the profit markups. If you look at the markups by the many handlers of coffee from the grower to your cup, the differences between them are startling. For local buyers, transporters, millers, baggers, processors, etc., the markup runs from as low as 2 percent to as high as 11 percent depending on the region. But the markup for the final marketer (for example, Kraft, Nestlé, Sara Lee) can be as high as 25 to 30 percent. By contrast, the new and promising "fair trade" business model buys straight from co-ops in the farming regions, and can thereby double, triple, and quadruple the incomes of the people at the lower levels of production. One of the reasons for the growing interest in fair trade coffee in churches and other houses of worship is just this "mission" opportunity to lift the incomes of poor coffee farmers simply by drinking coffee during "coffee hour." However, the fair trade concept is still young, and so far has only a tiny share of the market.

Victor and Hugo

In the summer of 2003 I took my last trip to Guatemala with Hugo. His doctor said the cancer was growing and didn't recommend he make the trip. But Hugo had to go. He had set aside some money in a trust to help the family, and wanted to go and tell them. We took several others from our church with us on that trip, and it was a good thing because he was in a lot of pain and more than once one of us had to help him in or out of the truck or down a hill. It was hard, but he was tough, and we managed to make the painful drive one last time up into the mountains in an old pickup with bad shocks so he could see his kids. They knew him well by this time and they all poured out to see him. He was in tears. He was in his glory.

I saw Victor off by the house, and I went over to him and asked how his coffee farming was going. He smiled but looked ahead at Hugo playing with the children, including their frail little girl, who looked better now but still not well. Too much damage had occurred at too early an age for her to ever be truly healthy. "Mister Hugo loves our children," he said. "And he wants to help us. But we can no longer farm here and we are going away."

"Where?" I asked.

"There are many of us. We cannot farm here and feed our families. We will ride on the bus into the city where there are jobs in the factories and they will hire men who are strong and work hard."

I looked at him with dismay. He was old and worn and would never be hired in a factory. What would happen is that his sons would get the jobs, they would take care of him, and Victor would be humiliated.

"When do you leave?" I asked.

"Soon," he said. "We cannot feed our families here anymore."

On the way home, I told Hugo about my conversation with Victor, and he was shocked. He had been so happy to see his sponsored kids again that he had forgotten to ask Victor how he was doing. He grew silent for some time, and finally said, "That Victor's a good man. He's a hard worker and doesn't deserve this." Both of them were farmers, and Hugo had often commented on the unfairness of his wealth and Victor's desperation. It was a shame that they couldn't have been able to communicate more easily. They had a lot in common. "I've got to do something," he said. "I've got to send them more money."

"I don't think that would help," I said. "Every year they make less money than the year before. You can't just pay for their whole lives."

"But I've got to do something. They can't just pack up and lose everything." His face tensed for a moment, like someone who was in pain, and he reached down and rubbed his thigh. "Tell me again about that fair trade thing. I've just got to do something."

"What Then Should We Do?"

Fair trade coffee is actually just one of many ways that people can get involved. Oxfam International, for example, has a whole package of policy proposals that it promotes under its "Coffee Rescue Plan," such as getting roasters to pay higher wages to farmers and reducing the stock of existing coffee. Other groups campaigned for years (successfully, it turns out) to get the United States to rejoin the International Coffee Organization, so that its influence could be used to reinstate something like the old coffee price stabilization agreement. The United States did rejoin the organization in 2004, but so far has refused to agree to any coffee revitalization program that is not based on laissez faire, free market principles. But nothing short of a complete reimagining of the meaning and purpose of international commerce will ultimately help the poorest farmers at the bottom of the trade ladder, an understanding that believes that all of God's children should have a place at the table and periodically "rigs" the rules of the market to ensure that that happens.

However, the fair trade movement is probably the most accessible way for most people in the United States to feel they are having an impact on the problem. When a company is practicing fair trade, it partners directly with farmer co-ops in developing countries and eliminates the layers of "middle people," and in so doing guarantees a stable living wage. In addition, to be certified as a fair trade company, the cooperative must also promote democratic principles of governance, gender equality, humane working conditions, and environmental sensitivity.

Many religious organizations have special arrangements with a very fine fair trade company called Equal Exchange, the oldest and largest in the United States. When a congregation or parishioner purchases one of their coffees, teas, chocolate, nuts, or cocoa, not only does the money help raise living standards of growers; a portion is also donated to a Small Farmer Fund, which is then spent on credit, training, and emergency aid to farmers, helping them become more self-sustaining. Equal Exchange also makes long-term commitments to their farmer co-op partners, not only offering the base purchase price when the market is good, but credit and other benefits when the market is bad, thus leveling out some of the punishing chaos of global trade.

By winter Hugo had gotten to the point where he was sick in bed most of the time and by summer he was far too frail to make the trip back to Guatemala again. Then, in the early winter, when our children were decorating the manger, the choir was preparing its annual cantata, and the church as a whole was preparing to welcome the birth of the Son of God, who fed the multitude, visited the poor, and healed the sick, Hugo died. He never found a way to solve all the problems for those kids he learned to love so much up in the mountains of Chiquimula.

Not long after that, our church became a "Jubilee Congregation" so we could work as a community toward canceling crippling third world debts, and we began selling fair trade coffee to help put food on the tables of poor farmers around the world. We put up a big display in the parish hall, bought huge bags of coffee from Equal Exchange, and have been selling it on Sundays ever since. I doubt that our little project will ever help Victor and María and their kids, who finally lost everything they had and had to move away and start over as poor and broken people. But I'm certain we've helped other people like them. And I'm certain that somehow in the mystery of pain and love and life and death that Hugo knows of our little coffee display, and wherever he is, I think he's glad.

SEVEN

Trade in Israel:
Samuel and Naboth

Then you shall have the trumpet sounded loud; on the tenth day of the seventh month — on the day of atonement — you shall have the trumpet sounded throughout all your land. And you shall hallow the fiftieth year and you shall proclaim liberty throughout the land to all its inhabitants. It shall be a jubilee for you: you shall return, every one of you, to your property and every one of you to your family. That fiftieth year shall be a jubilee for you.... — Leviticus 25:9–11b

The "Creation" of Israel

As many economists enjoy saying, economic globalization is not really a new thing. There have been periods of international integration of markets that go back thousands of years. One of the earliest stories of cross-border trade was in the Ancient Near East during the time of the settlement of what is now known as Israel, and it had a major impact on that nation's history, culture, and theology. Looking at what happened to the people in that region and how they responded to it can offer guidance to us today in responding to our own situation.

Even though the Bible begins with God creating the six-day work week, the story of Israel as a nation began in about 1200 B.C.E., when bands of liberated slaves following a man named Moses, fled oppression in Egypt, and settled in the hill country of eastern Canaan. There, for the most part, they became farmers. They joined with other groups of wandering ex-slaves, impoverished nomads, scavenger bands, and *hapiru*, "people of the land," later known as the "Hebrews." Their home in the eastern part of Canaan was far from the militarized city-states of the west, which were still heavily controlled by Egypt. In part because of their remoteness and in part because they were surrounded by weakened empires and kingdoms, they were able to establish a unique society. They consciously created a loosely structured nation that was a deliberate contrast to what they had known in Egypt and what they had found in the Egyptian-ruled city states in Canaan. ("You shall not do as they do in the land of Egypt, where you lived, and you shall not do as they do in the land of Canaan, to which I am bringing you," Lev. 18:3a.) Egypt, for example, had a powerful army, and the *hapiru* had none. Egypt had a hereditary ruler, a pharaoh, and they had prophets called "judges," who were both popularly chosen and temporary. Egypt had a steep hierarchical wealth structure, and the *hapiru* created perhaps the most egalitarian nation of the Ancient Near East. Egypt had a polytheistic cabinet of gods who lived in distant realms, and the *hapiru* worshiped Yahweh, who was one and lived with them daily.

Also in contrast to Egypt, which had a tightly organized and centralized economy, their economy and society were loose and interdependent and built on a theology of trust and mutual support. Economically, they were organized in great families or "tribes" (*mishpahah*), which understood that all land was to be held in common and shared with everyone, and nobody was ever to become poor. Ultimately all of the land was owned by Yahweh and only loaned to them for their stewardship and care. It is worth noting that in Genesis, the book written to retell their earliest history, the word for "poor" never occurs, not because everyone was rich, but because the gap between rich and poor was so small that the term was irrelevant. Israel was self-consciously more egalitarian than any of its nearby neighbors.[1]

Theologically, they believed in a God who purposefully identified with the poor and the oppressed[2] and who owned all the land upon which they lived and from which they obtained sustenance. "The Land is mine," their God told them, and you who live on it are "aliens (*gur,* resident aliens, protected foreigners) or tenants (*tosub,* temporary sojourners)" (Lev. 25:23b). Their central ethical principle, and the one they repeated to each other frequently, was that because they were once slaves in Egypt and because Yahweh had freed them from that slavery, therefore they should not oppress the poor, the widow, the orphan, the homeless, or the immigrant.

You cannot cheat the poor, they would say, and you cannot perpetually own slaves. You cannot do these things because you were once oppressed and slaves yourselves. Your very redemption forbids it.[3]

The Invention of Poverty

Beginning in about the tenth century B.C.E. and moving forward, Israel began to change. The egalitarian society, the large socially supportive communal farms, the loose, nonmilitaristic governance, all faded. The nation acquired a king, a standing army, a ruling royal class, an international trading system, and great wealth. At the same time it also gained oppression, militarism, poverty, and true hunger. In this period we begin to see stories of authentic deprivation in the biblical texts for the first time. Stories like that of the starving widow of Zaraphath (1 Kings 17:8–16) and the widow of a follower of Elisha (2 Kings 4:1–2), or of the Shunammite woman who had her land stolen from her while she was away (2 Kings 8:1–6). These stories would have been unheard of during Israel's earlier history.[4]

One very interesting way to visualize this devolution into an economically polarized society is to look at the changes in the types of houses that Israel built over time. When archaeologists excavated the important northern city of Jezreel, they found that the size and placement of homes changed over the centuries. Houses that were unearthed from the tenth century are generally small and uniform in shape, indicating that each family lived pretty much like its neighbors. But houses two hundred years later, in the eighth century, at the same site, vary greatly in size showing that something dramatic had taken place. Some are very large with land around them, and located in pleasant, spacious parts of town, while the majority are much smaller, closer together, and in tiny, cramped areas, walled off from their larger neighbors. Between these two centuries a major social revolution had taken place.[5] Israel's spiritual, covenantal, and communal understanding of itself had changed. For some, evidently, poverty was no longer considered an affront to the justice of Yahweh. No longer was inconceivable wealth considered evil. When a society makes a change that is that large, it isn't just making decisions about economics. It is making decisions about its deepest understandings of God and the meaning of human life. A decision to give vast wealth to the few and take it from the many is not merely politics; it is also theology, because it is an issue of values, not governance. It challenges and contradicts humanity's relationship with the One who is origin and creator of all that is. Unsurprisingly, as this gap between wealth and poverty widened, the great eighth-century prophets such as Amos, Hosea, the Isaiahs, and Jeremiah began to emerge on the scene, demanding justice with a conservative "back to the Bible" message of restoration of the oneness of all creation that God had intended.

It's also not surprising to learn that as the social fabric of Israel was being torn, so was its environment. During these two centuries, there was also tremendous environmental destruction in the Mediterranean region due to unchecked hunting, overproduction of crops, and overcutting of forests. The thirst for timber for export to Carthage and Rome and the massive building projects in Jerusalem devastated the forests of Lebanon and Ephraim (1 Kings 7:2). The firs on Mount Hermon disappeared (Ezek. 27:5). The lions that lived in the Jordan River valley became extinct. To a large extent, the land became "desolate," just as the prophet Micah had warned (7:13). In Jeremiah, God directly attributes the desolation to human actions:

> Many shepherds have destroyed my vineyard,
> they have trampled down my portion,
> they have made my pleasant portion
> a desolate wilderness.
> They have made it a desolation;
> desolate, it mourns to me.
> The whole land is made desolate,
> but no one lays it to heart. (Jer. 12:10–11)[6]

These things may not have been sufficiently severe as to threaten the future of the planet, as they do today, but even so, overfishing, overfarming, and overcutting of forests caused a depletion of food and resources for those living nearby. And they contributed to the rise in poverty in preexilic Israel.

What Made Israel Poor?

There were a number of factors that changed Israel and precipitated its rise in poverty and oppression. Two that have particular relevance for us today are the growth in the power of its kings and the growth in its cross-border trade, an early version of what we have been calling "economic globalization."

Israel Calls a King

Israel took on a king for the first time in response to a series of terrorist attacks by mysterious "Sea People" (later known as the Philistines) along their western borders in the early 1100s B.C.E. The more frightened that people grew of these attacks, the more willing they were to give up their freedoms in return for national security. Within a remarkably short time they moved from being a relatively egalitarian, relatively nonmilitary society to one that was substantially authoritarian and militarized. And each new ruling government—along with its wealthy elite allies—demanded more and more resources, wealth, and conscripts from the population.

An insightful story of this transition is found in 1 Samuel 8, where the prophet Samuel is forced to anoint Israel's very first king. The text as we have it was actually written many years after the events it relates, but it is telling in terms of how at least one segment of the society later viewed what they once had and what they were willing to give up. The story goes that, after suffering the deaths of over four thousand in one battle and even more in another, the people of Israel became terrified of their mysterious adversaries. Instead of the more traditional responses of repentance and recovenanting, they clamored for blood revenge led by an absolute authority, and the only way to have that, they believed, was by taking on a strong leader who could go to war with their adversaries and protect the homeland. A delegation of the "elders of Israel" came to Samuel, the last of the great prophet judges, and demanded that he anoint a king to rule over them. In a scene probably driven as much by fear as grief, they told him that they had had enough and wanted a ruler who would strengthen the military, increase national security, and protect them from foreigners.

Samuel opposed the move, so he took the issue to God, and God told him that their request constituted a failure of their faith and trust in God, and that by demanding a strong authority to rule over them, they were in fact demanding an idol instead of God. God begrudgingly told Samuel to give them what they wanted, but also told him to warn them in detail of all that they would lose in freedoms and wealth if they had someone rule over them, making decisions for them. But they didn't care. Sometimes when a nation is frightened by shadowy terrorist actors, it searches inward to ask what happened, but sometimes it lashes outward to exact revenge. "We are determined to have a king over us," they said (1 Sam. 8:19). They wanted a strong military and a strong ruler to protect them. They wanted someone to make them feel safe, who could inflict violent vengeance upon vague enemies. And personal losses, to them, were simply the worthy sacrifice for the cause. So Samuel looked around Israel until he found a deeply disturbed and possibly bipolar young farmer named Saul and anointed him as their first king. After that, Israel as a nation and as a people changed forever. Each successive king took on more and more of the trappings of a typical, brutal, authoritarian Near Eastern monarchy, in which the rich got richer and the poor were conscripted to fight in endless wars. Even if later kings were not interested in warring with their neighbors, they would have found it difficult to resist once the system and machinery of war had been put into place.

Trading for Poverty

A second factor contributing to the growth in Israel's poverty was an increase in trade. At first, trading was done just within their own tribal system. When they first settled in Palestine, they were mainly in the hills in the east of the region; but eventually as the population grew, some migrated down into the valleys of the west. With that migration came the first divisions in production (olives and wine in the west, and cereals and cattle in the east), and the first vestiges of market-based winners and losers. Those in the valleys who benefited from trade between the two groups aligned themselves with the Canaanite kings in the early years and Israelite kings later. They supported the kings' desires to build large standing armies, because their business deals needed protection from attacks, and stability is good for business. Those who didn't benefit tended to be the ones who lost their farms to big corporate farmers (see Mic. 2:1–2) and were conscripted to fight in preemptive defensive wars.[7]

The biggest impact on poverty from trade, however, was the result of a burgeoning business relationship between North Israel and the cities of Tyre and Sidon, the two main import-export centers of Phoenicia, and their immediate neighbor to the north. From roughly the eighth to the fourth century B.C.E, Phoenicia was the most globally connected economic power in the ancient world. It wasn't advanced capitalism as we know it today, but it did have a constantly expanding market system based on trade and accumulation and surplus, and its business arrangements demanded huge amounts of goods and cheap labor. And it also made a handful of families in Tyre and Sidon fabulously wealthy. (Think of the city of Dubai today for a modern parallel.)

From as far west as Tarshish in Spain the Phoenicians imported silver, iron, tin, and lead. From Beth-Togarmah in Armenia, they traded war horses and mules; from Rhodes in the Aegean, they traded in ivory tusks and ebony; from Edom, turquoise, purple, embroidered work, linen, coral, and rubies; from Arabia, lambs, rams, and goats; from Sheba and Raamah, spices and gold. And on and on. They were known as the "merchant of the peoples on many coastlands" (Ezek. 27:2). They were the "bestower of crowns, whose merchants were princes, whose traders were the honored of the earth" (23:8).

North Israel's proximity to this trading center meant that it evolved not only into a primary source location for raw materials (honey, wheat, oil, and agricultural goods) but also a near-equal business partner through trade agreements and royal marriages. As that relationship developed, it changed forever Israel's understanding of the economy (as family-based and Yahweh-owned) and its ethic (as gratitude for their liberation from slavery). From about 800 to 600 B.C.E., a handful of people were allowed to grow fabulously wealthy by capitalizing on the wealth of Tyre and Sidon's international trading system. Ezekiel says accurately, but somewhat sarcastically, of those involved in international trade, "By your great wisdom in trade you have increased your wealth, and your heart has become proud in your wealth" (28:4).

As these traders became ever more rich, they often aligned with (or were the same as) the emerging royal class. Their hunger for production and sales required more and more land and more and more work to be taken from the peasants. King Omri established Jezreel, the city of the archaeological digs described above, as the capital of Israel, right at the border with Phoenicia. Then he married off his son Ahab to Jezebel, daughter of Ethbaal, who was the king of Sidon and an important shipping entrepreneur. They in turn married their daughter Athaliah to Joram, heir to the throne of Judah, which opened even more trade routes to the south. North Israel and Judah shared two very important north-south trade routes, so their old animosities took a back seat to the need to make money from transport fees and tolls going through their respective countries. This increase in both trade and centralized power inevitably created an increase in wealth for the few at the top and poverty for the many at the bottom. One powerful story that illustrates the growth in global trade and the concentration of wealth in the hands of the wealthy is the illegal land deal that King Ahab and his wife, Jezebel, arranged in Jezreel to steal a vineyard from a farmer named Naboth (1 Kings 21). It is a quintessential example of the lengths to which the wealthy and powerful would go to acquire land for their own production. The story doesn't say, but it is likely that Ahab and Jezebel wanted Naboth's land because it was close to the border and anything grown there could be exported north to Tyre with lower transportation costs. The text says only that he wanted the land for growing "vegetables," but not what kind. It is very possible that he was interested in acquiring his own vineyards in the northern kingdom to compete with the major wine production region that was much further south and in Judah. In those days, the bulk of wine for export came from what has been called the "Bordeaux region" of Palestine, the fertile valleys around Gibeon, just north of Jerusalem.[8]

The story begins with Ahab and Jezebel on vacation up in their northern palace. One day they look out their window and see a vineyard right next door that is owned by Naboth. Ahab goes to him and offers to buy it for what is actually a reasonable price. In fact he makes two offers, the first being a trade for another piece of property and the second cash payment in that newfangled unit of exchange called "money."[9] But Naboth refuses both offers. He says he is simply unable to sell it at all because to do so would violate Torah teachings that it is God and not individual farmers who owns the land (Lev. 25:23). It is family property, what he calls an "ancestral inheritance," owned by the entire family and by God, and God would "forbid" his selling it (1 Kings 21:1–3).[10] The Hebrew word here translated usually as "inheritance" is *nahala* and could also be translated "sacred patrimony" or "sacred heirloom." It gives the clear sense that the ownership of this property has nothing to do with contracts and legal arrangements and everything to do with a family's relationship with the originator of it who gifted it to them. "The land shall not be sold in perpetuity," Yahweh had told them (Lev. 25:23).

The offer probably seemed like a simple business transaction to King Ahab — even more so to Jezebel, who was raised in a culture where religion was a wholly owned subsidiary of business interests. But when Naboth turned him down, Ahab remembered the teachings about land and property he'd learned in Sunday School and he went back home dejected. In fact he went to bed, turned his face to the wall, and refused to eat (1 Kings 21:4). Jezebel, on the other hand, would have none of that. She witheringly tells him that if he was any kind of king he would have just taken the land and have been done with it. So she constructs an elaborate scheme to bribe some politicians,[11] distort the courts, and steal the land herself. And she has poor Naboth killed in the process, completing a story that has great resonance in a number of countries around the world, including occasionally our own.

This story concludes with the prophet Elijah appearing on the scene and condemning the injustice of stealing and murder. However, clearly, as time went on Ahab and Jezebel's understanding of land and markets prevailed and Naboth and Elijah's did not. Money continued to flow upward into fewer and fewer hands, and land continued to be acquired by some and denied to others. The result of all this was that families and individuals began to slide further into debt to keep from starving, often losing their farms, often selling themselves and their family members into slavery and then losing their freedom altogether.

In the ancient world, peasants lived in a precarious balance under the best of times, barely able to support their families. But when something happened, such as an increase in taxes, drought, or military conscription, that balance would fail. They would be forced to take out loans from their wealthy landowning neighbors, the only source of credit in the ancient world, and then put themselves at even more risk than before. The wealthy were typically more than willing to make the loans, but usually (if not always) at usurious rates with an eye toward eventually foreclosing on the debtor's property. When poor farmers inevitably did get behind on payments, they would first have to give up their farm implements, then their livestock, then their land, and finally their freedom. They became slaves. Slavery of fellow Israelites within Israel was, with few exceptions, the result of economic indebtedness.[12] That's why the legal codes of the Torah eventually forbade the charging of interest on loans.[13] Payment of interest ordinarily comes out of a family's

Figure 10. Changes in Gini Index, 1947–2007

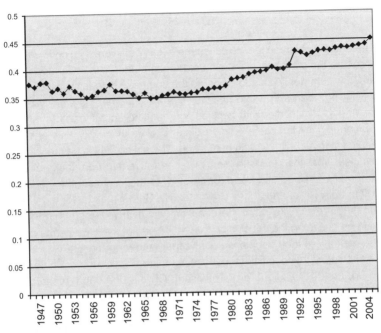

Source: Census Bureau, *www.census.gov/www/income/histinc/f04.html*

surplus. But what does a peasant family take it out of when there is no surplus? It's no surprise that the Hebrew word used to describe "interest" comes from the word *neshek,* meaning "a bite out of living flesh." It is telling that in the Hebrew scriptures, *neshek* is used far more often referencing a snake or serpent than a loan shark (though at times it is difficult to tell the difference).[14]

At the height of the 2008 international debt crisis, there was an odd parallel in the program known as "Debt for Equity Swaps," whereby a highly indebted country could literally trade some of its national productive capability away in exchange for a reduction in its debt load. Countries have turned over such things as state industries, national forests, and even the equivalent of their social security program to their creditors as payments on loans. The plan was very popular among the bankers in the creditor nations, but among the

INEQUALITY

There is a tool in economics called the "Gini coefficient," which is used to measure the statistical dispersion of numbers, that is, how far apart they are. It is commonly used to measure the degree of inequality in income or wealth between and within nations. The measurement is usually based on a zero to 1 scale, with zero being complete equality, with everyone owning exactly the same, and 1 being absolute inequality, with one person owning *all* of the wealth of a nation. There's no way to be precise, but it's clear from the stories in the biblical narrative that from the beginning of the era of kings and trade, on through to their demise, the inequality within both Israel and Judah grew steadily. Sometimes faster than other times, but it's unlikely that the direction was ever reversed. And there's also no escaping the conclusion that at the end of their two-century slide the majority of their people were less free, and more poor.

However, the coefficient *can* be measured in countries in today's world, and the results are not pleasant. On the one hand, researchers have found that countries with a narrow gap between rich and poor almost always do better and are more democratic than those with a wide gap. Countries with a small Gini coefficient have fewer people in prisons, more children in school (and with higher grades), fewer teen pregnancies, fewer cases of spouse abuse, fewer homicides, longer lives, and so on. Across the board in almost every measurement, the common thread for happier, more productive, more free, more wealthy nations is that there is less distance between the wealth and incomes of a nation's people.

---

people in the debtor nations the loss of sovereignty and the sense of being enslaved to a wealthy neighbor kept its implementation low.

Israel's story illustrates something we have noted before, that the growth of poverty is partly a story of how the powerful exercise their power over the weak, and partly of how expanding trade itself creates ever widening gaps between the wealthy and the poor (and how it gives the wealthy the power to abuse the poor). As land and people began being viewed as commodities, the vast tribal structure also began to lose its ability to protect the marginalized (widows, orphans, elderly) from falling into starvation. Peasants (a concept

On the other hand, they have also found that the United States has one of the highest measurements of inequality in the world. According to the CIA Fact Book for 2008, we are down at the bottom, just under Nigeria, Kenya, the Philippines, and Cameroon, and just above Uruguay, Jamaica, and Uganda. I'm sure there are lovely people in each of those countries, but is this really the company we would like to keep when we are promoting ourselves as the model of justice and equality around the world? According to research by scientists Richard Wilkinson and Kate Pickett, our descent into inequality began gradually in the late 1960s, but had rapid rises during the 1980s and the 2000s and has never reversed. Not coincidentally, the United States also ranks at or near the bottom of every social indicator. And when the researchers applied the same methodology to the fifty states, they found similarly that social well-being (happiness, low crime, low domestic violence, etc.) is higher in states with less income and wealth inequality.[15] Elizabeth Warren, the head of the Congressional Oversight Panel, has recently written that past eras of economic growth would raise the middle class, but today when the economy grows, the middle barely changes at all. In the boom of the 1960s, for example, the median income rose 33 percent (adjusted for inflation) but in the "boom" of the 2000s, it rose by 1.6 percent. Meanwhile basic expenses went up. By the early 2000s (before the explosion of home loans that caused the crash of 2008), the average family spent twice as much (adjusted for inflation) on mortgages than it did twenty years ago. And they spent it on houses that were only about 10 percent bigger and twenty-five years older. They also paid twice as much for health insurance.[16]

unknown only a few generations earlier) lived precariously, hand to mouth.

Responses from Israel's Activist Community

Israel's story is painful, but what wisdom can we draw from it to address our contemporary — and also sometimes painful — global trade? Here are four of their responses, plus some added guidance from Christian scriptures. Notice that in each of them a common thread is a conservative attempt to turn back the clock, to return

Israel to the egalitarian, communal society and economy that it had known before it acquired a king, a stratified society, and a market-driven economy.

Campaigns to Change Government Leaders

One attempt to counter abuses of power was to work on campaigns to change their national leadership. Many of us have done that ourselves on occasion, and sometimes the change was for the better and sometimes it was not. The prophet Jeremiah promoted and later supported the administration of King Josiah, who, though very young, turned out to be a great reformer, and historians consider his administration to be a positive, hopeful time. However, sometimes a change in leaders does not bring about what we want. Elisha, a bitter critic of the Omri dynasty (because, among other things, it had taken the land of small, free farmers), called for the anointing of Jehu as the new king. But when Jehu went to the palace in Jezreel to take over the reins of government, he slaughtered the entire royal family in a bloody massacre (2 Kings 9–10); and when he became king he took on all of the same trappings of monarchical power that Elisha had decried in his predecessors. Later, Hosea condemned the bloodshed involved in that transition, showing that even within the countercultural voices there was not always agreement on methods (Hos. 1:4–5). Similarly, years later during the Hellenist period, many people were outraged over the actions of King Antiochus IV, who in addition to heavy tributes and brutal suppression, also placed a statue of Zeus in the Jewish Temple and prohibited worship of Yahweh. Many then joined the Maccabean resistance movement and became guerrilla fighters against his despotic rule. However, when the war ended, the new leaders became just another Hellenist totalitarian royal family and utilized some of the same techniques of suppression and control as practiced by their predecessors.

Biblical scholar Ulrich Duchrow has argued that this event, which could be described as a victory in battles but defeat in values, devastated the underground resistance movement in Israel for generations. Some reformers, he says, dropped out of society altogether after that and moved to the desert to become a community that would later be called the Essenes. Others became members of or followers of the Pharisees, who tried to maintain alternative moral lifestyles, but within the status quo and avoiding making waves. A third group ceased believing in the possibility of the realm of God on earth in this life altogether and simply waited passively for the coming of God's intervention in history through a messiah.[17]

Campaigns to Write Progressive Laws

Another response was through the work of legal scholars, mainly in the progressive High Court in Jerusalem, who drafted a number of "antipoverty" laws to be placed in the Torah, to help the poor and to curb abuses. Even though some of the legislation was idealistic and could never be implemented, overall this was one of the most productive methods of social reform in Israel. Among the laws were:

1. Prohibitions on charging interest (Exod. 22:25; Lev. 25:36–37; Deut. 23:19–20; 24:17; Neh, 6:6–13);

2. "Gleaning" of harvests for the poor (Lev. 19:9–10; 23:22; Deut. 24:19–21; Ruth 2);

3. The *go'el,* or "next-of-kin," which offers protection from foreclosure on one's property or slavery for oneself when one inevitably gets behind on loan payments, by giving the nearest living relative the first option to purchase either the person or the property (Lev. 25:25–28; Ruth 2:17–20; Jer. 24:6–13);

4. Curbing the power of the king by, for example, limiting the size of the army he could raise, the amount of money he could make, and requiring him to obey the law ("Signing statements" had not yet been invented, Deut. 17:14–20);

5. The Sabbath (seventh year), and Jubilee (fiftieth year) systems for the release of slaves, cancelation of debts, and return of stolen property.

These last two demand a larger comment.

Sabbath and Jubilee

Sabbath and Jubilee are important but often overlooked in biblically based visions for political activism. Sabbath itself, the older of the two, is found in no early culture but Israel's and had a profound impact on the Israelites' theology and moral sense of who they were.

The exact origins of Sabbath are now lost, but it probably began as a worshipful response to Israel's slavery in Egypt, a way of ethically honoring their time of bondage (Deut. 5:12–15), and only later was applied to the idea of rest for the land.[18] Its root, *shabbậth*, is the intensive noun form of the verb *sabbath*, "to rest," "desist" from work. It is a strong, forceful word meaning to cease and desist from all work, not just to pause mildly from it for one day, go to church, and then lunch at the mall. The double "b" in the name gives it an intensive force, implying a complete cessation forever, which probably originally only applied to slavery. So it is very likely that "Sabbath" was originally an activist, antislavery spiritual practice, which evolved over time in response to the terrible rise in the number of slaves in Israel. Walter Brueggemann says that it symbolizes "an occasion of public amnesty [when] the world is restored to its rightful posture, and society is reorganized according to covenantal relations."[19]

Every seven years (a Sabbath year) all slaves would be released ("When you buy a male Hebrew slave, he shall serve six years, but in the seventh he shall go out a free person," Exod. 21:2), and debts would be canceled ("Every seventh year you shall grant a remission of debts," Deut. 15:1). They were eventually expanded into the Jubilee Year, which occurred every fifty years (seven Sabbath years times seven, plus one), when all debts, slaves, or property that had not been returned, released, or restored through other measures would be included. They both arose out of the same egalitarian worldview, but the Jubilee was the most radical. To enact a Jubilee implied that the "reset button" on all of life's evils and injustices would be pressed, and all would be returned back to the world as God had originally intended it.[20]

In a broad theological sense, the authors of the Jubilee "reset" probably saw it as a return to the condition of the Garden of Eden, though in practical terms they more than likely had the egalitarian lives of their early tribal system in their minds as a model.[21] That age was communal, relatively classless, and premonarchial. It was an age in which it was believed that all had what they needed, and one was not expected to abuse one's neighbor in order to get ahead. It is the notion of *dayenu,* the Hebrew word in the Passover *Haggadah* for "enough," or "sufficiency," or "abundance" (see Deut. 15:8; Exod. 36:7; Prov. 25:16; Lev. 5:7; 12:8). Israel was challenged by God to construct a society with *enough* for all and to reject one that supported wealth for the few and deprivation for the many.[22] The very real connection between "enough" and Sabbath is found in their stories of the wilderness experience, where they survived abundantly on the gift of manna that Yahweh sent to them daily. Then, on the seventh day, the Sabbath, they would be liberated from work and would share what they had gathered on the previous day. When everyone shared, everyone had enough. "Those who gathered much had nothing over, and those who gathered little had no shortage; they gathered as much as each of them needed" (Exod. 16:18). If someone tried to hoard, steal, barter, or otherwise take more than his or her share, that person's allotment of manna would spoil and go bad (Exod. 16). If someone wanted to keep a portion and leverage it for a larger portion, or hedge it against future profit failures, or invest it in shaky mortgages for tent construction, and then use the proceeds to buy credit default swaps on potential bad manna investments, they would find that at the end of the day, all of their "spoils" had spoiled.

The structure of today's global economy requires high levels of poverty in order to lower labor costs and increase profits for the few at the top; for ancient Israel that would have been inconceivable and intolerable. The clear, though metaphorical, message of the manna story is that God's creation is sufficient for all of our needs, and if we try to take more than our share, the creation is spoiled. This is a *dayenu* message, but also a *Sabbath* message, and was important for Israel's own understanding of itself as an ethical nation. A line in the communion liturgy of many faith groups reads, "Sharing for all means scarcity for none." It is, however, a fact of our fallen existence that we have so often done the opposite. We have broken the relationship, and hoarded, stolen, and abused our gifts. If we would but have faith and trust in God's abundant gift of life, we would be happy, but we don't. And most of us, most of the time, live our lives not experiencing nor understanding God's *dayenu*.

Admittedly, many of these and other "legislative" proposals were opposed by the wealthy and royal classes and never enacted, most notably the Jubilee Year. But that doesn't mean that they were not helpful to the overall cause of justice for the people and the land of Israel. Writing them down, arguing about them, putting them into the Torah, altogether made them a part of the moral fiber of Israel; and they formed the basis of reform movements for millennia to come. The Jubilee, for example, while never being allowed to be put into practice,[23] went underground as a word and emerged as one of the most powerful metaphors for God's reign of justice in the Bible (see Isa. 61, Luke 4, and others). In a very real sense the Jubilee became even more powerful when the official powers denied its implementation. It became a cosmic measuring stick by activists and peasant organizations for God's vision of shalom, against which all of the corrupt structures of the world were to be judged. Countless prophets, marginalized Israelites, and even Jesus found strength in it. The themes of returning land, liberating slaves and debt prisoners, and "good news to the poor" are maintained and woven through them all. Ezekiel refers to it as the "Year of Liberty" (46:17). The so-called "Second" Isaiah (author of roughly the middle portion of the book of Isaiah) calls it the "time of favor" and "day of salvation" (Isa. 49:7a–9). "Third" Isaiah calls it the "year of the Lord's favor" (Isa. 61:2). Jesus' use of Jubilee traditions is remarkable, in no small measure because so few Christians even know that he did it. In his "inaugural address" in Luke 4, he not only cites Isaiah's poetic reformulation of it (Isa. 61:1–2 in Luke 4:16–21), but also claims that by the very event of their hearing Isaiah's words, the Jubilee's liberating justice has become alive for them.[24] He takes the notion of the Jubilee and reformulates it into his key teaching as the coming kingdom (or "realm") of God.

The Jubilee contained a picture of life that was very different from the individualizing, stratifying world of Israel, Babylon, Persia, and Rome, but was very much like the world of shalom that God had created and intended for humankind. Over and against the physical brutality of human existence, it became an ideal to be strived for, a radical vision for social change. The inhumane course of history forced the theologians of the Jubilee traditions to see the Jubilee increasingly as an activist spiritual vision of what the real world should look like, a world that was hidden in the cruel chaos of their physical social situation. For them, the Jubilee became a symbol, not in the sense of fantasy or "not real," but in the sense of something that stands for and pulls us toward that which was unseen, yet "truly real."[25]

Prophetic Protest

The prophets were the most famous of those who protested against poverty and injustice. They didn't focus solely on economic causes of poverty (and there were more causes than trade and kingship, of course), but when they did, it was often on the abuses of those who were winners, the rich, and on the theological roots of their abuse, which most often was idolatry. They argued that when one ceases to worship Yahweh, or begins to worship a neighboring god, one almost automatically begins to oppress and abuse others. Oppression, as we have said, is not just an economic or political act; it is a theological one, and for the prophets the two were inseparable. The grisly battle of the gods on top of Mount Carmel (1 Kings 18) is partly an indictment of the people who have turned their backs on the old ways of cosmic care and mutual support, but it is also and more importantly a statement that it was their worship of Baal that had turned them away. "How long will you go limping with two different opinions?" Elijah asks. "If the Lord is God, follow him; but if Baal, then follow him" (18:21; or as Jesus would put it later on, "You cannot serve both God and mammon").

In the eighth century, Amos and Hosea, two great prophets in the north, and others in the south railed against the increasing abuse of the poor by the wealthy (see Hos. 12:7–8; Amos 2:7–8; 4:1–7, 11; 8:4–6; also Mic. 2:1–2). And they too melded the two themes. Amos condemns Israel "because they sell the righteous for silver, and the needy for a pair of sandals" (Amos 2:6b) but says they commit that sin because "they lay themselves down beside every altar" (2:8a). And, though he is the most relentless of all of the prophets in condemning injustice, the cure remains in turning back to God. "Seek the Lord and live," he reminds them (5:6a), and "Seek good and not evil, that you may live; and so the Lord, the God of hosts, will be with you" (5:14).

Seeking justice and seeking God are closely related. It is difficult to do one without the other being closely at hand. Similarly with Hosea, there are great sins throughout the land, "swearing, lying, and murder, and stealing and adultery...bloodshed follows bloodshed" (4:2), and yet their cause is that "there is no knowledge of God in the land" (v. 1b). The root of the sin of the wealthy is that "with their silver and gold they made idols of silver and gold for their own destruction" (8:4) and that they worship their gold like an adulterer worships a lover. He, too, combines condemnations of physical sins with a theological, spiritual solution, "Return O Israel, to the Lord your God, for you have stumbled because of your iniquity" (14:1).

Nonviolent Defiance

There are many examples of defiance throughout the Bible, but one of the most symbolically powerful is in the third chapter of the

> In 1997 the IMF decided to change its charter to push capital
> market liberalization. And I said, Where is the evidence this is
> going to be good for developing countries? Why haven't you
> produced some research showing it was going to be good? They
> said: We don't need research; we know it's true. They didn't say
> it in precisely those words, but clearly they took it as religion.
> —Joseph Stiglitz, *Globalization and Its Discontents*

book of Daniel, written following the desecration of the temple by
Antiochus IV in 167 B.C.E.[26] The story is about nonviolent resistance to idolatry in the form of worship of a combined political and
economic power. The king (symbol of political power) announces
that the entire nation must turn from Yahweh and worship a new
god made of gold (symbol of economic power).[27] Anyone refusing
to worship the economic power will be destroyed by the political
power.

When the big day for the dedication of the statue arrives, the
king brings out the national "musical ensemble" to play for the
festivities and invites dignitaries from all over the country to come
and bow down. "All the peoples" of Babylonia gather around, sing
along, bow in worship, and make nice for the king. Everyone is
happy until someone tells the king that three low-level government
officials in some of the distant provinces did not show up. Shadrach,
Meshach, and Abednego have sent word that they had more important things to do than take part in a ceremony that they view as
idolatry. They are immediately brought in for questioning and the
king gives them an ultimatum. In this country, he says, we worship
gold. No exceptions. "So when the band starts playing, if you aren't
down worshiping gold with the rest of us, you'll be thrown into a
fiery furnace and burned alive" (see Dan. 3:14–15).

They refuse the generous offer, but do it in a way that has profound implications. They say that even if God is unable to deliver
them from the fire, they would still resist because worshiping a
global God that is in and beyond all things, and not worshiping
tangible, divisive, polarizing, alienating, stratifying gods is worth
it, even if it means losing their lives. "Even if God will not [save

JOSEPHUS AND THE IMF

Even though the Jubilee laws existed in some form from Israel's earliest days, the national rulers never allowed them to be implemented, and only the prophets and marginalized of the religious community spoke of them (and even then, in the guarded, disguised forms we've discussed). One interesting exception to that is the Jewish historian Flavius Josephus who wrote shortly after the death of Jesus. In his book *The Antiquities of the Jews* (Book 3, Chapter 12.3), he goes into great detail to describe the complex rules by which people would have their debts canceled and their land returned under a declaration of Jubilee. Interestingly, his description is so ponderous and so detailed and so complicated, that in the end one wonders whether the rules were intended not to help the process but to block it. Josephus himself came from moneyed classes, and from the perspective of his class, he may never have noticed the irony that these rules for the implementation of the Jubilee in fact kept it from being implemented. In the mid-1990s, the public uproar against what appeared to be inhumane monetary practices of the World Bank and the IMF caused the Fund to establish a program of debt relief called the "Highly Indebted Poor Country" (HIPC) initiative. In it some forty-one countries were to receive cancelations of huge amounts of their international debt loads. However, the IMF made the rules for qualifying so stringent, so complicated, so draconian, that for years very few countries received debt relief. The IMF was pushed and prodded by activists of faith and conscience, and eventually a few more countries were added to the list. Today they are pushing for even more, but every step of the way, the IMF and its friends in the finance ministries of the supporting countries have been dragging their feet and adding more rules and regulations. It is hard not to wonder if today the class blindness that struck Josephus might not also be infecting the eyes of the policy makers in the international lending institutions which monitor and control the flow of world wealth.

us]...we will [still] not serve your gods and we will not worship the god of gold that you have created" (Dan. 3:18). They are making the startling statement that even if their nonviolent defiance of the gods of power and markets takes their lives, they will not give in. A just and equitable society is worthy even if they lose their lives in support of it. They know that military and economic power cannot exercise its strength unless it is worshiped and therefore they take away its strength by refusing to worship it. They refuse to allow it to frighten them and control them. Their vision is of an alternative world, one based on the great Torah equality of early Canaan and against the commodification of people and the worship of wealth. Their God is a stark alternative to the one established by the union of economic and political power.

They reject the government's claim to absolute power over their lives by standing *against* the power and gold and *for* a simple faith. And they win, simply by proclaiming the unity and radicality of a God that transcends human distortions of the oneness of creation. The market is not God, the military is not God, the nation is not God, and gold is not God. Only "God" is God.

Guidance from Christian Scriptures: Acting Like It Is So

Many of the themes we have discussed are also found in the Christian scriptures: denouncing the powerful, nonviolent resistance, etc. Jesus was born in those same Hebrew traditions and freely applied them to his own teachings and ministry. For example, the central ethic of gratitude for liberation we saw above in Deuteronomy can be found in his parable of the Unforgiving Servant (Matt. 18:23–35), where a king frees a slave and cancels his debts and expects him to treat others the same way. In this case, however, the slave ignores his own liberation and begins to throw fellow servants in jail for not paying him the paltry sums of money they owed him. When the king hears of it, he is outraged and rescinds the first slave's emancipation and throws the slave back in jail. The judgment seems harsh, but the message of the king is clear, "I freed you, and your job was to free others, and you didn't do it," a theme that resonates strongly with the liberation-from-slavery ethic of the early Hebrews. Likewise, in Luke 4, when Jesus gives his "inaugural address," mentioned above, he preaches from the text in Isaiah 61 that calls for enacting the principles of the Jubilee, and Luke portrays him as self-consciously claiming that his ministry is in fact that Jubilee: "Today this scripture has been fulfilled ["has become real and alive"] in your hearing" (Luke 4:21). He even intensifies its radicality by adding the phrase "to let the oppressed go free" from Isaiah 58:6d to the text.

In subtle and not-so-subtle ways, he returns to this theme many times. For example, when the followers of John come to him and ask him if he is in fact the Messiah who is expected, he repeats portions of this sermon, and gives Jubilee provisions for the poor as his answer (Luke 7:22). In the "Lord's Prayer," he explicitly calls for the sharing of bread and the "release" from debts (Matt. 18:24–33; Luke 11:2–4).[28] This Greek word, usually translated "forgive," is *aphiemi,* the technical term used by the LXX (the first-century Greek translation of the Hebrew scriptures available to Matthew and Jesus) in Leviticus 25 for "release" of slaves and "release" from indebtedness. There are a number of other Greek terms that could have been used if the intention was simply to say *forgive,* for example, *paúô* (to stop, quit); *katapaúô* (to cease); *katargéô* (to render inactive); *charízomai* (to forgive); *apolúô* (to release, dismiss); *egkataleípô* (to forsake, abandon); *apotíthçmi* (to put away); *chôrízô* (to separate); and many others, but none were used here. The fact that this particular word, with its ancient Jubilee symbolism, was chosen for the most central prayer of Jesus, is enormously significant.

Other parts of Jesus' concern for "the poor" also resonate with the vision of the Jubilee. Recall that one of the primary threads in the Torah's Jubilee legislation (and later prophetic denunciations of the rich based on it) was the call to return to the age when all was shared in common, when God was the owner of the land (Lev. 25:23), and there were no people who were truly poor. With Jesus, the call to redeem or lift the poor is a major theme of his ministry and is probably intended to call his listeners back to the lost Jubilee ideal when the poor were cared for by the larger society. "Blessed are you who are poor" (Luke 6:20; Matt. 5.1–12), "The poor have good news brought to them" (Luke 7:22; Matt. 11.2–19); "Invite the poor, the crippled, the lame, and the blind" (Luke 14:13); " 'Go out at once into the streets and lanes of the town and bring in the poor, the crippled, the blind, and the lame' " (Luke 14:21; Matt.

22:1–14); "Sell all that you own and distribute the money to the poor, and you will have treasure in heaven" (Luke 18:22; Matt. 19:16–30; Mark 10:17–31); the parable of a "poor man named Lazarus" (Luke 16:19–31). It's hard to avoid the conclusion that Jesus was trying to remind them of an age, long lost, when their community and political economy were structured in such a way that the poor and oppressed were taken care of and didn't need the teachings of someone like him telling them to do it.

Some scholars believe that Jesus' feeding the multitude (Matt. 14:13–21; Mark 6:30–44; Luke 9:10–17; John 6:1–14) also reflects elements of the Jubilee, this time as an *enacted* parable. That is, in the feeding, Jesus may be modeling the oneness of humanity implied in the Jubilee and calling upon the gathered multitude to make it a reality by doing the same. Notice that John's version places the incident on the shore of Lake Tiberias.[29] This is significant because the nearby city of Tiberias had only recently been developed by Herod Antipas as a resort town (famous for hot baths), and it quickly became the largest city in Israel, surpassing even Sepphoris, which had been founded only a generation earlier and until then was the largest.

This meant that in less than a hundred years Israel grew to have three major cities, with wealthy — frequently foreign — populations, all requiring food and resources from the surrounding farms and villages. Their growth put increasing demands on the food supply in the region and contributed to a rise in hunger throughout Israel. This trend was in turn exacerbated by the pro-city economic policies of Antipas, which forced rural farmers to either give up some of their produce to feed the cities or pay a tribute to the government on what they did not give. So in effect, the more the farmers grew, the more they had to pay in tribute to the powerful urban centers. Farmers could lower the amount of tax they paid by not growing as many crops, but that would also lower the amount of food they had for their own personal consumption. They lost either way. Incidentally, this is not unlike the policies of a number of developing countries today that push their farmers to grow crops for export in order to raise the hard currency needed to pay on international debts. The more they grow and send away, the more precarious becomes their own situation, often driving them from their farms and into the cities, where they are then available as hungry, desperate, and inexpensive labor for the multinational sweatshops making even more products for export.

When food production went down in ancient Israel, it did two things. First it simply lowered the amount of fruits, vegetables, and grains that were available for consumption and made the whole region grow incrementally more hungry. Second, and more interestingly, when this large percentage of grains was taken out of the system, the price for what remained went up. It was simple Econ 101: when supply goes down price goes up. There was less food to go around, and the food that was still grown cost more to purchase for the families who didn't have direct access to it themselves. That also means that there is a high likelihood that the masses of people who begged from Jesus in the cities and followed him in the countryside were people who had been driven off of their land by poverty and hunger and the economic policies of their rulers.[30]

To get a sense of the level of poverty in Palestine in the first century, the average annual income per person was about fifty *denarii*. Subtract from that about 20 percent for taxes (Roman tax, temple tax, levies, etc.), and most people then lived off around forty *denarii* a year. However, most reasonable estimates say that it actually required a minimum of two hundred *denarii* to stay alive and support a family of five or six.[31] So what did people do? Well, mainly they died young. They starved or were taken down by poverty and malnutrition-related diseases. Josephus, an ancient historian and contemporary of Jesus, noted that starvation was so common that some rabbis could recognize it by the smell of someone's breath.[32] Some lived behind government buildings, or under bridges, or in boxes or caves or fields — not unlike many in poor countries like Haiti today, even before earthquakes and floods destroyed their sheltering buildings and bridges. And when they heard that an itinerant preacher from Nazareth had just arrived by boat on the sea of Tiberias, teaching, healing, and feeding, they flocked to him.

In light of their huge numbers, his disciples think first of using market forces to feed them (just run into town and pick up a few things for supper). But in many ways it was the market (and the market's failures) that drove so many to hunger in the first place, so Jesus says no. Instead he very sacramentally takes the bread that is already present among them, blesses it, breaks it, shares it, and miraculously there is enough to go around for all. It is a miracle and once again a symbol of the Jubilee, the eschatological feast on the mountaintop and Sabbath manna in the desert, embodied in physical actions and now rebranded as the arrival of the "kingdom (or better: *realm*) of God." It models the sharing of the great families in early Canaan, before their economy fell apart and before greed drove them into hoarding.

More miraculously, it is also possible that Jesus' actions actually drew the reality of the realm of God *out of* the recipients of the miracle. That is, it is possible that when the participants saw him share his meager offering of bread, they produced their own food from their private supplies. Perhaps one person said, "Well, the wife did make me this sandwich and packed me this thermos of coffee, and I probably don't need all of it." Another said, "You know, I do have this banana that I forgot to check at the gate when I came in, and I don't need all of it." And the guy who picked up the box of Oreos at the Seven Eleven that morning on the way out of town to the rally. And the one who won the turkey at the meat raffle at the Grange meeting last night. And the one who remembered he still had a piece of that fruitcake left over from the office party a couple of years ago that never went bad. And so on, all down the line, until all the loaves and fishes had been passed around and the "twelve" disciples (representing the twelve tribes of early settlements in Canaan) gathered up twelve baskets full of leftovers and snacks. And suddenly the Jubilee had become flesh and dwelt among them. The engine of growth in the economics of Jubilee is not greed or self-interest or even market forces, it is sharing.[33]

The Greek word for "sharing," *koinônía*, has a double meaning of both "to share *in*," as in fellowship, community, and communion (Acts 2:42; 1 Cor. 10:16) and "to share *with*," as in sharing of one's abundance with the poor (Rom. 15:26; 2 Cor. 9:13; Heb. 13:16). Clearly Jesus is portrayed as doing both by the lake in John 6. Later, when Jesus brings his disciples together in an "upper room" and shares with them in their last supper, he reenacts the feeding story and pointedly tells them to make that act a present reality ("in remembrance," *anamnesis*, "to make present") every time they break bread together. They took him seriously, and following his resurrection the apostles created a sacramental feeding program for the poor of Jerusalem that even Paul re-created in his foreign churches. Acts 2:42–47 and 4:32–37 show the disciples modeling their new church on that image. They shared all of their possessions in common and "there was not a needy person among them"

(4:34). Through what became known later as "the Eucharist," they broke bread, blessed it, and shared it with their communities, just as Jesus had done at Lake Tiberias, and hundreds of hungry people were fed. The ministry in fact grew so large that it expanded to the Greek-speaking populations, and they had to enlarge the number of servants (*diakonos,* root of "deacons") at the tables because poor widows and others "were being neglected in the daily distribution of food" (Acts 6:1).

Paul believed in the feeding-and-equality ministry he saw taking place in Jerusalem, and he helped finance it through collections in Corinth, Galatia, Macedonia, Achaia, and probably Rome (Acts 24:17; Rom. 15:25–32; Gal. 2:9–10; 1 Cor. 16:1–4; 2 Cor. 8–9). He also patterned his house churches at least in Corinth, and probably Galatia, after the Jerusalem model and celebrated the Eucharist as an act of both sacrament and sharing with the poor. The breaking of bread was done to make present the spirit of Jesus, and the bounty of the table was to be shared with those who had little. The act was a radical alternative vision of an economy based on family and sharing, not competition and abuse. It symbolized Jesus feeding the multitude with bread on the hillside, and the feeding of the Hebrews with manna in the desert. It was a symbol of *dayenu,* the sufficiency of God's creation where all is shared among the "family," and a statement against the powers that separated winners from losers in a toxically stratified economy. The Eucharist is a symbol of God's grace (from *charis* "giving thanks," Luke 22:17, 19; 1 Cor. 11:24), a free and undeserved gift from God that when shared is sufficient for all of the community.

But true to our fallen natures, it did not always work. On at least one occasion Paul chastises the rich leisure-class members of the church who were able to arrive early at the Eucharistic meal because they didn't have to work, and then ate up all of the food, leaving none for the poor people who had to arrive late because they had jobs. "What!" he says, "Don't you have homes to eat and drink in? Or do you show contempt for the church of God and humiliate those who have nothing?" (1 Cor. 11:22a; see also 2 Pet. 2:13). Because of the human propensity toward denying the meaning of God's gifts, the Eucharistic meal and sharing with the poor were separated in the second century into two separate and unequal acts, and finally even the celebration of the Eucharist as a meal at all was banned in the seventh century. It occurs only on sporadic special occasions today. Today's highly structured ceremony symbolizes community and fellowship for Protestants and salvation and sacrament for Catholics, but very, very few ever acknowledge, or even are aware of, its roots as a radical economic model for constructing God's good society, God's Jubilee.

"What Then Should We Do" Today?[34]

There's a story in John Steinbeck's epic novel *East of Eden* that speaks to the sense of inadequacy that comes over us when trying to craft a world less brutal and cold than the one we have now, and I'll close with it. There is a young man who falls in love and marries a woman who, for complicated reasons, actually hates him. Just after she gives birth to their first children, twins, she announces that she is leaving him. When he protests she takes a gun out and shoots him in the chest and then leaves, stepping over his bleeding body. He survives the ordeal with the help of a servant, who also takes care of his babies, but it's a lifeless, hopeless life. He has no energy in him, no reason to live, nothing to live for. Eventually an older neighbor hears about what happened and comes over and pulls the young man out of the house, slaps him around, and demands that he come back to life again. He says he can't. He says he's just living a death. No life left in him; no hope to create one. The death that is in him is too deep and real, and there is nothing in him that could even *believe* in life again.

Then the older man says something, just a few words, but words that speak to people of faith and conscience and their constant, ongoing struggles to make a world more humane and more fair than the one we live in. He says simply, "Go through the motions." The younger man doesn't get it, so he repeats, "Go through the motions! Act out being alive, like a play. And after a while, a long while, it will be true."

I don't think that Jesus, standing by the lake of Tiberius, really imagined that by feeding the masses of homeless people before him that day that suddenly the kingdom, or the "kindom," or the realm of God was going to burst open full grown and wonderful. I don't think Paul thought that either when he was chastising his parishioners for not sharing their food with the poor. Or Isaiah when he said that the spirit of the Lord was upon him to bring good news to the poor, or Jeremiah or Amos, or the scribes behind Leviticus and Deuteronomy in calling on their fellow Israelites to care and sacrifice in ways that embodied an egalitarian, loving world. I do think, however, that they thought that if one person and another and then another began to act as though the Jubilee and the year of the Lord's favor had come upon them, then in a mysterious inexplicable way, for those people it had indeed arrived. Act like it is true and eventually it will become so.

I believe that when you step into the footsteps of the giants of faith and justice who came before us and live out their hardnosed acts of justice and love, then in a small way for you and for the people whose lives you touch and heal, the realm of God's reconciliation will have arrived. In your deeds it will have become so. "The kingdom of God is within you," Jesus is said to have announced. And he meant it.

So now at the conclusion of this book, you have a job. Your task is to go and write a letter to your congresspersons. Or better yet, go pay them a visit. Take a hunger action briefing paper from Bread for the World with you when you go. Then write a letter to the editor of your local newspaper. Sign up with Habitat to build a house, perhaps in Haiti, but at least in your own neighborhood. Buy fair trade coffee — and also sell it. Go with Witness for Peace to a town in southern Mexico to see what two-thirds of the planet lives like, and then come back and tell rich America what you saw. Then attend a demonstration at the World Bank with Jubilee USA to urge it to adopt more fair, just, and transparent lending practices for poor countries. Feed the hungry, shelter the homeless, welcome the immigrant, liberate the oppressed (whether far away or close at home), and more. Know that with each task you perform, each step you take, you may never see the heavens open up and a new era of peace and harmony fall down upon you and change everything. But you will see a little cloud of grace swirling around what you are doing. And for you — and the people in Haiti or Zambia or Mexico, or Dorchester, Massachusetts, or Heavener, Oklahoma, or East St. Louis, whose lives you lifted or saved — the day of the Lord's favor will have come upon you. It will have become a reality. The Jubilee will have arrived. If you *act* like it is true, then after a while, for those whom you touch and help, it will *be* true.

Notes

1. An Introduction

1. David Segal, "$100 Million Payday Poses Problem for Pay Czar," *New York Times*, August 1, 2009, A1.
2. Ulrich Duchrow, *Alternatives to Global Capitalism: Drawn from Biblical History, Designed for Political Action* (Utrecht: International Books, 1995), 12, 15–16.

2. Globalization: The Greatest Story Oversold

1. "Wal-Mart and Sweatshops," *www.nlcnet.org*, October 22, 2002.
2. Mark Weisbrot, Dean Baker, and David Rosnick, "The Scorecard on Development: 25 Years of Diminished Progress," DESA Working Paper No. 31, ST/ESA/2006/DWP/31, September 2006, 3–5. China and India are the two largest countries to grow while avoiding globalization dogma. See pp. 14–16.
3. Marc Auboin, "Boosting the Availability of Trade Finance in the Current Crisis: Background Analysis for a Substantial G20 Package," *Policy Insight*, no. 35 (Centre for Economic Policy Research, June 2009): 1.
4. Doug Henwood, "The Americanization of Global Finance," *NACLA Report on the Americas* 33, no. 1 (1999): 13–20; Gerd Häusler, "The Globalization of Finance," *Finance and Development* 39, no. 1 (March 2002).
5. Louise Story, Landon Thomas Jr., and Nelson D. Schwartz, "Wall St. Helped to Mask Debt Fueling Europe's Crisis," *New York Times*, February 13, 2010.
6. Landon Thomas Jr., "Is Greece's Debt Trashing the Euro?" *New York Times*, February 6, 2010, BU 1.
7. Donald Worster, *Dust Bowl: The Southern Plains of the 1930s* (New York: Oxford University Press: 1982), 44–45.
8. Robert Weissman and Harvey Rosenfield, *Sold Out: How Wall Street and Washington Betrayed America* (Washington, D.C.: Wall Street Watch/Essential Information, March 4, 2009), 155ff.

Matthew Benjamin and Christine Harper, "Glass-Steagall's Specter Returns to Haunt Wall Street" March 10, 2009, see online at *www.bloomberg.com/apps/news?pid=20601087&sid=ad_KRWTbPsJw& refer=home*.

9. Anthony DePalma and Diana B. Henriques, "Lawsuit Says Del Monte Sale Was Rigged," *New York Times,* December 19, 2002.

10. Daniel Gross, *Dumb Money: How Our Greatest Financial Minds Bankrupted the Nation* (New York: Free Press, 2009), 80.

11. See, for example, the AOV Philippines Outsourcing Service, which until 2008 was the fastest growing company in Manila: *www.aovphilippinesoutsourcingservice.com/outsourcing/hire-a-graphic -artist-at-aov-outsourcing-service*.

12. Kathleen Madigan, "Outsourcing Jobs: Is It Bad?" *Business Week,* August 25, 2003.

13. Sarah Anderson and John Cavanagh, *The Top 200: The Rise of Corporate Global Power* (Washington, D.C.: Institute for Policy Studies, 2000), 2.

14. R. C. Longworth, "Globalization Survey Reveals U.S. Corporations Prefer Dictatorships," *International Herald Tribune,* November 19, 1999.

15. Gerard Greenfield, "Vietnam and the World Coffee Crisis: Local Coffee Riots in a Global Context," *Sand in the Wheels* 121, ATTAC (March 27, 2002).

16. Nuria Molina and Javier Pereira, *Critical Conditions: The IMF Maintains Its Grip on Low-income Governments* (EURODAD, April 2008), 4.

17. John Williamson, "What Should the World Bank Think about the Washington Consensus?" *World Bank Research Observer* 15, no. 2 (August 2000): 4.

18. Description from an unpublished speech at Brandeis University, October 2002.

19. Words like "rules" and "requirements" are occasionally placed in quotes because, while the wealthy countries and financial institutions would argue that they are merely prudent fiscal policies suggestions, they certainly *feel* like requirements from the perspective of the poor countries that have had the rules forced upon them.

20. Tim Weiner, "Corn Growing in Mexico 'Has Basically Collapsed' as U.S. Imports Flood Country," *New York Times,* March 8, 2002.

21. *The Other Side of Mexico* 69 (September–October 2000), cited in "Towards an Economy of Hope: Proclaiming Jubilee!" *Economic Justice Report* 22, no. 1 (April 2001).

22. Bhuwan Thapaliya, "India's Dilemma: Farmer's Rising Suicide Rate," *Global Politician,* December 9, 2007; *www.globalpolitician.com/23847-india.*

23. William Eubanks, "A Rotten System: Subsidizing Environmental Degradation and Poor Public Health with Our Nation's Tax Dollars," *Stanford Environmental Law Journal* 28, no. 213 (May 6, 2009): 226; *http://ssm.corn/abstract=1287408.*

24. Presbyterian Church in the USA, *Food, Agriculture, and Democratic Participation,* 2005.

25. Sarah Cohen, Dan Morgan, and Laura Stanton, "Farm Subsidies over Time," *Washington Post,* July 2, 2006.

26. Floyd Norris, "As Bank Profits Grew, Warning Signs Went Unheeded," *New York Times,* November 16, 2007, B1. On Amos and market tricks, see Amos 8:5b; Deut. 25:13–15.

27. See, for example, Alexander Cobham, "Capital Account Liberalisation and Poverty," Working Paper Number 70, Finance and Trade Policy Research Centre (April 2001). "While the growth benefits of liberalisation are far from clear for poorer countries, there may be significant costs in poverty terms."

28. See Cobham above and also Mark Weisbrot and Dean Baker, "The Relative Impact of Trade Liberalization on Developing Countries" (Washington: Center for Economic and Policy Research, June 12, 2002).

29. "Capital Flight, Tax Havens and Development Finance," EURODAD, 2006; *www.eurodad.org/debt/?id=2190.*

30. Christian E. Weller and Adam Hersh, "The Long and Short of It: Global Liberalization, Poverty and Inequality" (Economic Policy Institute, June 2003).

31. Milton Friedman, *Public Schools: Make Them Private,* Cato Institute Briefing Paper No. 23, June 23, 1995. Also see Naomi Klein, *The Shock Doctrine: The Rise of Disaster Capitalism* (New York: Henry Holt, 2007), 69.

32. John Williamson, "What Should the World Bank Think about the Washington Consensus?" 4.

33. Joseph Stiglitz, *Globalization and Its Discontents* (New York: Norton, 2002), 72.

34. Klein, *The Shock Doctrine,* 300.

35. Ibid., 320–24.

36. Stiglitz, *Globalization and Its Discontents,* 54–59.

37. Tellingly, this past chief economist for the World Bank criticizes the work of the IMF far more frequently than he does the World Bank.

38. Stiglitz, *Globalization and Its Discontents,* 153.

39. William Finnegan, "Leasing the Rain: The World Is Running Out of Fresh Water, and the Fight to Control It Has Begun," *New Yorker* (August 8, 2002); Jim Schultz, "Bolivia: The Water War Widens," *NACLA: Report on the Americas* 36, no. 4 (January–February 2003): 34–35. See also Wallace H. Ryan Kuroiwa, "Privatizing Water: Profits over People," in *Privatization: A Challenge to the Common Good* (Cleveland: United Church of Christ, Justice and Witness Ministries, 2003), 4–5.

40. In *The Lexus and the Olive Tree* Friedman devotes one chapter to what he calls the "backlash" against what he believes to be the obvious values of globalization and then goes on to address how we who know of globalization's values need to listen to the complainers or else someday they may be strong enough to "destabilize" its *inevitable* march forward (329).

41. You may recognize names like Jagdish Bhagwati, C. Fred Bergstrom, and Thomas Friedman as frequent cheerleaders on the interview circuit.

42. Measuring the health of a society by the growth of its GDP has often received criticism because it measures all sales as being equal, even those done for disaster reconstruction as happened following Hurricane Katrina, and because it measures the total wealth of a nation and not its constituent parts. For example, if Carlos Slim, the wealthiest man in the world and a resident of Mexico City, has a 10 percent increase in income, the total national GDP will go up, even if the income of the vast majority of the citizens went down (Mark Weisbrot, Robert Naiman, and Joyce Kim, *The Emperor Has No Growth: Declining Economic Growth Rates in the Era of Globalization* [Washington, D.C.: Center for Economic Policy and Research, 2000], 4).

43. Weller and Hersh, "The Long and Short of It," 2.

44. Ibid., 4. Emphasis added.

45. Mark Weisbrot, Dean Baker, Egor Kraev, and Judy Chen, *The Scorecard on Globalization 1980–2000: Twenty Years of Diminished Progress* (Washington, D.C.: Center for Economic and Policy Research, 2000), 2–3.

46. Mark Weisbrot, "The Mirage of Progress," *American Prospect,* Special Supplement (Winter 2002): A10.

47. World Bank numbers up through 1997, cited in Robin Hahnel, *Panic Rules: Everything You Need to Know about the Global Economy* (Cambridge, Mass.: South End Press, 1999), 10.

48. Marc Bacchetta, Ekkehard Ernst, and Juana P. Bustamante, *Globalization and Informal Jobs in Developing Countries: A Joint Study of the International Labour Office and the Secretariat of the World Trade Organization* (Lausanne, Switzerland: 2009).

49. Ibid., 88–89.

50. Weisbrot, "The Mirage of Progress," A10.

51. "Amnesty Focuses on Globalization," Associated Press, May 30, 2001.

52. Schultz, "Bolivia: The Water War Widens," 34–35. See also Kuroiwa, "Privatizing Water," 4–5.

53. See the collection of documents uncovered by the National Security Archive on CIA involvement in the coup at *www.gwu.edu/~nsarchiv/news/20000919/index.html*.

54. Klein, *The Shock Doctrine*, 109.

55. Ibid., 102.

56. Ibid., 94. The most famous study that has come out that documents the ravages of the Pinochet years is from the "National Commission on Political Imprisonment and Torture Report," known as the "The Valech Report," because it was chaired by Bishop Sergio Valech. It is the culmination of testimonies of over thirty-five thousand people taken over a five-year period following the return of Chile to democracy. Its first part was released on November 29, 2004, and the second on June 1, 2005. For excerpts translated into English, which first appeared in the *Miami Herald*, see *www.onpedia.com/encyclopedia/Valech-Report*.

57. Williamson, "What Should the World Bank Think about the Washington Consensus?" 251–64.

58. Quoted in Wayne Elwood, *No-Nonsense Guide to Globalization* (Oxford: New Internationalist Publications, 2001), 17.

59. Interview with author and economist Thomas Frank, *Now*, Public Broadcasting System, broadcast February 1, 2002.

60. Peter Drucker, *Managing the Next Century* (New York: Truman Talley Books/St. Martin's Press, 2002), 149–50, cited in Robert White, *Biblical Economics: Economic Myths versus Biblical Values* (Lanham, Md.: University Press of America, 2006), 4. Italics added.

61. "Calling for a More Just, Humane Direction for Economic Globalization," United Church of Christ, 24th General Synod.

62. H. Richard Niebuhr, *Radical Monotheism and Western Culture, with Supplementary Essays* (Louisville: Westminster John Knox Press: 1960), 17–18.

63. Most of her story can be found in Anthony Faiola, Ellen Nakashima, and Jill Drew, "What Went Wrong?" *Washington Post*, October 15, 2008, A1.

64. Michael Hirsh, "Chasing Stiglitz: Obama's Economic Team Is Missing the One Guy Who's Been Right all Along," *Newsweek*, December 8, 2008, 22.

65. Dani Rodrik, "Faith-based Economics," March 3, 2008, *http:// rodrik.typepad.com/dani_rodriks_weblog/2008/03/faith-based-eco.html.*

66. B. B. Price, ed., *Ancient Economic Thought,* Routledge Studies in the History of Economics (London: Routledge, 1997), 152.

67. See also Ulrich Duchrow and Franz Hinkelammert, *Property for People, Not for Profit: Alternatives to the Global Tyranny of Capital* (New York: Zed Books, 2004), 5–6.

3. International Debt: Pat and Elaine

1. "A Silent War," Jubilee 2000/UK.

2. Joe Nocera, "Can a Vision Save All of Africa?" *New York Times,* June 16, 2007.

3. "A Silent War," paper of Jubilee 2000/UK.

4. Marina Ottaway, *Less Is Better: An Agenda for Africa,* Carnegie Endowment for International Peace, 1, no. 2 (December 2000): 3.

5. "Zambia's Debt History," *Debt and Aid,* Jesuit Centre for Theological Reflection (2000): 7. "Voice from the South: A Country's Inheritance," interview with Zambian debt activist, Muyatwa Sitali, p. 2 (2007), *www.jubileeusa.org/resources/debt-resources/policy-papers/ southvoicesitali.html.*

6. Cited in *Enlace,* the newsletter of the Christian Commission for Development (CCD), of Honduras.

7. *www.worldcentric.org/stateworld/debt.htm.*

8. From the U.S. General Accounting Office, and the *New York Times,* November 22, 1998, respectively; cited in "Proclaim Jubilee: Break the Chains of Debt," background paper by Church World Service.

9. Ben White, "Wall Street's Pay Is Expected to Plummet," *New York Times,* November 5, 2008, B1.

10. "Merrill Lynch Bonuses Totaled $3.6b," *Boston Globe,* February 12, 2009, B1.

11. "Nigeria: The Cement Block," *Time Magazine,* October 27, 1975; Esther Pan, "The Pernicious Effects of Oil," *Foreign Affairs,* Council on Foreign Relations (October 10, 2005): 51.

12. Michael L. Ross, "Blood Barrels: Why Oil Wealth Fuels Conflict," *Foreign Affairs* (May–June 2008): 3.

13. Noreena Hertz, *The Debt Threat: How Debt Is Destroying the Developing World* (New York: Harper, 1994), 61.

14. To be fair, the United States, the World Bank, the IMF, and others have made their share of destructive loans to dictators to keep them happy and voting with us in the United Nations, but perhaps one could say they

were not as frequent as the banks (at least in the early days of loans) and less blatant about it.

15. Hertz, *The Debt Threat*, 61.

16. A good survey discussion of how the money from OPEC "oil shocks" moved to unregulated loans to the Third World can be found in Robert Devlin, "Growth and Transformation of International Banking," in *Debt and Crisis in Latin America: The Supply Side of the Story* (Princeton, N.J.: Princeton University Press, 1989), 8–55.

17. Hertz, *The Debt Threat*, 60.

18. Cited in ibid., 61, though the story could not be independently corroborated.

19. The norm, however, was closer to 20 percent, still a horrific drain on the economy. See Oscar Ugarteche, "The Structural Adjustment Stranglehold: Debt and Underdevelopment in the Americas," *NACLA: Report on the Americas* 33, no. 1 (July–August 1999): 23.

20. See online *http://jubileeusa.typepad.com/blog_the_debt/2008/10/fast-track-for.html.*

21. Hertz, *The Debt Threat*, 77.

22. Cited in Richard Peet, *Unholy Trinity: The IMF, the World Bank, and the WTO* (London: Zed Books, 2003), 104.

23. Ibid., 103.

24. Hertz, *The Debt Threat*, 103–4.

25. Dani Rodrik, "The Rights and Wrongs of Globalization," lecture delivered at the Princeton Colloquium on Public and International Affairs, Woodrow Wilson School of Public and International Affairs, Princeton University, "The Return to Morality in International Affairs: A World of 'Good and Evil'?" April 25–26, 2003, 59–60.

26. Joseph Stiglitz, *Globalization and Its Discontents* (New York: W. W. Norton, 2002), 76.

27. Peet, *Unholy Trinity*, 103.

28. The list is adapted loosely from John Cavanagh, Sarah Anderson, and Jill Pike, "Behind the Cloak of Benevolence: World Bank and IMF Policies Hurt Workers at Home and Abroad," in Kevin Danaher, *Corporations Are Gonna Get Your Mama* (Monroe, Maine: Common Courage Press, 1996), 82.

29. For his discussion of the debt cancelation guidelines, see Josephus, *Antiquities of the Jews*, Book 3, chap. 12.3.

30. Sarah Williams and Trisha Rogers, *Unfinished Business: Ten Years of Dropping the Debt* (London: Jubilee Debt Campaign, 2008), 12.

31. Peet, *Unholy Trinity*, 100.

32. Hertz, *The Debt Threat*, 122.

33. "Did the G-8 Cancel the Debt? Myths and Realities about International Debt after the G-8 Deal," *Jubilee USA Issue Brief* (April 2006).

34. "The Concept of Odious Debt"; see online *www.jubileeusa.org/de/ truth-about-debt/dont-owe-wont-pay/the-concept-of-odious-debt.html.* Also see the discussion of the history of odious and illegitimate debt and the various suggested expansions of the concept in Cephas Lumina, *Effects of Foreign Debt and Other Related International Financial Obligations of States on the Full Enjoyment of All Human Rights, Particularly Economic, Social and Cultural Rights.* Report of the UN Human Rights Council to the General Assembly, August 12, 2009, 8–11.

35. Interview with Zambian debt activist Muyatwa Sitali, "Voice from the South: A Country's Inheritance," interview with Zambian debt activist Muyatwa Sitali (2007), *www.jubileeusa.org/resources/debt-resources/ policy-papers/southvoicesitali.html.*

36. Adapted from David J. Miner, "Called to End Hunger," a sermon preached at St. Alban's Episcopal Church, Albany, California, February 22, 2009, and David Beckmann, "Building Political Will to End Hunger," 2006 McDougall Lecture, Food and Agriculture Organization of the United Nations, November 19, 2005.

4. NAFTA: Why Does Nikolas Dance?

1. Ohio Conference on Fair Trade, February 28, 2008, see online *www.citizenstrade.org/pdf/OCFT_%20PresPrimaryTradeQuestionnaire _Obama_022008.pdf.*

2. For more on the problems in international coffee production, see chapter 6, "Coffee: Victor and Hugo."

3. Carlos Marichal, "The Vicious Cycles of Mexican Debt," *NACLA Report on the Americas* 31, no. 3 (November–December 1997): 27.

4. Walden Bello, "Manufacturing a Food Crisis," *The Nation* (June 2, 2008), 16.

5. $1.7 billion loan from the IMF, $2.3 billion loan from the World Bank, and $1.6 billion loan from the "Paris Club" (wealthy countries who loan to poor countries). In addition to these loans, this was also the time when U.S. Treasury Secretary Nicholas Brady was arranging the "Brady Bonds" we discussed in chapter 3. With them, some of Mexico's larger loans were to be repackaged as discounted U.S.-backed bonds, guaranteeing income for buyers and lower interest payments for Mexico (Marichal, "The Vicious Cycles of Mexican Debt," 27).

6. "How the International Monetary Fund and the World Bank Undermine Democracy and Erode Human Rights: Five Case Studies" (San Francisco: Global Exchange, 2001), 4.

7. Noreena Hertz, *The Debt Threat: How Debt Is Destroying the Developing World* (New York: HarperCollins, 2004), 76.

8. Roberto Sanchez-Rodriguez, *NAFTA Ten Years After: The Legacy of the North American Commission for Environmental Cooperation* (Riverside, Calif.: Department of Environmental Sciences, University of California, 2006), 2.

9. *Wall Street Journal* (October 15, 1997), cited in Kevin P. Gallagher, "Tracking the Economy: Paying for NAFTA," *NACLA: Report on the Americas* (July–August 2004): 47.

10. NAFTA Part Two: "Trade In Goods," chap. 3: "National Treatment and Market Access for Goods," Annex 302.2, *www.NAFTA-sec-alena.org/ DefaultSite/index_e.aspx?DetailID=103#An302.2.*

11. David Bacon, "Displaced People: NAFTA's Most Important Product," *NACLA: Report of the Americas* (September 3, 2008). Also see David Bacon, *Illegal People: How Globalization Creates Migration and Criminalizes Immigrants* (Boston: Beacon Press, 2008), 59.

12. Anne Vigna, "NAFTA Hurts Mexico, Too," *Agence Global* (June 1, 2008); see online *http://election-news-usa.blogspot.com/2008/04/mcm-mexico-devastated-by-free-trade.html.*

13. Marla Dickerson, "Placing Blame for Mexico's Ills," *Los Angeles Times,* July 1, 2006, C-1.

14. Eduardo Zepeda, Timothy A. Wise, and Kevin P. Gallagher, *Rethinking Trade Policy for Development: Lessons from Mexico under NAFTA* (Policy Outlook, Carnegie Endowment for International Peace: December 2009), 6.

15. Ibid., 11.

16. Ibid., 12.

17. One of the ironies of the NAFTA story is that it was sold by the Clinton administration as a way of helping Mexico "export goods, not people," while twenty years later the opposite has become true. Their export of goods has gone down, while their export of people has gone up.

18. Julie Jette, "NAFTA at Ten: Did It Work?" Harvard Business School: Working Knowledge, Archive, April 12, 2004; see online *http://hbswk.hbs.edu/archive/4056.html.*

19. William Greider, "A New Giant Sucking Sound," *The Nation* (December 31, 2001).

20. Hertz, in researching for her book *The Debt Threat,* interviewed day traders in the midst of their work. She asked one of them if he was

concerned that their cumulative decisions affect the well-being of countries and people all over the world. He said no. "The thing is," he told her, "capital has no soul" (77).

21. "The Broken Promise of NAFTA," *New York Times,* January 6, 2004.

22. Adam Liptak, "Review of U.S. Rulings by NAFTA Tribunals Stirs Worries," *New York Times,* April 18, 2004.

23. "Mondev vs. the City of Boston," *NAFTA Chapter 11 Investor-to-State Cases: Bankrupting Democracy, Lessons for Fast Track and the Free Trade Area of the Americas* (Public Citizen, 2001), 29.

24. Liptak, "Review of U.S. Rulings by NAFTA Tribunals Stirs Worries."

25. Ibid.

5. Immigration: Jasmine and Daniel

1. "National Statistics Online," *www.statistics.gov.uk/cci/nugget.asp?id=1312.*

2. John Gibler, "Mexico's Ghost Towns: The Other Side of the Immigration Debate," *In These Times,* May 29, 2008.

3. Editorial, "Enforcement Gone Bad," *New York Times,* February 22, 2009.

4. Julia Preston and Steven Greenhouse, "Immigration Accord by Labor Boosts Obama Effort," *New York Times,* April 14, 2009.

5. Susan B. Carter and Richard Sutch, "Labor Market Flooding? Migrant Destination and Wage Change during America's Age of Mass Migration," *Border Battles: The U.S. Immigration Debates* (Social Science Research Council, March 12, 2007); *http://borderbattles.ssrc.org/Carter_Sutch/printable.html.*

6. Mike Mcgraw and Laura Bauer, "U.S. System to Find, Help Victims of Human Trafficking Is Broken," *Kansas City Star,* December 12, 2009. Originally cited in SojoMail@sojonet, December 17, 2009.

7. Tina Rosenberg, "Why Mexico's Small Corn Farmers Go Hungry," *New York Times,* March 3, 2003.

8. Laura Carlsen, "Food Insecurity: The World Needs Its Small Farmers," *CounterPunch,* October 24, 2006; see online *www.counterpunch.org/carlsen10242006.html.*

9. Personal interview, January 29, 2009. See also *Dumping without Borders: How U.S. Agricultural Policies Are Destroying Mexican Corn Farmers* (London: Oxfam UK, 2003), 3.

10. Bread for the World Institute, *Hunger 2007: Healthy Food, Farms and Families* (Washington, D.C.: Bread for the World, 2007), 3.

11. Bill Malone and Shawnda Hines, "Bread for the World Calls 2008 Farm Bill 'Half a Loaf,' " press release, Bread for the World, May 14, 2008; *www.bread.org/press-room/releases/bread-for-the-world-calls-2008-farm -bill-half-a-loaf.html*.

12. Miguel Pickard, "In the Crossfire: Mesoamerican Migrants Journey North," special report, IRC Americas Program (Silver City, N.Mex.: International Relations Center, March 18, 2005), 1. These numbers are from before the 2008–9 recession, during which they slid downward temporarily. By the middle of 2010, the numbers of people leaving Mexico for work in the United States had begun to move back up again.

13. *Hunger 2007: Healthy Food, Farms, and Families*, 5.

14. Anthony DePalma, "How a Tortilla Empire Was Built on Favoritism," *New York Times*, February 15, 1996.

15. Tom Philpott, "Tortilla Spat: How Mexico's Iconic Flatbread Went Industrial and Lost Its Flavor," *Grist Magazine* (September 13, 2006).

16. The quote is from Megan Feldman, "El Tren de la Muerte: Central American Migrants Risk Life and Limb on the Death Trains to Texas," *Dallas Observer*, July 25, 2007; *www.dallasobserver.com/2007-07-26/ news/el-tren-de-la-muerte/1*.

6. Coffee: Victor and Hugo

1. Gregory Dicum and Nina Luttinger, *The Coffee Book: Anatomy of an Industry from Crop to the Last Drop* (New York: New Press, 1999), 61.

2. Justin Coburn, Jeff Atkinston, and Bruce Francis, "What's That in Your Coffee?" *www.oxfam.org.au/oxfamnews/february_2003/coffee.html*.

3. Charis Gresser and Sophia Tickell, *Mugged: Poverty in Your Coffee Cup* (London: Oxfam International, 2002), 9.

4. Coburn, Atkinson, and Francis, "What's That in Your Coffee?"

5. Paul Jeffrey, "Depressed Coffee Prices Yield Suffering in Poor Countries," *National Catholic Reporter*, February 7, 2003.

6. *Khat Fast Facts: Questions and Answers*, National Drug Intelligence Center, Department of Justice, 2002; accessed at *www.usdoj.gov/ndic*.

7. William Wallis, "Farmers of Ethiopia Turn to Khat as World Coffee Prices Tumble," *Financial Times*, December 8, 2003, C2.

8. Gresser and Tickell, *Mugged*.

9. Gerard Greenfield, "Vietnam and the World Coffee Crisis: Local Coffee Riots in a Global Context," *Sand in the Wheels* (ATTAC, no. 121, March 27, 2002).

10. Alexandra Seno, "Trouble Brewing: Behind the Turmoil in the World's Coffee Economy Is the Collapse of the Cold-War Cartel That Once Regulated It," *Newsweek,* October 29, 2007.

7. Trade in Israel: Samuel and Naboth

1. Ulrich Duchrow, "Israel's Emergence as a 'Contrast society,' " *Alternatives to Global Capitalism: Drawn from Biblical History, Designed for Political Action* (Utrecht: International Books, 1994), 144.

2. See Exodus 3:7–8a: "Then the Lord said, 'I have observed the misery of my people who are in Egypt; I have heard their cry on account of their taskmasters. Indeed, I know their sufferings, and I have come down to deliver them from the Egyptians, and to bring them up out of that land to a good and broad land, a land flowing with milk and honey....' " The phrase, "God of the Hebrews" implies God's identification with the poor of the land.

3. See Deuteronomy 24:17–22: "You shall not deprive a resident alien or an orphan of justice; you shall not take a widow's garment in pledge. Remember that you were a slave in Egypt and the Lord your God redeemed you from there; therefore I command you to do this. When you reap your harvest in your field and forget a sheaf in the field, you shall not go back to get it; it shall be left for the alien, the orphan, and the widow, so that the Lord your God may bless you in all your undertakings. When you beat your olive trees, do not strip what is left; it shall be for the alien, the orphan, and the widow. When you gather the grapes of your vineyard, do not glean what is left; it shall be for the alien, the orphan, and the widow. Remember that you were a slave in the land of Egypt; therefore I am commanding you to do this."

4. Duchrow, "Economy in the Ancient Near East," 127–35.

5. Roland de Vaux, *Ancient Israel* (New York: McGraw-Hill, 1965), 2:481.

6. Norman C. Habel, *The Land Is Mine: Six Biblical Land Ideologies* (Minneapolis: Augsburg Fortress Press, 1995), 84–85.

7. Duchrow, *Alternatives to Global Capitalism,* 149.

8. See "Search for Phoenician Shipwrecks," *Biblical Archaeology Review* 12, no. 5 (September–October 1999): 16; and D. N. Premnath, *Eighth Century Prophets: A Social Analysis* (St. Louis: Chalice Press, 2003), 58–62.

9. *Kesep,* also "silver," or coins made from silver (see Gen. 20:16, Lev.25:50). Nadav Na'aman has discovered almost identical conditions for land purchase in Assyria under Sargon II, indicating that swap or cash

was a fairly common offer for the times. "Naboth's Vineyard and the Foundation of Jezreel," *Journal for the Study of the Old Testament* 33, no. 2 (2008): 211.

10. See Walter Brueggemann, "The Prophet as a Destabilizing Presence," in *A Social Reading of the Old Testament: Prophetic Approaches to Israel's Communal Life,* ed. Patrick D. Miller (Minneapolis: Fortress, 1994), 221–44.

11. Literally, "sons of Belial," translated variously as "scoundrels" (NRSV and NIV), "worthless men" (ESV), "villains" (NET), and "base fellows" (RSV). So "politicians" is probably an accurate modern equivalent.

12. See Genesis 47:13–22, the story of Pharaoh, through Joseph, acquiring all the land of Egypt and enslaving all its people, through a series of loans made during times of drought. The story takes place in Egypt, but was most likely written by the "Elohist" writer of the eighth century and reflects a storyline more representative of that era.

13. Deuteronomy 23:19; Exodus 22:25; Leviticus 25:35–37; see also Ezekiel 18:8, 13, 17; 22:12. More precisely, interest itself was allowed, just not at usurious rates.

14. See "*Nešek,*" *Theological Wordbook of the Old Testament,* ed. R. Laird Harris, Gleason L. Archer Jr. and Bruce K. Waltke (Chicago: Moody Press, 1980).

15. "The Importance of Economic Equality," interview with Richard Wilkinson and Kate Pickett, authors of *The Spirit Level: Why Greater Equality Makes Societies Stronger. Time,* December 22, 2009, 43. Their research can be found at *www.equalitytrust.org.uk/node/130.*

16. Elizabeth Warren, "America without a Middle Class," *Huffington Post* (*www.huffingtonpost.com/elizabeth-warren/america-without-a -middle_b_377829.html?view=print,* accessed January 4, 2010).

17. Ulrich Duchrow, "Biblical Perspectives on Empire: A View from Western Europe," *Ecumenical Review* (January 1994): 3.

18. Walter Brueggemann, *The Land: Place as Gift, Promise, and Challenge in the Biblical Faith,* 2nd ed. (Minneapolis: Fortress Press, 2002), 59.

19. Ibid., 60.

20. Richard Lowery, *Sabbath and Jubilee* (St. Louis: Chalice Press, 2000), 5.

21. Duchrow, *Alternatives to Global Capitalism,* 153–54.

22. Lowery, *Sabbath and Jubilee,* 38.

23. Possible exceptions might be Nehemiah 5, Jeremiah 34:8–22, and an example in the writings of Josephus, where, like Zedekiah, during a

siege of Jerusalem — this time by Rome — a general cancelation of debts is proclaimed. The word "Jubilee" is used in the ancient world only rarely, as when the "Book of the Jubilees" uses it as a term for measuring time, and when Josephus speaks of it as a historical artifact.

24. *Peplērōtai.* Perfect passive indicative of *pleróō,* "to come alive," "to be made real," "manifested," "fulfilled," Luke 4:21.

25. Walter Harrelson, *The Ten Commandments and Human Rights* (Philadelphia: Fortress Press, 1980), 79–92. Harrelson says cleverly that there is no rational way to explain how and where Israel came up with the "sabbath," except that maybe God told them to do it.

26. It should be noted that although the stories of Daniel are set during the period of the Babylonian captivity (587–539 B.C.E.), they were actually written much later during the reign of Antiochus IV (175–164 B.C.E.) and target his contemporary audience and his contemporary situation. It should also be noted that while the faith community of Daniel supported active defiance, it did not support armed resistance (see 1 Macc. 1:29–38), that would be a fifth option, and one which we are not discussing here.

27. There is some debate as to whether the untitled statue is to a god, a king, or to a king that is to be worshiped as though he were a god. For our needs, however, the fact that the population was required by the king to worship something gold, in the same manner that one would worship a god, is the important core to the story. See the discussion in Victor Matthews, Mark Chavalas, and John Walton, *The IVP Bible Background Commentary: Old Testament* (Downers Grove, Ill.: InterVarsity Press, 2000).

28. Scholars suggest that Matthew's version of the prayer holds more closely to the earliest words, while Luke's seems to retain the earlier structure. So regardless of how the total prayer was structured, if Jesus actually said it, the terms we're quoting here for "release" and "debts" are most likely correct and not "forgive us our *sins*" (Luke 11:4).

29. The Greek of verse 1 is awkward, seeming to say that the lake was called both Galilee and Tiberias. Other ancient manuscripts add *eis tà mere Tiberiás* after *Galilaias,* giving something like "across the sea of Galilee to the area around [the city of] Tiberias." That is much smoother, but is probably a gloss. More likely double names are a result of the town and sea names being in transition since Tiberias was such a new city. The old folks knew the area as "Galilee," and the new folks knew of it as "Tiberias." John, the latest of the Gospel writers, was more aware of this than the Synoptics and included both names.

30. See Amy-Jill Levine, "Visions of Kingdoms," *The Oxford History of the Biblical World,* ed. Michael D. Coogan (New York: Oxford University Press, 1998), 364.

31. Ekkhard Stegemann and Wolfgang Stegemann, *The Jesus Movement: A Social History of Its First Century,* trans. O. C. Dean Jr. (Minneapolis: Fortress Press, 1999), 89–90.

32. Joachim Jeremias, *Jerusalem in the Time of Jesus* (Philadelphia: Fortress, 1969), 116.

33. See also the many expressions of sufficiency in the Sermon on the Mount (Matt. 6:19–21, 24, 33).

34. From Luke 3:10–11. John has just baptized a river of people into a new and volatile movement that was enriching the masses and terrifying the authorities. And the first thing they asked when they came up out of the water was, "What then should we do?" Now that we have been baptized into the new order, what are we supposed to do about it? His answer was clear and blunt, and not bad advice even for us today: "Whoever has two coats must share with anyone who has none; and whoever has food must do likewise."

Further Resources
and Tools for Action

Books from a Religious Perspective

Beckmann, David, and Arthur Simon. *Grace at the Table: Ending Hunger in God's World.* New York: Paulist Press, 1999.

Cobb, John B., Jr. *Sustaining the Common Good: A Christian Perspective on the Global Economy.* Cleveland: Pilgrim Press, 1994.

Daly, Herman E., and John B. Cobb, Jr. *For the Common Good: Redirecting the Economy toward Community, the Environment, and a Sustainable Future.* Boston: Beacon Press, 1989.

Duchrow, Ulrich. *Alternatives to Global Capitalism: Drawn from Biblical History, Designed for Political Action.* Utrecht: International Books, 1995.

Heslam, Peter, ed. *Globalization and the Good.* Grand Rapids: William B. Eerdmans, 2004.

Kinsler, Ross, and Gloria Kinsler. *The Biblical Jubilee and the Struggle for Life: An Invitation to Personal, Ecclesial, and Social Transformation.* Maryknoll, N.Y.: Orbis Books, 2000.

————. *God's Economy: Biblical Studies from Latin America.* Maryknoll, N.Y.: Orbis Books, 2005.

Lerner, Michael. *The Left Hand of God: Taking Back Our Country from the Religious Right.* San Francisco: HarperCollins, 2007.

Lowery, Richard H. *Sabbath and Jubilee.* St. Louis: Chalice Press, 2000.

Massaro, Thomas, S.J. *Living Justice: Catholic Social Teaching in Action.* Lanham, Md.: Rowman and Littlefield, 2008.

McFague, Sallie. *Life Abundant: Rethinking Theology and Economy for a Planet in Peril.* Minneapolis: Fortress Press, 2001.

Moe-Lobeda, Cynthia D. *Healing a Broken World: Globalization and God.* Minneapolis: Fortress Press, 2002.

Peters, Rebecca Todd. *In Search of the Good Life: The Ethics of Globalization.* New York: Continuum, 2004.

Richard, Pablo, et al. *The Idols of Death and the God of Life: A Theology.* Maryknoll, N.Y.: Orbis Books, 1983.

Schreiter, Robert J., ed. *Mission in the Third Millennium*. Maryknoll, N.Y.: Orbis Books, 2001.

Tanner, Kathryn. *Economy of Grace*. Minneapolis: Fortress Press, 2004.

Ucko, Hans, ed. *The Jubilee Challenge: Utopia or Possibility*. Geneva: WCC Publications, 1997.

White, Robert. *Biblical Economics: Economic Myths versus Biblical Values*. Lanham, Md.: University Press of America, 2006.

Books from a Nonreligious Perspective

Anderson, Sarah, John Cavanagh, and Thea Lee. *Guide to the Global Economy*. New York: The New Press, 2000.

Barber, Benjamin R. *Jihad vs. McWorld: How Globalism and Tribalism Are Reshaping the World*. New York: Ballantine, 1995.

Barry, Christian, Barry Herman, and Lydia Tomitova. *Dealing Fairly with Developing Country Debt*. Malden, Mass.: Blackwell Publishing, 2007.

Brown, Lester R. *Eco-Economy: Building an Economy for the Earth*. New York: W. W. Norton, 2000.

Cavanagh, John, and Jerry Mander. *Alternatives to Economic Globalization: A Better World Is Possible*. San Francisco: Berrett-Koehler Publishers, 2002.

Dicum, Gregory, and Nina Luttinger. *The Coffee Book: Anatomy of an Industry from Crop to the Last Drop*. New York: New Press, 2006.

Frank, Thomas. *One Market under God: Extreme Capitalism, Market Populism, and the End of Economic Democracy*. New York: Doubleday, 2000.

Friedman, Thomas. *The Lexus and the Olive Tree*. New York: Farrar, Straus and Giroux, 2000.

George, Susan. *The Debt Boomerang*. San Francisco: Westview Press, 1992.

———. *A Fate Worse Than Debt*. New York: Grove Weidenfeld, 1990.

———. *How the Other Half Dies*. Montclair, N.J.: Allen Osmun, 1977.

Hertz, Noreena. *The Debt Threat: How Debt Is Destroying the Developing World*. New York: HarperCollins, 2004.

Hahnel, Robin. *Panic Rules: Everything You Need to Know about the Global Economy*. Cambridge, Mass.: South End Press, 1999.

Klein, Naomi. *The Shock Doctrine: The Rise of Disaster Capitalism*. New York: Henry Holt, 2007.

Korten, David. *When Corporations Rule the World*. San Francisco: Berrett-Koehler Publishers, 1995.

Lamfalussy, Alexandre. *Financial Crises in Emerging Markets: An Essay on Financial Globalization and Fragility.* New Haven: Yale University Press, 2000.

Mander, J., and E. Goldsmith. *The Case against the Global Economy and for a Turn toward the Local.* San Francisco: Sierra Club Books, 1996.

Millman, Gregory J. *The Vandal's Crown: How Rebel Currency Traders Overthrew the World's Central Banks.* New York: Free Press, 1995.

Wallach, Lori, and Michelle Sforza. *The WTO: Five Years of Reasons to Resist Corporate Globalization.* New York: Seven Story Press, 1999.

Magazines and Journals
That Frequently Carry Articles on Globalization

The Christian Century: www.christiancentury.org/. An ecumenical Christian magazine in the mainline Protestant tradition that attempts to nurture faith and examine issues of politics, culture, and theology.

The Progressive Christian: www.tpcmagazine.org/. The Progressive Christian is a bimonthly magazine for people of faith seeking the common good through reflection, dialogue, and action.

Sojourners Magazine: www.sojo.net. Sojourners' mission is to articulate the biblical call to social justice, inspiring hope and building a movement to transform individuals, communities, the church, and the world.

Tikkun: www.tikkun.org. A progressive interfaith magazine with Jewish roots. Edited by Rabbi Michael Lerner. Promotes a "Global Marshall Plan," a "New Bottom Line" based on a "politics of meaning," and is one of the founders of the Network of Spiritual Progressives (see below under organizations).

Other Magazines and Journals

The American Prospect: www.prospect.org.
1710 Rhode Island Avenue NW, 12th Floor
Washington, DC 20036
888-678-8732

Dissent: www.dissentmagazine.org
310 Riverside Drive, #1201, New York, NY 10025

Dollars & Sense: www.DollarsAndSense.org
P.O. Box 3000, Denville, NJ 07834

Multinational Monitor: www.multinationalmonitor.org/
P.O. Box 19405, Washington, DC 20036
202-387-8030

NACLA: Report on the Americas: www.nacla.org
475 Riverside Drive, New York, NY 10115

The Nation: www.thenation.com/
33 Irving Place, New York, NY 10003
212-209-5400

The New Internationalist: www.newint.org
P.O. Box 1143, Lewiston, NY 04192

Z Magazine: www.zmag.org/
Z Communications, 18 Millfield Street
Woods Hole, MA 02543
508-548-9063

Online Resources

(Most organizations have an online focus. The following are primarily online.)

Economic Policy Institute: www.epinet.org
1660 L Street NW, Washington, DC 20036
EPI is a nonprofit, nonpartisan think tank that seeks to broaden the public debate about strategies to achieve a prosperous and fair economy. Founded in 1986 by a group of economic policy experts, EPI was established to broaden the discussion to include the interests of low- and middle-income workers.

Fifty Years Is Enough: www.50years.org/
A coalition of over two hundred U.S. grassroots, women's, solidarity, faith-based, policy, social- and economic-justice, youth, labor and development organizations dedicated to the transformation of the World Bank and the International Monetary Fund (IMF).

Focus on the Global South: www.focusweb.org/
Focus is in Thailand, the Philippines, and India. It combines policy research, advocacy, activism, and grassroots capacity building in order to generate critical analysis and encourage debates on national and international policies related to corporate-led globalization, neoliberalism, and militarization.

Foreign Policy in Focus: www.foreignpolicy-infocus.org
733 15th Street NW, Suite 1020, Washington, DC 20005
  A joint project of the Interhemispheric Resource Center and the Institute for Policy Studies, Foreign Policy in Focus is dedicated to forging a new foreign policy agenda for America emphasizing the country's role as a more responsible global leader and partner. FPIF provides policy briefs, op-ed pieces and essays, and media interviews in an attempt to bring analysts, advocates, and scholars together with constituency groups.

Organizations

(Note: some of these groups also have journals or newsletters and some of the journals above are also from organizations. All of them also have an online presence.)

Religious

Bread for the World: *www.bread.org*
50 F Street NW, Suite 500
Washington, DC 20001
202-639-9400
  Bread for the World is an ecumenical collective Christian voice urging our nation's decision-makers to end hunger at home and abroad. By changing policies, programs, and conditions that allow hunger and poverty to persist, it provides help and opportunity far beyond the communities in which its members live.

Church World Service: *www.churchworldservice.org*
475 Riverside Dr., Suite 700
New York, NY 10115
Phone: 212-870-2061
  Founded in 1946, Church World Service is the relief, development, and refugee assistance ministry of thirty-five Protestant, Orthodox, and Anglican denominations in the United States. In partnership with indigenous organizations in more than eighty countries, CWS works worldwide to meet human needs and foster self-reliance. Within the United States, CWS assists communities in responding to disasters, resettles refugees, promotes fair national and international policies, provides educational resources, and offers opportunities to join a people-to-people network of local and global caring through participation in CROP Hunger Walks, the Tools & Blankets Program, and the Kits Program.

Jubilee USA Network: *www.jubileeusa.org*
212 East Capitol Street NE
Washington, DC 20003
202-783-3566

Jubilee USA Network is an alliance of more than eighty religious denominations and faith communities, as well as human rights, environmental, labor, and community groups working for the definitive cancelation of crushing debts to fight poverty and injustice in Asia, Africa, and Latin America. The Network brings together people to turn a disparate reality around by active solidarity with partners worldwide, targeted and timely advocacy strategies, and educational outreach.

NETWORK: *www.networklobby.org*
25 E Street NW, Suite 200, Washington, DC 20001-1630
202-347-9797

NETWORK has been a progressive voice within the Catholic community, influencing Congress in favor of peace and justice, for more than thirty years. Through lobbying and legislative advocacy, it attempts to close the gap between rich and poor and to dismantle policies rooted in racism, greed and violence.

Network of Spiritual Progressives: *www.spiritualprogressives.org*
2342 Shattuck Avenue, Suite 1200
Berkeley, CA 94704
510-644-1200

Related to *Tikkun* magazine, and co-founded by Rabbi Michael Lerner, Sister Joan Chittister, and Protestant theologian Cornel West, NSP is an interfaith organization dedicated to a "healing" progressive response to global social and political issues. It sponsors workshops, conferences, and local chapters, in addition to the many programs and projects of *Tikkun*.

SERRV: *www.serrv.org.*
500 Main Street, P.O. Box 365
New Windsor, MD 21776
800-422-5915

SERRV International was one of the first alternative trade organizations in the world and was a founding member of the World Fair Trade Association (WFAT). It is a nonprofit alternative trade and development organization whose mission is to promote the social and economic progress of people in developing regions of the world by marketing their products in a just and direct manner. Its goal is to alleviate poverty and empower low-income people through trade, training, and other forms of capacity building as they work to improve their lives.

Witness for Peace: *www.witnessforpeace.org/*
3628 12th Street NE, 1st Floor
Washington, DC 20017
202-547-6112
  Witness for Peace is a politically independent, interfaith, grassroots organization whose mission is to support peace, justice, and sustainable economies in the Americas by changing the United States.

Nonreligious

Amnesty International: *www.amnestyusa.org*
5 Penn Plaza, New York, NY 10001
212-807-8400
  Amnesty International is one of the oldest and largest international nongovernmental human rights organizations. It monitors the abuses of nations and mobilizes public opinion to put pressure on governments that they have found to be abusers.

Center for Economic Policy Analysis: *www.newschool.edu/cepa*
80 Fifth Avenue, 5th Floor, New York, NY 10011
  The center is the research arm of the Department of Economics at the New School University. CEPA was established in the fall of 1995. It is the goal of CEPA to build an active forum for debates on macroeconomic policy, wage inequality, and globalization.

Financial Markets Center: *www.fmcenter.org*
P.O. Box 334, Philomont, VA 20131
  The Financial Markets Center is an independent nonprofit organization devoted to providing information and analysis about the Federal Reserve System and financial markets to the public and to policy makers. The Web site includes the Fed Archive (with important documents related to monetary policy), as well as materials dealing with basic education and public participation. The center is especially concerned with promoting accountability and democratic values.

Global Development and Environment Institute: *http://ase.tufts.edu/gdae/*
Cabot Center, Fletcher School, Tufts University
Medford, MA 02155
  The G-DAE Institute is a research institute at Tufts University dedicated to promoting a better understanding of how societies can pursue their economic and community goals in an environmentally and socially sustainable manner.

Global Exchange: *www.globalexchange.org/*
2017 Mission Street, 2nd Floor
San Francisco, CA 94110
415-255-7296

Global Exchange is an education and action resource center organized for global change. It has campaigns from the War in Iraq to oil consumption and global climate change, from the exploitation of the global economy to the creation of the local green economy.

Global Trade Watch: *www.citizen.org/trade/*
1600 20th Street NW, Washington, DC 20009
202-588-1000

Global Trade Watch promotes democracy by challenging corporate globalization, arguing that the current globalization model is neither a random inevitability nor "free trade."

Halifax Initiative: *www.halifaxinitiative.org*
153 rue Chapel St. Suite 104
Ottawa, ON K1N 1H5, Canada

A coalition of Canadian non-governmental organizations doing public interest work and education for fundamental reform of international financial institutions, namely, the World Bank and the International Monetary Fund. It is a coalition of development, environment, faith-based, human rights, and labor groups.

Institute for Economic Analysis: *www.iea-macro-economics.org*
4 High Street #4–6, Brattleboro, VT 05301

IEA's basic aim is to develop tools for macroeconomic analysis and policy that can maintain stable full-employment growth, low inflation, low interest rates, and equitable distribution of income and wealth. Its innovative conceptual framework integrates GDP and financial accounts for more systematic coordination of monetary and fiscal policy. Special focuses are Fed monetary policy, federal budget deficit/surpluses, Social Security, consumer credit, and world economic recovery.

Institute for Policy Research: *www.nwu.edu/IPR*
Northwestern University, 2040 Sheridan Road, Evanston, IL 60208

IPR's mission is to stimulate and support excellent social science research on significant public policy issues and to disseminate the findings widely — to students, scholars, policymakers, and the public at large. Institute research now falls broadly into seven program areas that include poverty, race, and inequality; child, adolescent, and family studies;

communications, media, and public opinion; community development; law and justice; philanthropy; and environmental policy.

The International Monetary Fund: *imf.org.*

Pew Center on Global Climate Change: *www.pewclimate.org*
2101 Wilson Boulevard, Suite 550, Arlington, VA 22201
The Pew Center on Global Climate Change is a nonprofit, nonpartisan, and independent organization dedicated to providing credible information and innovative solutions in the effort to address global climate change.

Tobin Tax Initiative: *www.tobintax.org*
CEED/IIRP, P.O. Box 4167, Arcata, CA 95518
1-707-822-8347
Tobin Taxes are excise taxes on cross-border currency transactions. The revenue should go to global priorities: basic environmental and human needs. Such taxes will help tame currency market volatility and restore national economic sovereignty.

TransFairUSA: *www.transfairusa.org*
1500 Broadway, Suite 400
Oakland, CA 94612
info@transfairusa.org. 510-663-5260
A nonprofit organization that provides independent certification of Fair Trade products in the United States. It is the main certification organization for fair trade products in the United States.

United Students Against Sweatshops: *www.usas.org.* 1150 17th Street NW
Washington, DC 20036
202-667-9328

World Bank: *www.WorldBank.org.*

World Trade Organization: *www.WTO.org.*